the
mama
sutra

. . . . .

A STORY OF LOVE, LOSS, AND THE PATH OF MOTHERHOOD

Anne Cushman

Shambhala
BOULDER
2019

Shambhala Publications, Inc.
4720 Walnut Street
Boulder, Colorado 80301
www.shambhala.com

9 8 7 6 5 4 3 2 1

First Edition
Printed in the United States of America

⊗This edition is printed on acid-free paper that meets
the American National Standards Institute z39.48 Standard.
♻This book is printed on 30% postconsumer recycled paper.
For more information please visit www.shambhala.com.

Shambhala Publications is distributed worldwide
by Penguin Random House, Inc., and its subsidiaries.

Designed by Claudine Mansour Design

LIBRARY OF CONGRESS CATALOGING-IN-PUBLICATION DATA
Names: Cushman, Anne, author.
Title: The mama sutra: a story of love, loss, and the path of motherhood /
Anne Cushman.
Description: First edition. | Boulder: Shambhala, [2019] | Includes
bibliographical references.
Identifiers: LCCN 2018035342 | ISBN 9781611804638 (pbk.: alk. paper)
Subjects: LCSH: Cushman, Anne. | Motherhood. | Loss (Psychology) | Buddhism.
Classification: LCC HQ759 .c984 2019 | DDC 306.874/3—dc23
LC record available at https://lccn.loc.gov/2018035342

For my mother
Nancy Troland Cushman
1924–2015

and my daughter
Sierra
May 9, 1999

Sutra is the Sanskrit name for a short spiritual teaching in the yogic and Buddhist tradition. It comes from the same root as the English word *suture*, a verb that means "to stitch."

The stories in this book are not sutras in the traditional sense. They are an homage to the long threads that run through all human lives, stitching up what's shredded in our hearts.

Contents

Author's Note

The stories in this book are crafted from the raw material of my life—as imperfectly preserved in my memory and my journals. To protect their privacy, I've sometimes omitted or changed people's names or identifying details, including the names of my son, his father, and my partner's daughter.

the mama sutra

Introduction

If my baby daughter had lived past her birth she would have had her eighteenth birthday last Mother's Day. I wonder what she would have been like. I picture her with skin still creamy and luminous, the dark hair she had as a newborn baby now grown long and shiny—maybe caught back in a ponytail, maybe cascading loose over her shoulders. I never saw her eyes—her lids were closed by the time I held her, already dead, in my arms—so I invent them: green, like mine, rather than golden brown like her younger brother's. But they are light-filled and sparkling, like his.

I imagine my daughter texting me from school like her teenage brother just did: "I just got cast as 'Moist' in 'Dr. Horrible's Sing-Along Blog!'" "Mom, I'm not feeling so good, can you pick me up today?" I envision the way she would roll her eyes at my haphazard outfits, the clothes of a writer and meditator who works at home in sweatshirts and yoga pants—"*God*, Mom, can you at least put on matching socks before you leave the house?" (Her brother doesn't even notice what I wear, but I'm sure she would.)

In these daydreams, my daughter is always dropped into the house that I am living in now. It is *this* honey-colored couch we are snuggling into together, reading *Big Little Lies* (me) and *Twilight* (her) in front of the fire as the fog rolls in over the mountain out the window. It is *this* kitchen where I'm scrambling eggs for her, her brother, and her stepsister in the morning, the sink still piled high with dishes from last night's vegetable miso soup.

Of course, in this fantasy, her brother and stepsister are here too—how could they not be? The three of them are spotting jackrabbits and bobcats in the drought-baked hills above our house or arguing about whether to watch *Bridesmaids* or *Star Wars* on family movie night. The girls are singing along as their brother plays "Hysteria" by Muse on his electric guitar.

But, of course, that's not the way it would be. Because if she had lived everything would have been different.

. . .

This book is a collection of stories about motherhood as a path to awakening. I've been writing them for almost two decades. Some of them I have published before. Others have felt too raw to share past the confines of my journals. All of them together—I want to reassure you—culminate in a happy ending.

When I first found out I was going to have a baby, at age thirty-five, I started a journal of my pregnancy. I was a writer, an editor, and had been a practitioner of yoga and Buddhist meditation for almost sixteen years. I had just published *From Here to Nirvana*, a guidebook for modern pilgrims to spiritual sites in India. I thought recording my passage through pregnancy and birth would be like documenting another kind of pilgrimage—a journey of transformation and awakening, the deepest yoga of all. I had the arrogance, and ignorance, to think that I knew in advance how the story would go.

By that time, I'd spent months on meditation retreats where I sat cross-legged on a cushion for hours each day, walked back and forth in slow motion, and took ten minutes to savor a single raisin. I'd worn out a dozen yoga mats—the rubber scraped into holes by the pressure of my heels—as I breathed and sweated and bent my body into backbends, handstands, and splits.

I'd backpacked from the Himalayas to the Arabian Sea, my only outfits two baggy *salwar kameez* that I washed out every night in sinks in cheap hotels where the drain emptied straight onto the gritty clay floor. I'd meditated under the Bodhi Tree in Bodh Gaya, on the very spot where the Buddha had attained enlightenment. Trapped by an unexpected Himalayan snowstorm while hiking to the source of the Ganges River, I'd spent the night shivering on the rocky floor of a hermit yogi's cave, watching the rats scurry by and listening to avalanches crash as the yogi chanted, *"Jai, Sita Ram!"*

But when I sat cross-legged on my living room floor and watched a big pink plus sign appear at the tip of my pregnancy test stick, I suspected that I was setting off on a journey wilder, deeper, and more transformative than anything I had ever tasted before.

I was sure it would be a journey of love, adventure, and spiritual awakening. I didn't know, yet, that it would also be a journey of heartbreak.

Hidden somewhere in my mind, unacknowledged, was the illusion that my yoga and meditation practice was a magic talisman that would protect me from disaster. I would eat organic food, do yoga every day, and have a virtually painless home birth that would be like a slightly more strenuous *vinyasa* practice. I would carry my baby with me everywhere in a sling, like the Mayans, and sleep with her in a family bed—and therefore she would not have colic, not cry all night, not even spit up. Parenthood would add a whole new spiritual dimension to my relationship with my baby's father. Our days would be a festival of family meditations and pancake breakfasts, and after we tucked our little one into bed each night, we'd fall into each other's arms in passionate gratitude for our good fortune.

When I was four months pregnant, I put on a little black dress with a stretchy waistband and trotted into the office of a New York editor to pitch her my new book idea.

"A Buddhist yoga mom's journey into motherhood," I told her. "A cross between Anne Lamott and the Dalai Lama."

"It's a great idea," the editor told me, leaning back in her chair. She was in her sixties, with forty years of publishing experience and a couple of children of her own. Later, I would realize that she had probably seen plenty of book proposals—and lives—that didn't go as planned. "Send me a draft when the baby is a year old."

But the story I thought I was telling ended before that.

I tried a few years later to tell the story again.

By that time my one-year-old son was toddling through my house, clutching a blue baby blankie and a stuffed lion. My daughter's footprints were framed on an altar beside his diaper changing table, next to a statue of Kuan Yin, the Buddhist goddess of compassion who is said to hear the cries of the world.

I thought that this new story would be a transformational tale of death and rebirth. I would write about how yoga and meditation helped me transform grief into love and wisdom—and the tale would end with me and my husband and son living happily ever after together.

I wanted to use that story to highlight the power of mothering as a meditative practice in its own right. Since my son had been born, it had become achingly clear to me that the classical yogic and Buddhist canon didn't have much to say about mothering—or intimate relationships in general. Over the centuries, meditation and yoga had primarily been paths for renunciate men. "How can a person who is attached to family life, with his senses uncontrolled and bound by strong ties of affection, liberate himself?" asked one ancient yoga text.

Intimate relationships were dangerous because they inflamed desire—"It is better that you enter the mouth of a hideous cobra or a pit of blazing coals than enter a woman," Buddhist monks used to be warned. They could ensnare the practitioner in family life, leaving no time to meditate. The young prince who would become the Buddha named his son Rahula, meaning "fetter." In order to pursue spiritual awakening, he had left both wife and son behind, slipping out of the house in the middle of the night and galloping off on horseback, apparently to avoid a nasty scene.

Early Buddhist nuns wrote poems about their lives, recounting how they'd turned to spiritual practice after their children were carried away by hawks, buried in mudslides, or swept away down rivers. Their poetry sings of the freedom that lay on the other side of unfathomable loss: "I have seen the jackals eating the flesh of my sons in the cemetery. My family destroyed, my husband dead, despised by everybody, I found what does not die." Such texts offered me little guidance for how to find that profound awakening while still caring for children, or still grieving ones who had died, and nothing at all about negotiating the complex, ever-changing constellation of intimate relationships that make up a family.

Sure, the selfless compassion of a mother for her child was presented as the model for loving-kindness meditation. But that was a metaphor. Actual moms—cursing in childbirth, leaking milk, kissing bruises, pounding a wall in the middle of the night so they didn't pound their babies—as spiritual practitioners? My search of the classical yoga and Buddhist sutras came up empty.

But those were the things I wanted to write about. I wanted to tell the story of a real mother, finding awakening with her shirt stained with peanut butter. I wanted to write about how the lofty ideals of spiritual practice intersected with the wild, chaotic, hilarious, heartbreaking details of everyday life. I filled my journal with notes about parenting.

But then my marriage went down in flames. Grief overtook my journals too.

I wanted to write a story that turned out well. So I set this one aside.

Instead, I published a novel about a young woman looking for love—and enlightenment—in all the wrong places. I enjoyed raising my son and hammered out a new and healthy relationship with his father. I published personal essays about parenting and spiritual practice in yoga and meditation magazines. I eventually taught mindfulness retreats and directed a yoga and meditation teacher training at a Buddhist meditation center. I fell in and out of lust and love.

I knew that my daughter's life and death had not just shattered my heart, but they had also rebuilt it, wider and deeper and more tender than it had been before. I knew that the path I was walking with my growing son was opening me in ways that no meditation retreat or yoga practice ever had.

I wanted to write a book about mindfulness and parenting as a spiritual practice—but how could I reveal the ragged details of my own life? Surely someone truly mindful wouldn't be screaming at her soon to be ex-husband and then kicking a wall so hard she broke her toe. An enlightened being wouldn't have a tantrummy toddler whose first words to another child would be "go away." She wouldn't have a boyfriend who would climb through her window in a drunken rage in the middle of the night, thinking she had been out carousing with another guy, when in fact she had been sipping chamomile tea at her former mother-in-law's eighty-fifth birthday party.

I figured I better keep my mouth shut about this whole motherhood-as-spiritual-practice idea.

Now, years later, I finally understand—waiting for a happy ending isn't the point of writing, or of life. Don't misunderstand me. As I write this, my life is filled with joy. My son is a radiant high-school student with a pack of friends and a passion for environmental science, creative writing, and theater. I share my home and my heart with a beloved partner—a musician and martial artist who plays guitar with my son and teaches him to spar with wooden swords on our deck.

My son's father is happily married to a beautiful, raven-haired woman whom I don't know well but who I know loves my son. Last Father's Day I helped my son pack up a picnic lunch of salmon salad and sparkling apple juice and sent the three of them all off for a walk around a nearby lake. Then I went on a different hike with my partner and his daughter, who has become my child too—a twenty-something artist with creamy, luminous skin, and long dark hair that cascades over her shoulders like a waterfall.

I know this happy moment is not the end of the story. If there's one thing that my journey into motherhood taught me for sure, it's that life swirls and eddies on and on like a river. Oceans evaporate into mist. Clouds rain into mountain streams. Streams sing their way back to the ocean again. Love always walks hand in hand with impermanence. All human stories of love are the stories of loss, eventually.

But here's the other side of that truth—love doesn't end when someone we love is gone.

Long before I got pregnant with my first baby, I was on a meditation retreat in the south of France. The Vietnamese Zen master Thich Nhat Hanh began a dharma talk one morning with these words: "She was just eighteen years old when I met her." We retreatants were riveted as, over the course of our three-week retreat, he told us the story of how as a young novice monk he had fallen in love with a nun. He never touched her—"I didn't even place my hand upon the top of her head." The war swept them apart, and she eventually left the order of nuns. But that love changed the trajectory of his practice, his teachings, and his entire life.

At the end of the retreat, a woman raised her hand and asked, "Did you ever see her again?"

"Have you not understood what I have been telling you?" Thich Nhat Hanh asked. "She is here in the room with us. I see her every moment of every day. You hear her whenever I speak."

Letter to a Daughter
Who Didn't Live to Be Born

· · · · ·

DEAR SIERRA,

I thought we would have more time together.

I thought there would be diaper pails, and mobiles, and breast-feeding at midnight in a rocking chair upholstered in stars and moons. I thought there would be *Goodnight Moon*, and *Winnie the Pooh*, and *Misty of Chincoteague*, and *Harriet the Spy*. I thought there would be braces, bikes, spaghetti, tampons, arguments about cleaning your room. And that sometime in the faraway future I'd be hugging you goodbye in a college dorm and crying, even though I'd know you'd be home for Thanksgiving.

But as it turned out, the time that you lived inside my body was the only time we had. So I want to tell you some pieces of the story of your life and what you taught me. Because your story is one of the ways you stay alive, even as I let you go.

Who knows when any story begins? Tug on the dangling thread of any moment and the whole universe begins to unspool. The present is the fruit of the past and the seed of the future. Look into a young girl's eyes and you see a great-grandmother gazing back at you. In a boy's hello, you might hear the echo of his father's voice—just as it sounded the first time he said your name.

Where does a story begin? Here's one place I might begin yours, Sierra: the day I met your dad, the first day of freshman week at Princeton University, eighteen years before you were born.

Just hours before, I'd said goodbye to my parents, watched them drive away, and set out to explore my new dorm. I wound my way through a maze of empty corridors in a dorm that smelled like years of stale pizza and spilled beer. In front of a door with music playing behind it, I paused.

As I was lifting my hand to knock, I heard a voice. "Are you looking for me?"

I turned to see your half-naked dad walking toward me, dark, curly hair still wet from the shower, a towel wrapped around his waist.

I had just spent four years in a barely coed boarding school where the girls' campus was on the top of a mountain, a five-mile bus ride from the boys' campus in the valley, and where being caught in a boy's bedroom was grounds for expulsion. I was a brainy high-school-newspaper editor who'd only recently traded her thick glasses for contact lenses.

I had never been this close to a guy with no clothes on.

"I guess I am," I said.

He invited me into the room whose door I'd been about to knock on. The walls were hung with madras-print bedspreads; the single twin bed had been replaced with a queen-size air mattress. In one corner was a homemade water-balloon bazooka for firing into the courtyard below. In another corner were piled the disassembled parts for an automatic plant-watering machine he was inventing.

We stayed up most of the night together, roaming the campus and comparing notes about our lives.

I was a seventeen-year-old freshman from a Connecticut prep school renowned for its demanding international baccalaureate program. He was a nineteen-year-old junior from a California beach school renowned for its popular P.E. class, "Bike and Surf."

I was the daughter of a Catholic three-star Army general whose Puritan ancestors were on the Mayflower. When I was ten years old, our family car had a bumper sticker on it that read "We Do Things Right," which was the slogan my father had coined for the 101st Airborne Division when he was its commander.

He was descended, he said, "from a long line of atheists, conscientious objectors, and horse thieves." He had been raised by his single mother, who had refused to let him join the Boy Scouts on the grounds that it was the training ground for a paramilitary organization.

He'd had his first live-in girlfriend when he was sixteen. He was philosophically opposed to monogamy and said that the only interesting people he knew came from broken homes—although he was willing to give me the benefit of the doubt because my father had been gone in Vietnam for so much of my childhood.

I had never been in love with anyone who wasn't a character in a novel: Laurie from *Little Women* was high on my list, as was Rhett Butler from *Gone with the Wind*. I didn't admit this to him that night, but I had never even been on a date, unless you counted the time I went to "A Presidential Classroom for Young Americans" in Washington, DC, and a fellow overachiever from a high school in Vermont asked me to sit next to him on the bus on the way to the tour of Capitol Hill.

Nor did I tell him how I used to open like love letters my end-of-term envelopes full of grades and comments, reading and rereading the litany of As and praise that let me know I was admired. And I definitely didn't tell him about my failed attempt to find a table to eat at in the boys' dining hall my senior year. I had gone from half-empty table to half-empty table, asking if I could join them. Boy after boy looked me over and told me there was no room. I fled to the girls' bathroom and hid in a stall until it was time for English class. The rest of the year I spent lunch in the bathroom, eating handfuls of dry Grape-Nuts I'd stashed in my blazer pocket at breakfast.

Later, Sierra, I would discover that there were things your father hadn't told me either. He hadn't told me that after a brutal divorce when he was two, his father had gotten custody of him and his big sister. His mother had climbed over a fence to kidnap them back. She changed her name and disappeared with them. He had never seen his father again.

He didn't tell me that some mornings before he left for elementary school, his mother told him she didn't want to live anymore. He would come home not knowing whether he would find her dead or alive.

Together we were an emotional ship made of toothpicks, sailing through an ocean of submerged icebergs. But we didn't know that, that night as we walked across the golf course toward the tower of the graduate school, looming above us like a medieval prison. "According to surfers," he told me, "getting tubed in a breaking wave is the greatest pleasure the world has to offer. The next is taking LSD. The next is having sex. They're the only people in the world who rate sex so low."

I looked up at the sky. This was the first night in my life that no one was checking to see what time I came home. My life, which had proceeded in black and white, had suddenly burst into color.

All I said was, "I've never surfed."

A few weeks after we met, we began collaborating on an article about what the graffiti in the campus bathrooms revealed about male-female relationships at Princeton. When we started comparing our research notes I discovered to my chagrin that I didn't know the meaning of most of the terms used in the men's bathrooms. He was happy to tutor me.

It turned out that no campus publication would print an essay that began with the words "Her pubic hair was jet-black"—a reference to the full-size image of a naked woman we discovered on the wall of the art department's bathroom, with a three-dimensional vulva sculpted out of clay and a head the size of a pencil dot. But it didn't matter that we remained unpublished. Our relationship was off and running.

Over the next four years, here's some of what happened: We began spending every night twined in each other's arms in dorm beds barely big enough for us to roll over. Your dad commissioned the university glassblower at the chemistry lab to blow us a giant bong. He built a system to shine a laser beam through a multifaceted glass ball rigged up to a speaker woofer, so we could dance in his dorm room to a private light show that pulsed to the beat of Brian Eno and the Grateful Dead.

While your dad wrote short stories (avidly) and Chaucer papers (belatedly) for his English lit degree, I signed up for a class in world religions because it didn't meet too early in the morning. Captivated by the lectures on yoga and Buddhism—paths that pointed toward the possibility of happiness in a world I already knew could be painful—I switched my major from creative writing to comparative religion. I became the campus stringer for a local newspaper.

After he graduated, your dad stayed in town to try to launch a video production company.

My senior year, I got us both a National Endowment for the Humanities grant to produce a documentary on Zen Buddhism for my senior thesis. We spent a month shooting video and meditating together at the Zen Center of Los Angeles, an urban community where we heard occasional gunshots in the neighborhood and the Japanese Zen master had just been packed off to an alcoholism treatment center after his followers discovered that he had been having affairs with his senior students. "I am not a perfect teacher," the Zen master told me in an interview when he returned, "but the dharma is a perfect dharma."

The term *dharma*, I knew from my studies, referred to the teachings of the Buddha—and, in broader sense, the truth about how things really are. Your dad and I were so inspired by everything that we were learning about spiritual practice that on the plane home, we took turns slipping into the bathroom to smoke a joint.

Or here's another place your story could begin, Sierra: the day your dad and I decided to have a baby together.

By then we had been best friends and an on-again, off-again couple for eighteen years. He was my first love and my heart's imperfect gold standard for measuring all those that followed. We had played together, worked together, fought each other, traveled the world together. But by the time I passed my thirty-fifth birthday, we hadn't spoken for months. Then he came to visit me in my funky one-bedroom cabin in a one-intersection, one-bar town an hour north of San Francisco, where I'd moved to the last time we'd broken up.

Your dad maneuvered his ancient, unreliable, cream-colored sports car—which he'd nicknamed Creampuff—up my rutted driveway. "Do you realize that in all the years I've known you," he asked as he got out, "you've never chosen a home that didn't have a sign on the driveway saying, 'Not a City-Maintained Road'?"

"Just playing hard to get," I said, leaning in for a hug. His arms wrapped around me, my head rested against his chest, and the circuitry that bound us together sprang alive again, as if we had just slept through our morning classes wrapped in each other's arms on a twin dorm mattress; as if we had forgotten the time I threw a mug at him that just missed his head and dented my bedroom wall.

We sat in front of the smoky fire in the living room, curled up on the futon sofa we'd bought together in college.

"I like what you've done with your workspace." He nodded at the custom-built desk and bookshelves fitted into an alcove to the right of the fireplace. "You must think you'll be living here a while."

"Unless I decide to go back to India." I had just spent a year there, researching the spiritual guidebook that was about to come out that month.

"Is that an option?"

"I'm tossing a coin. Go to India or have a baby?"

He looked at the sputtering fire, not at me. "You're thinking about having a baby?"

"Well—I'm thirty-five." I stared at the bloodstain in the middle of the rug where my cat Kali had decapitated a rat. "If I'm going to do it, it's time."

He picked up a poker and adjusted the logs. "It doesn't scare you, the idea of doing it on your own?"

"The idea of not doing it at all scares me more."

"I know exactly what you mean."

At one end of a smoldering log a flame leaped up.

I looked up at your dad and said something I hadn't been planning: "You're the only person I've ever met who I want to have a baby with."

"I feel the same way," he said. "I've never wanted to have a child with anyone else. And I've never stopped wanting it with you, even when I thought we were never going to speak to each other again."

"Are we insane to be even talking about this?"

"I told my mother I was going to see you. She said, 'It's not too late yet. But it's *almost* too late.'"

Your dad and I had never even lived together. I had just quit my job as an editor at *Yoga Journal* to try to make it as a freelance writer. This cottage—with wood rats in the walls, a smoky fireplace for heat, a propane-fired stove, and a hole burned in the kitchen linoleum where a previous tenant had tried to do a Vedic prosperity fire ritual—was the first home that I hadn't shared with roommates. I'd invested a lot in personal growth workshops and nothing at all in a savings account. Having a baby was a crazy idea.

But as I watched the flames spreading from log to log, I felt you with me for the first time. You were a passionate, intense, stubborn little presence, neither polite nor convenient. You weren't a winged cherub. You were more like a ball of fire. And you were hammering on the door of our lives, demanding that we let you in.

The classic myth of the spiritual journey always begins with a call. In the traditional male version of the story, that's generally a call to *leave*. In India, I'd met yogis living in caves in the Himalayas; meditating naked and ash-smeared by the funeral pyres in Benares, the city of death; wandering as beggars from town to town, their only possessions a staff and a metal lunch tin. To prove their scorn for the body, they took ascetic vows—sleeping in slings hung from trees or holding a hand in the air for years at a stretch until the arm withered to a twig. They left their families, changed their names, and never spoke of their pasts.

But what if there were another kind of spiritual call—a call to *stay*? What if I could hear it as I hacked through the tangled jungle of human relationships, riddled with fear and delusions, graced with tenderness and passion? And what if that path of awakening took me deeper into that jungle rather than away from it?

"Let's do things in the conventional order for once," your dad said. So we decided we'd wait a few months before getting pregnant, and we started to plan a wedding instead. But before we'd even picked out a venue, you were on your way. I was just beginning a three-month stint as a writer-in-residence at the Kripalu Center for Yoga and Health in western Massachusetts, on the other side of the country from your dad. So to welcome you, he sent an email.

Dear Sprout:

As you currently are smaller than a tadpole and lack even rudimentary sensory apparatuses, I shall ask your mother to read this aloud to you. Despite your surprise arrival, your mother and I already love you very much. I have to confess to a little bit of nervousness about meeting you. Of course I want to make a good impression, though I suspect that all you'll notice about me for the first couple years is that I have no breasts. I don't know much about your kind either, but I'm very interested in learning from you.

I have many powers and abilities, and I shall use them all to keep you safe from harm for as long as I live. I shall help you grow in ways you feel are important, even if I don't fully understand the point of your efforts.

Like me, you'll probably have to make a lot of mistakes.

Love always,

Daddy

At my first prenatal visit, at a clinic in the Berkshires not far from the ashram, the doctor told me that I was an "elderly *prima gravida*"—a woman having her first baby over age thirty-five. "We'll have to keep a close eye on you," she said.

The term was a shock. I thought of myself as just getting started in life. Packing for this trip to the East Coast I'd included a sweater that still had my name tag from boarding school sewn in it.

I opened my mouth to tell the doctor that she didn't have to worry. I'd been eating organic vegetarian food since I was nineteen and doing yoga every day since I was twenty-one. In my mid-twenties, I'd taken the "five wonderful precepts" in a ceremony with the Zen Buddhist teacher Thich Nhat Hanh—and to honor the vow to avoid intoxicants, I hadn't so much as sipped a glass of wine since. I wanted to assure her that my idea of getting wild and crazy was putting butter on my toast instead of olive oil.

But before I could say anything, the doctor was rubbing a cool jelly on my abdomen. "Would you like to hear the baby's heartbeat?" she asked, gliding a plastic wand over the flat surface of my belly.

"You mean, I can already hear it?"

"Absolutely. Nice and strong." She passed me the Doppler. "Fun fact: When the heart first forms, it's actually on the outside of the embryo. It takes a few weeks for the rest of the body to form around it."

So we all start out with our hearts outside our bodies? That sounded about right to me. The protective shell on top of them comes later. And sooner or later, if we are really alive, we feel as if our heart is back on the outside again, undefended.

I slipped the Doppler over my ears and heard your heartbeat for the first time: *Whoosh. Whoosh. Whoosh.*

I'd been a Zen student for almost two decades. I'd sat on a black cushion, chanting over and over an ancient sutra called "The Identity of Relative and Absolute" while incense rose in spirals before the statue of a serenely smiling Buddha: "Light and darkness are a pair, like the foot before and the foot behind in walking. Ordinary life fits the Absolute like a box and its lid."

What could be more ordinary than a pregnancy? Every human being who has ever been born started out that way: a speck of multiplying cells inside a woman's womb. I had started keeping a journal of my pregnancy, but so far it seemed as if nothing was happening, other than the fact that my yoga pants were getting tighter and I felt queasy when I looked at the baked beans in the dining hall buffet.

And yet, as I heard your heartbeat, I felt as if I were bowing down at an altar. I was connected with the mystery that pulses at the heart of every moment: Where does life come from? Not just an individual life, or the life of humanity, or even life on earth—but this entire cosmos of stars and jellyfish, bombs and telephones, coral reefs and mitochondria?

Whoosh. Whoosh. Whoosh.

Every morning, in my suite overlooking a lake and an autumn forest of crimson and gold, I did an hour of yoga and meditated for twenty minutes. Then I went for a slow jog—the grass crisp with frost, wild geese shrieking overhead, the water gunmetal gray in the dawn light. I had to stop to pee a lot—squatting under the birch trees, the acrid smell of the steaming leaves so intense to my hormone-enhanced senses that it made me sneeze.

After my run I'd stop by the breakfast buffet and pile a tray with granola, yogurt, bananas, muffins, soymilk, oatmeal, eggs—ridiculous amounts of food, as if stoking a blast furnace. I sprinkled nutritional yeast on everything: vitamin B for your developing nervous system. Flax oil—omega-3s for your brain. Organic prenatal vitamins. A smoothie of fresh fruit and vegetable juices.

Then I'd sit at my computer, fighting the progesterone tide of sleepiness that tugged me under. I was supposed to be writing a novel about spiritual practice, but I was having a hard time staying awake long enough to come up with a plot.

Instead, I freewrote—mainly about you. *As I peed this morning, I wondered if Sprout could hear me. It's a good thing he/she doesn't have an ego yet, doesn't get impatient or insulted. What a marvel it is that tucked between my bladder and my bowels is the cradle where a whole new human being is forming— who will emerge just between the holes for the piss and the shit.*

I wrote down random dreams: *I give birth to my baby and it is a kitten. It runs under the bed and hides. "Don't worry," says my sister. "Lots of babies start out that way."*

I wrote down random insights:

Any story can be summed up in a few pages. If getting to the end were what was important, the CliffsNotes of Hamlet *would be as good as the play. But what art and yoga are about is slowing down to pay attention—to honor what's below the surface; to give the gift of bhakti, or devotion, to every passing moment.*

Ultimately—whether with a pregnancy or a novel—it has to be the process that matters; it has to be the process that we care about deeply. It's the process, not the result, that works its deep alchemy in our soul. It is the process that releases the prana, not the pose.

In between pregnancy musings, I also typed pages and pages of my habitual, familiar whining and ranting. Sometimes I felt as if I were keeping two separate journals—but maybe it wasn't that. Maybe it was that the profound and the ordinary are braided together in every moment, and that it just takes a shift of focus to switch from seeing one to seeing the other. Maybe the sacred shines through whenever the fog in the mind starts to lift, like the sun breaking through the clouds, illuminating a lake full of wild geese.

Every day on my yoga mat, rolling my hips from side to side, I tuned in to your presence—a boiling energy, nested between my navel and my pubic bone.

As a yoga student, I'd learned about prana, the great life force that flowed through and sustained the physical form, permeating the body but radiating beyond it. Pregnant with you, I could viscerally sense how the universe itself could have been birthed from this energy, a tiny seed of potentiality exploding forth into galaxies whirling through space.

I let myself open to prana as I flowed through the poses, spiraling around the forms like a vine twining around a trellis. I felt myself softening, opening, bursting into blossom.

Whoosh. Whoosh. Whoosh.

Dear Sprout Daddy,

I can feel Sprout moving!

I know I'm not supposed to be able to feel it yet—the books say most women don't feel anything until eighteen to twenty-two weeks, and I'm not yet at sixteen—but it's so obvious to me, this little flutter inside, like a goldfish brushing against the edge of its bowl. The books say most women mistake it for gas at first, but what are most women thinking? It's in a completely different place, clearly not intestinal. My mom says the doctors always insisted that she was making it up, that she couldn't be feeling it that early, but that she always did—she described it as a gentle stroke on the inside of her uterus, like someone brushing a finger against her cheek.

Love and kisses and butterfly wings,

Sprout-Mama

Dear Sprout:

Daddy bought a guitar today.

A guitar is a six-stringed instrument for making music. Music is an arrangement of sound that expresses emotion. Sound is . . . Daddy's not sure whether you have ears yet. This will all be a lot clearer after you are fully incarnated.

Anyway, Daddy bought a guitar today. A good one. (Yes, the money came out of your college fund, but college is years away.) As Daddy was trying out the different guitars in the store, he kept thinking of you and how much he looks forward to playing music for you, to singing you lullabies and love songs.

Hugs and kisses and songs,

Daddy

"If you look deeply into the palm of your hand, you will see your parents and all generations of your ancestors," writes Thich Nhat Hanh. "All of them are alive in this moment. Each is present in your body. You are the continuation of each of these people."

With you beginning to kick inside me, Sierra, I understood

this as never before. You carried your ancestors inside you like Russian nesting dolls. You were made of their stories, as surely as you were made of blood and bones, carbon and calcium, sunlight and water.

So as you grew, I wrote their stories to tell you.

I wrote the story of my father's birth at a US military hospital in China in 1921. His father, an Army officer, was stationed there with his young bride. The military doctors didn't know that she was pregnant with twins, although her Chinese ayah had told her so again and again. My grandfather had already left the hospital to announce the news of his son's birth when the doctors discovered another little boy inside the womb. By the time they extracted him, baby Bernard was dead. "I was so happy," my grandmother wrote later in a letter home. "I always wanted twins." My grandfather added a terse PS: "'We buried him in a corner of the churchyard reserved for unbaptized babies. Poor little chap. But it's not as if he had ever really lived."

I wrote the story of your dad's mother, your wild and free-spirited Grandma Joan—and how, as a teenager in the 1930s, she dived off a cliff into Echo Lake in the High Sierra, holding a rock in her hands to pull her deeper. She hit her head on the rock and passed out underwater. If a friend hadn't dived in after her, she would have drowned.

I wrote the story of how my father met my mother—in 1942, at Fort Benning, Georgia, where his class of West Point cadets were to study engineering at the Officer Candidates School. The United States had just entered World War II. Engineering would mean building bridges, laying and disarming mines.

A hop at the Polo Hunt Club welcomed the cadets. At one end of the room stood the row of young men in khaki uniforms. At the other end clustered a bevy of officers' daughters in party dresses—including my nineteen-year-old mother, in lavender organdy, home from Connecticut College for the summer. The band started playing "The Dipsy Doodle." Nobody knew what to do.

My mother stepped forward. "Let's all find someone to dance with!" she called and offered her hand to the first cadet she saw—the man standing next to my father. Everyone began the jitterbug, and my father promptly cut in to dance with my mother. Then he cut in again. They danced to "Blue Moon" and "Don't Sit Under the Apple Tree (with Anyone Else but Me)." After the dance, they sat together on the steps in the warm Georgia twilight. My mother pointed to the outline of the trees against the dimming sky and said, "This is the silhouette hour." A week later, on the train to Fort Knox—where the cadets were going to study armor and tanks— my father said to the cadet sitting next to him, "I just met the girl I am going to marry."

Thich Nhat Hanh writes in *No Mud, No Lotus*, "If you have suffering in you and you don't know where it comes from, looking deeply you may see that this is the suffering of your ancestors, handed down from one generation to another, because no one knew how to recognize, embrace, and heal it. It's not your fault, nor is it their fault. . . . The suffering of the parent is the suffering of the child. Looking deeply is a chance to transform and heal this suffering and stop the cycle." So many times in the zendo I'd chanted it: "All my ancient twisted karma . . . I now fully avow."

What was the legacy we were passing on to you, Sierra? How could we heal it best we could?

When I was five months pregnant, I flew back to California. I went shopping for a wine-red maternity wedding dress for our ceremony at Green Gulch Zen Center. Your dad created a flip-book for the invitation—a black-and-white image of my hand entering from one side of the frame, while his hand entered from the other. At the end of the book, the hands were joined.

On Christmas morning, your dad made me a cup of raspberry leaf tea—good for the uterus, I'd read—and brought it to me in bed. Then he went to the closet and pulled out a pile of wrapped presents. "They're mainly for Sprout. I got a little carried away."

The note on the first package said, "Welcome to a strange, strange world." Inside was a goofy little rattle shaped like an elf.

The next two packages I opened contained tiny T-shirts. "You know these won't fit her for five or six months, right?"

He looked stunned. "You mean she'll be tinier than *that*?"

Next, I unwrapped a clear plastic Super Ball with tiny dolphins embedded in the center, leaping through the waves. "They remind me of her," he said. "So joyful, so playful, so brave. She's the culmination of so much. She makes up for all our mistakes."

"She heals everything." I hugged him. "All the ways we have hurt each other are erased by this one huge thing we are doing right."

Every time I blow my nose, the tissue comes away red with blood. That's normal, my new midwife, Johanna, tells me, when I visit her in her home office in San Francisco. Apparently, all my mucus membranes are swollen and extra sensitive. There's almost double the blood volume coursing through me, plus I'm hauling around thirty extra pounds of baby, placenta, amniotic fluid, blood, and fat. My skin is like a drum over the twitching mound of my belly. The arches of my feet ache. The flesh under my left armpit is bulging out in an old-lady wad—Johanna tells me there is mammary tissue there that is swelling, along with my breasts, as the pregnancy progresses. She asks me, seriously, if I have an extra nipple.

"Some women have them," she says. "Sometimes they even have a whole line of nipples, extending up into the armpit."

I was six months pregnant, and my armpit was preparing to nurse my baby, like a dog preparing to nurse a litter? *I can't believe how animal this whole experience is. After the appointment, when I come home and do yoga, I find myself prowling around the room on my hands and knees, roaring and snarling. I rock and wriggle and moan. I growl and bark.*

After our wedding, your dad and I moved in together. We found a house in a sheltered, wooded valley about ten minutes north of the Golden Gate Bridge. In the grassy backyard was a play structure with a corkscrew slide we imagined you squealing down.

We painted our bedroom yellow and your room pale lavender. We moved in our hodgepodge of possessions—a hand-me-down couch from his parents, my king-size bed, his television. A wooden coffee table made by his mother's father and a small rug my parents had picked up when they were stationed in Korea. A clutter of mismatched forks and knives inherited from various roommates. A muffin tin and a blender we had been given as wedding presents.

I knew that this stage of pregnancy was called the nesting phase, and my hormones were screaming at me to gather together my twigs: diaper tables, rakes, breast pumps, fire alarms, a sponge mop and bucket. I felt as if I were preparing my life for a new arrival the way a pujari at an Indian temple prepares the altar for a ritual.

But pregnancy wasn't just preparation, it was an experience in itself. Sitting on a pile of crates at the Home Depot, resting my aching feet while your dad rounded up garden hoses and shower curtains, I remembered a meditation retreat I had done years earlier with Thich Nhat Hanh at his monastery in the south of France. I was doing walking meditation along a path that wound by a field of sunflowers into a wood when I passed a small wooden sign: "You have already arrived."

You were not in the future, Sierra. You were already here. I knew when you slept and when you woke up. I sensed your personality— bright, curious, active, playful.

You had already arrived.

Seven and a half months pregnant.

Sprout is stronger every day. I can't even call her Sprout anymore—she is Sierra to me now. She has a new move—she reaches out with her feet deep into my right side while simultaneously burrowing her head down toward my crotch. I can feel her just beneath the surface of my skin—squirming, kicking, rolling, pressing out as if she wants to break through the surface.

My belly juts out preposterously over my feet. "You look like a building by Frank Lloyd Wright," her daddy says.

He puts his face up against my navel and croons, "Who's your daddy? Who's your daddy?"

Sierra kicks him in the nose.

In April, a month before my due date, our midwife, Johanna, came to our house to inspect the room for our home birth.

Johanna was a tiny German woman, both stern and warm—a cross between an earth goddess and a drill sergeant. She had delivered over a hundred babies. I could feel my whole body relax every time I saw her—*Thank God, finally, someone who knows what's going on here.*

"You could probably do most of your labor outside if you want," she told me, looking around our yard, bright with daffodils and irises. "But it's probably not warm enough to actually give birth out here."

Letting go of my hopes of giving birth under a redwood tree, like a deer, I followed her and your dad back into my bedroom.

We all sat down on the bed, and Johanna explained the stages of labor to us, from the early "prodromal" stage—"Sounds like something to do with camels," quipped your dad—to the "ring of fire" at the end.

"If early labor comes in the evening, I may just tell you to have a beer and go to bed," she told me.

"That's never going to happen. Anne doesn't drink beer even when she isn't pregnant," said your dad. "*I'll* have a beer, though!"

"And if the early labor starts in the morning, then—" Johanna continued.

"Then I've got all day to drink!" He leaned over, put his face against my belly, and told you, "When you're born, Daddy's going to be drunk, drunk, drunk."

Johanna pulled out some educational props: a plastic model of a pelvis; a baby doll whose arms and legs snap into a fetal position; a stuffed placenta and cord, trailing a web of amniotic sac. She slipped the baby's head in the ankle-piece of a cut-off sock to show how the cervix dilates and effaces in preparation for labor and delivery.

How was it, I wondered, that in all the pages and pages of Buddhist and yogic texts, there was so little about this miraculous passage, this incredible practice of giving birth, of arriving in life? Most of the texts were, of course, written by men—monastic men, at that. There is a lot about death, and instructions to the dying on how not to get born again. But as far as I knew, there were no instructions given on how to bring new life into the world, and how that can lead to awakening.

"Your baby is riding low in your pelvis," Johanna told me after my exam. "That's perfectly normal. It's good—she knows where she is going."

All was just as it should be, she said: my cervix was closed but soft and ripe; there was plenty of space all around it for a baby's head.

"Perfect," she repeated. "Perfect."

When I left the room, I heard her say something softly to your dad. Later that day, he repeated it to me: "I have such a good feeling about this birth. I hardly ever have such a good feeling," she had whispered to him. "But she shouldn't hear this. I'm not supposed to say such things."

Eight months pregnant.

I no longer want the angular forms of traditional yoga—the military precision, the silver stars shining on the shoulder of my uniform. I want to move into the deep territory of dreams, wild and untidy like the grass growing outside my window. I want both my yoga and my life to be a celebration of the sacred feminine, a celebration of flesh and spirit both—a way to bow down to each moment. So that my meditations, my movements, my words, and my life sing of the mystery of birth and death.

Monks think of incarnation as suffering, a trap. It's better to free yourself from this cycle of birth and death, they say. Get off that spinning wheel of samsara. But this little life coming through—this is no trap! She is coming in full of enthusiasm. Despite all the suffering in the world, she is coming in bright with hope. She wants to be born. And I cannot embrace any spirituality that thinks of this as a bad thing. This tethering of spirit to incarnation is not a trap. It is a weaving into the divine dance. It is a celebration. It is a song.

As you got bigger, my yoga practice changed. Everything in my practice had to be geared toward the marathon of labor that lay ahead.

I focused on deep squats to open my hips and pelvis. I practiced *mula bhanda*—drawing in and releasing the muscles of my pelvic floor and perineum again and again. My attention returned again and again to that vessel of my pelvis where you were rolling—preparing to be born but already clearly, fully incarnate. I was preparing the great mobilization of energy in my lower chakras, what the Chinese call the *tan tien* and the Japanese the *hara*.

Giving birth, I could feel, was not about drawing the energy upward, as in the classical yoga models developed by generations of men—the energy ascending up through the chakras to the third eye, out the crown of the head, and beyond. Rather, it was an organic inward drawing of the power downward and into the low belly. It was an awakening of that sweet inner source of power, of sensuality, of sexuality, of life itself.

When I showered after yoga, I rubbed my nipples with a rough washcloth as Johanna had instructed, toughening them up to prepare for your mouth.

A month before you were due, my mother—your Granny—sent me a care package containing a soft white chenille towel and washcloth with an embroidered pink flower. On the phone she told me that it had belonged to her own mother. "All through my childhood, these were hanging in our bathroom, so they are entwined with happy memories for me. I want you to use them to bathe your baby."

I made a list of the things I still needed: *Diaper bag. Onesies. Booties. Diaper pail.* It reminded me of the lists I'd made before an eight-month trip to India a few years earlier: *Grapefruit seed extract for digestive disturbances. Inflatable meditation cushion.* I remembered how prepared I had felt as I loaded my backpack and consulted my guidebook, clinging to the illusion that I knew what my trip would be like—and how, when I got to India, it felt as if the top of my head had been blown right off. As I wandered down an alley filled with cows and rickshaws, utterly lost, my grapefruit seed extract was no help at all.

As we browsed the aisles at the baby store, I told myself how glad I would be, in a few weeks, that we had bought that blue gingham-checked diaper bag with the side flap that pulls out and makes a little clean surface to change your baby on. As I pondered the relative advantages of bureau-top versus shelf-top diaper tables, I told myself that we were preparing an altar—except that altars don't have to be covered in fitted rubber sheets so the Buddha doesn't poop on them.

Your dad insisted on buying a small electric baby wipe warmer. "I don't want her little bottom to be cold."

"Could we also use it for heating up tortillas?" I asked.

He turned to his mother—your Grandma Joan—for support. "Is this ridiculous?"

"Yes," she said emphatically.

But then, your Grandma Joan thought *all* this shopping was ridiculous. When she gave birth, apparently, everything was much simpler. "Caps?" she snorted as I lifted up a tiny pink knitted one.

"I didn't have any caps for my babies! What is this nonsense?"

When I selected a cozy, glider-style rocking chair with a cheerful pattern of stars and moons, she told me that all that machinery underneath it made it look like a medical instrument.

"It's safer than the old style with wooden rockers," your dad told her.

"No one has ever gotten injured by a rocking chair," she informed us. "In the whole history of the world."

Eight and a half months pregnant.

I can feel that all systems are go—Sierra is full term and could arrive any time. It's like waiting for a big date, or for Christmas when I was a child.

I am aware that Sierra is done—like cookies that are done baking. Although she will not really be done until she is ready to emerge, she is viable, she is just below the surface of my skin, a fully formed baby. The impulse is so strong to take her out now and hold her in my arms!

Ten days before my due date I went to see Johanna.

We mainly just chatted—there was not much more to do at this point, she told me. My urine tests were normal. My blood pressure was normal. "The baby has dropped—her head is engaged in the pelvis. She's a little baby—probably only six pounds now, probably no more than seven when she is born."

"Should I be eating more?"

"No, there's nothing to worry about."

There was so much squirming going on inside me I could hardly listen to Johanna. A foot jabbed out under my right rib; a lopsided dome rose to the right of my belly button. My belly hardened, then softened.

"I don't think you'll go past your due date," Johanna said. "You're not that kind of person. Some people need a little extra time to do everything. You do things on deadline."

Afterward, as your dad was driving me home, a song came on the radio. "Unbreak my heart," the singer wailed. "Uncry these tears . . ." He took my hand.

"I feel like that is what we have done," he told me.

One week before due date.

Sierra is asleep inside me now. Earlier she was squirming, poking uncomfortably—extending one foot, then another. Bursting with life. It is so mysterious—so utterly ordinary yet so completely incomprehensible—that this baby grew from one tiny sperm, one tiny egg.

We walk around in the midst of this incredible, throbbing mystery—the huge Don't-Know at the center of our lives—and act like it's not even there, like we know what we're doing here.

I just opened Peter Matthiessen's book Nine-Headed Dragon River *and read the quote from the fourteenth-century Zen master Dogen: "This life of one day is a life to rejoice in. Because of this, even though you live for just one day, if you can be awakened to the truth, that one day is vastly superior to an eternal life."*

Two days later, everything ended.

Oh, Sierra. I thought we would have so much more time. But I want you to know this: You changed our lives. And the fact that yours was short does not make it less precious.

Love,
Mommy

Into the Heart of Sorrow

· · · · ·

ON A COOL, brilliant summer morning, high thunderclouds just gathering over distant peaks, my husband and I hiked into the Desolation Wilderness to scatter our baby daughter's ashes.

His family owned a tiny cabin on Echo Lake, high in the Sierra Nevada mountains, where we had been going for vacations together for almost twenty years. His grandfather built the cabin as a refuge when he came back from World War I: no electricity, a woodstove for heat, propane for cooking, kerosene lamps. The only access was by boat. We had gone there for a week to grieve and heal: nights a requiem of stars and wind and woodsmoke; days of chilly sun and wildflowers.

On our fourth day there, we tucked into my daypack the little urn of Sierra's ashes, a ceramic jar painted with forget-me-nots that we had gotten for a wedding present. We rowed our canoe across Echo Lake and hiked for an hour into the pine forest. We climbed over a rocky ridge to a tiny, deserted lake set in a basin of mountains, with snowy peaks and blue sky reflected in its dark waters. At one end, a waterfall rushed in, a ribbon of foaming white. This is where we wanted Sierra's body to return to the earth.

Sierra had died while she was still inside me, a few days before she was due to be born. Doctors induced labor, and I gave birth to her body early on the morning of Mother's Day. My midwife washed her, dressed her, and brought her to me and my husband, wrapped in a soft blue blanket. She had a round face; dark brown hair; a sweet, sad mouth; the delicate, long-fingered hands of an artist. Her eyes were shut, as if she were taking a nap.

No one could tell us why Sierra had died. Her body was in perfect condition, with no sign of any problem whatsoever. An autopsy revealed a healthy placenta, a healthy umbilical cord, a healthy baby. It was possible, the obstetrician said, that her umbilical cord had somehow become pinched as she dropped into position for birth, cutting off the flow of oxygen. But in the end, all anyone could offer us were statistics: that about one in 250 pregnancies ends in a full-term stillbirth. And that about half the time, no one can figure out what went wrong.

In Buddhist teachings, the first noble truth is that life inevitably holds suffering. In a world where everything that exists is impermanent, there's no way to escape the eventual loss of what we hold most dear.

To remind themselves of this inexorable truth, yogis in India meditate in cremation grounds, covering their bodies with ashes as they watch corpses burn. Tibetan monks meditate in charnel grounds, watching bodies decay in front of them, vultures pecking out the eyes.

Spiritual practice can also lull us into the illusion that we are safe from suffering: do your daily yoga, and you and those you love will never get sick; meditate every morning, and you will keep the dogs of grief at bay. When asked what the greatest mystery of all was, the god Krishna said this: That people see other people dying all around them, and yet no one believes that it will happen to them.

But sooner or later loss will find you. You don't have to go to a charnel ground to see impermanence. Just gaze at the faces of your friends and family.

If you quarrel with your beloved, look into their eyes, I once heard Thich Nhat Hanh say. Picture both of you in a hundred and fifty years. Then you will know what to do.

My husband had taken a picture of me doing yoga on our patio just two days before Sierra died. I'm sitting on my mat with my legs stretched wide, wearing maternity leggings and a purple T-shirt stretched snug over my bulging belly. I am reaching toward the camera, my arms wide as though I want to embrace the whole world. I am laughing. I look unbelievably happy.

I had done yoga daily throughout my pregnancy. I'd had no

morning sickness, no back pain, no swollen feet, no varicose veins. It felt natural to lift up into an elbow balance at five months or to flow through a modified sun salutation at eight and a half, legs spread wide to make room for my baby.

I modified every pose to serve the child kicking and squirming inside me. My practice became softer, gentler, more meditative; my awareness spiraled deep inside, centering on the warm glow in my heart and belly. With every posture, I felt as if I were bowing down in awe before the mysterious power of life.

In classic yogic thought, the only way to achieve lasting happiness is to break our attachment to the world of flesh and bones—to cease chasing after the taste of strawberries, the smell of roses, the touch of a lover's mouth on the skin at the base of the neck. All these things will die and rot, the yogis remind us; the body is just a temporary vehicle, discarded like worn-out clothes when the spirit moves on. We should seek our refuge in a larger Self, beyond our personal identities, cravings, fears, and dreams.

But as I sat in meditation, hands cupping my belly, I knew that once you've felt that hurricane of life swelling up from nowhere inside your womb, you can't speak the same way about detachment from the world. Nor would you want to.

Following an impulse I couldn't quite name, I temporarily retired the Buddha statue from my altar. Driving home in the pouring rain from a daylong meditation retreat, I stopped at a garage sale in my neighborhood and spotted a statue of Kuan Yin, the graceful Buddhist goddess of compassion, her arms outstretched in blessing. Sierra wants this, I thought, and I took it home to her room, where it sat overlooking the car seat and bassinet that awaited her arrival.

My husband and I spent the last day of Sierra's life getting ready for her birth.

I met with a pediatrician to discuss new-baby care. I stopped by a used baby store to select a secondhand crib. "You're so full of energy!" the woman behind the counter said. "I wouldn't be surprised if you had your baby tonight."

I had already rounded up the home birth supplies my midwife

had ordered: cord clamps, sterile gloves, plastic king-size sheets, hydrogen peroxide, hot water bottle, cotton balls, olive oil, sanitary pads, sitz-bath herbs. I planned to labor in our garden, attended by lavender, irises, hummingbirds, and quail. I planned to deliver in our bedroom, with the view of the giant eucalyptus through the window. "The room you give birth in," my midwife told me, "will forever be a little piece of heaven."

When I came back from shopping, my husband and I lay on the bed and played our favorite game: Watch Anne's Belly. My skin rippled and bulged like a sheet pulled over a kitten. Little knobs—feet? hands? knees?—cruised the surface. Wherever we pressed our hands, we were met with eager pokes of curiosity and greeting.

We marveled at how much we already loved a person whose face we had never seen. We felt as if we knew her. Her rhythms were simple, predictable, unencumbered by intellect: she loved to play when her dad tapped my belly; she perked up when I ate a cookie; she fell asleep during yoga, rocked by the gentle sway of my body.

As the day went on, I noticed that Sierra was not moving as much as she usually did. But I wasn't worried. I'd heard that babies move less once their head is engaged in the pelvis. And I'd never heard of something going wrong this close to the birth.

At home that night, I cooed over the new crib, which my husband had assembled in Sierra's bedroom. Then I curled up in our bed and put my hands on my belly to talk to her. "Are you still sleeping, sweetheart?" I asked. "Say hello to mommy." Under my hand, I felt a little hand lift and move against mine, in a feeble but unmistakable salutation.

I thought it was a sleepy hello. It didn't occur to me that she might be summoning the last bit of her energy to say goodbye.

I was doing my morning yoga when I first suspected that something had gone wrong.

I was lying on my side on my yoga mat on our patio, gently stretching in the pale gold sun. Just a few more days, I was thinking. Just a few more days until I can hold her in my arms.

It wasn't unusual for Sierra to sleep through my yoga practice.

But it struck me that I hadn't felt her move since I woke up. I put my hand on my belly, pressed gently on a little knee.

It didn't push back.

An hour later, I was in the hospital, lying on an examining table, a lab technician sliding a transducer back and forth through the cold jelly on my abdomen. The doctor peered at the ultrasound screen.

"There's no evidence of movement," he said. He looked at the screen, not at me. "I can't find a heartbeat." Through my fog of terror, it took me a while to understand what he was saying. I kept hoping he meant something else.

I sat on the table and shuddered, silent, for the last minutes it took my husband to get to the hospital. He burst into the examining room, his face wrenched with fear and hope. That's when I finally said it: "Our baby's dead."

We clung to each other and wailed.

A baby who is dead must still be born.

The labor and delivery room was on the fifteenth floor of the hospital. My husband told me it had a view of trees and the ocean; I couldn't see them because I had cried my contact lenses out of my eyes.

The doctor painted my cervix with misoprosotol to start it dilating. The induced contractions came on fast and hard, with a drugged intensity—every two minutes a deep convulsion of pain, a vice tightening in my belly.

As soon as the epidural kicked in I went numb from the waist down. An IV in my arm dripped Pitocin to keep my contractions coming; fentanyl, to help me relax.

I labored all night, drugged, in the dark, my legs numb weights on the table, the contractions faint sensations, a physical report from a distant country. A catheter tube dangled between my legs; a rubber cuff on my arm swelled to take my blood pressure automatically every fifteen minutes. My husband sat in the chair beside me, intermittently holding my hand.

By dawn I was fully dilated. A nurse propped me up with my

feet in stirrups, an electronic contraction monitor strapped to my belly. "I don't know how I am going to get through this," I told my midwife, Johanna. She said, "You will just have to gather up the pieces of your heart in your two hands and hold them."

"Push," the nurse and the midwife chanted. "Push, push, push, push, push—stop. Now push. Push, push, push . . ." I held my breath, drew my belly in hard, reached my hands to the sky for strength, as in a yoga pose. I kept my eyes closed. I didn't want to see what was happening.

Afterward, my husband told me, "I watched her come out. She was covered in water and blood. The cord was amazing: thick and strong and dark and coiled. I kept hoping they would say they had made a mistake, it was a medical miracle, she'd just been in some sort of neonatal coma. I was still hoping that when she came out, she would start to cry."

In the dreadful silence afterward—with no baby crying—the doctor who had delivered her carried her body away, without showing her to me. Johanna followed them out.

What seemed like a long, long time later, Johanna came back to the room without her.

"Anne, they did an examination. There is nothing wrong with her," she said, as if that would make me feel better. *Nothing wrong. Except she is not alive.* "She is a beautiful little girl. Shall I bring her to you?"

I shook my head. I was afraid it would hurt too much to bear.

"Would you like us to take a picture of her for your baby book?" asked a nurse.

I shook my head again. I wanted to remember her as she was—a joyful dolphin, kicking and surfing the waves inside me.

They waited, and eventually I agreed. Johanna brought Sierra to our room. She put a sign on the door: Do Not Disturb Under Any Circumstances. My husband took our baby in his arms and placed her in my lap.

She was dressed in a baby-blue onesie and a little blue cap—not the clothes we had picked out for her. She had a round, round face, bruised from her passage through the birth canal. She had a delicate rosebud of a mouth. She had dark hair like mine and hands with long, long fingers like her dad's. She had perfect shells of ears. She looked like she was asleep.

I couldn't believe that this was the baby who had been kicking inside me. I couldn't believe that I was not still pregnant, waiting for her to arrive.

I don't remember if I stroked her hair. I don't remember if I kissed her forehead. I do remember that I said, "I love you." At least, I hope I said that.

After a few more minutes, her dad put her back in the bassinet in the corner. He tucked a little blanket up over her, as if to keep her warm.

I lay on my bed in stunned silence for a long, long time while my husband fell asleep on the chair beside me.

An hour or so later, a nurse arrived to take Sierra's body away for the autopsy. She picked her up quietly, not wanting to wake me up.

But through half-open eyes I watched her walk out the door. I turned over to watch my baby daughter being carried away.

I called out softly, "Goodbye."

We came home from the hospital without Sierra, leaving her body behind in the hospital morgue. In the middle of all the grief and rage and horror and disbelief—that persistent feeling that the universe had made a terrible error, that I'd somehow been sent somebody else's life and that my own wonderful life was actually waiting for me somewhere, if only I knew who to call—in the midst of all that, I was stunned at how viscerally, physically I missed her. My belly was shriveled and empty, like a deflated balloon. I was bleeding as if I had had a baby, but there was no baby, and my body did not understand where she was.

They forgot to remind me in the hospital that my milk would come in. My breasts were swollen with milk. I was stunned when I looked in the mirror and saw them, immense and blindly eager. To stop the milk, Johanna came to the house and bound them tightly to my chest.

She told me to sip sage tea, a bitter brew that tasted like an evergreen forest, but I wasn't allowed to drink more than two cups of liquid a day. I lay on the couch with icepacks piled on my chest, thirsty and cold and heartbroken.

I asked my best friend to call the hospital to find out if I could hold Sierra again before the cremation. But they told her that the autopsy had been very thorough and that Sierra was "not viewable."

That night I dreamed that her body had been brought to me in a cardboard box, all in pieces, and I was trying to put her back together again.

A friend who is a woodworker built us a tiny redwood casket, held together with wooden pegs instead of nails, so it would burn completely. He carved three intersecting circles on the lid, a traditional Japanese symbol of Buddhism's Three Treasures: the Buddha, the awakened heart; the Dharma, the path of truth; and the Sangha, the loving community. My husband took the casket into his workroom and slowly, painstakingly outlined the carving with black paint, so it stood out like a brand.

The crematorium was a huge, industrial hangar: unpainted cinderblock walls, gritty cement floor, a row of steel ovens the size of garages. The oven we'd been assigned was already roaring because they have to be preheated; it was like standing next to a jet about to take off. The huge rolling steel doors were plastered with orange signs: "Danger! Hot!"

We were met there by Wendy and Fu, the two women Zen priests who had performed our wedding at Green Gulch Zen Center. They set up a small altar outside the mouth of the oven, with flowers and a redwood seed and a statue of the Jizo Bodhisattva, the guardian of children who have died. They lit incense and chanted while my husband and I wept.

Then he and I put our hands on Sierra's casket and told her how much we loved her and how much joy she had brought us.

"You have been such a happy, bright spirit," I said. "I'll see you in everything happy and bright for the rest of my life." My husband traced the entwined spirals on the casket lid.

"This is me," he said. "This is your mommy. And this is you. And this"—tracing the big circle around the outside—"is love. You will always be part of our family."

Then my husband and I stepped inside the railing, up to a panel of lights and buttons and dials next to the oven door. I pushed the green button labeled "Door Open." The steel door rolled up to a blast of heat and an orange glow. A man in a plexiglass safety mask and heat-blocking mittens picked up the casket and placed it in the oven.

We all began to chant the *Heart Sutra*: "Form is emptiness, emptiness is form. Form is not other than emptiness, emptiness not other than form." It's Buddhism's fundamental creed, a statement of impermanence and interdependence: All forms are temporary, and nothing is separate from anything else. Clouds become rain, water is sucked up by plants, plants are eaten by people, people disintegrate back into water and dirt. Things that seem separate dissolve into one another and disappear.

The chant is a somber, slow, monotone drone: "Therefore in emptiness there is neither form, nor feelings, nor perceptions, nor mental formations, nor consciousness. No eyes, or ears, or nose, or tongue, or body, or mind. No form, no sound, no smell, no taste, no touch." I had forgotten to close the oven door. The attendant touched a button, and the great steel doors rolled down.

The end of the chant is a mantra in Pali, the vernacular language of India at the time of the Buddha: "*Gate, gate, paragate, parasamgate, bodhi svaha* . . . Gone, gone, all gone beyond, gone beyond the beyond; hail the goer."

We chanted the *Heart Sutra* over and over as Sierra burned. Then, at my request, we changed to a different kind of chant. "You are my sunshine," we sang, "my only sunshine. You make me happy when skies are gray . . ."

She was just a baby, after all; I couldn't bear the thought of sending her off into the great beyond with only monastic texts to sing her to sleep. We sang "Rock-a-Bye Baby," and "Row, Row, Row Your Boat," and "Yellow Submarine," and "Frére Jacques," and "Itsy Bitsy Spider."

This is an image I will never forget: the Zen priest, Fu, in her black robes and shaved head, with one hand on her hip and the other arm arced like a spout, singing "I'm a Little Teapot"—"just tip me over and pour me out"—as the crematorium oven roared behind her.

. . .

There's a Zen story about an enlightened master weeping at the death of his baby son. His disciples came to him, bewildered. "Master," they said, "why do you weep? I thought you told us that this world was an illusion."

"Yes," the teacher replied. "And the death of a child is the saddest illusion of all."

I used to think that spiritual practice would be a way of lessening the pain of grief—that I could escape into some Self, some detached witness consciousness that is beyond the world, from which I would watch my life dispassionately, like a movie I could turn off at any moment.

But, in fact, we are attached to life by a tie as primal as the umbilical cord, thick and dark and coiled and throbbing with blood. Now I know that I would never want to be so detached, so cut off from that primal pulse, that I did not mourn my daughter's death.

And I no longer even believe that's what the yogis meant—that we should use practice as a kind of spiritual epidural to anesthetize us from the pain of our lives.

For me, as it turned out, practice was not a way of stepping out of the pain but a way of walking right straight into it, of feeling it fully, of letting it rip through my body and heart. And this is how I want my practice to be. This is where I want to practice: not just on a cushion in a temple smelling of sandalwood, not just on a synthetic mat in a mirror-walled studio, but in every moment of this animal body, oozing blood, tears, and mother's milk.

"Are you doing your yoga?" my friends would ask, in the weeks after Sierra died. "Are you doing your meditation?"

I didn't know whether to answer "No, not at all" or "Yes, all the time."

The truth is that I was spending very little time on the mat. There's nothing like death to put an asana practice in perspective. In the face of unimaginable loss, I could derive little comfort from the perfection of my Triangle Pose.

But my years of practice had given me one simple gift: the power of the intention to rest in the moment with what is happening, breath by breath. For years I've asked myself, through meditation and yoga, to rest in sensation: to hold an intense pose and feel the burn of the muscles without moving away from it, to sit without moving in the meditation hall as waves of anger or fear or boredom crashed over me. Now I could use this training to receive the grief welling up inside me—and let it tear on through me.

For me, grief wasn't a constant pain; it came in vast, convulsing contractions, like labor. A florist's truck would arrive with another bouquet of flowers, the delivery man averting his eyes as he handed them over, escaping as fast as he could because he knew by now that they didn't mean good news. I'd look at that bunch of roses or amaryllis or orchids, exquisite, sweet-scented. I'd look at my whole house filling up with flowers in glass vases, already starting to die, instead of with smelly diapers and the sound of a baby crying. I'd remember the unbearable beauty of Sierra's face and her tiny curled hands. And I'd want to smash the vase of flowers against the wall.

So I'd let in that wave of pain—even though it was so intense I thought it would split me in two—because I learned that, like vomiting, it was better to let it happen than to try to avoid it. I found that I could feel that, breath by breath—one breath at a time—it was bearable. Then the wave would pass, and I'd be lying on the beach, gasping and exhausted, but more alive than before.

"Look deeply, and you will see that you are weeping for that which has been your delight," writes the poet Kahlil Gibran. In those wrenching moments I'd see that grief and joy are inextricably intertwined. My sorrow was a way of touching a truth: that the world is both fleeting and infinitely precious. The Zen master Issa wrote this poem after the death of his child: "Dew evaporates, and all the world is dew; so dear, so refreshing, so fleeting."

I once heard Thich Nhat Hanh say, "I would not want to live in a place where there is no suffering, because suffering breeds compassion." Yes, our grief is magnified by the way we cling to things that are impermanent by nature. But grief also reveals the glorious truth that we are woven into the fabric of the world, that we are linked to everything that is.

In the wake of Sierra's death, I discovered this: I don't believe my true Self is outside the world. I believe it is part of it. I believe my true Self shines in the apple trees, in the hummingbirds, in my baby's body, in the blood and sweat of childbirth, in the tears that come when I lose someone I love. It shines in the compassion that springs forth in a human heart in the presence of pain, as naturally as a mother's milk lets down when a baby cries.

For my spiritual practice, I don't want to step away from the world. I want to step closer, take it in my arms, cradle it close to my heart, like a mother holding her child. My loss is one little drop in a world full of pain. Around the world the week that Sierra died, human beings were facing unimaginable suffering. Bombs were falling on Kosovo. Mothers and fathers were mourning their lost children in Bosnia, in Rwanda, in Littleton, Colorado. They were mourning their children blown apart by bombs, drowned in flooded rivers, shot in gang warfare, wasted away on drugs.

In the weeks and years after Sierra's death, I heard the stories of countless grieving parents. I heard of babies who lived a few hours and died in their mother's arms. I heard of babies who stopped breathing in their cribs, and no one ever knew why. I heard of children taken by cancer, by car wrecks, by murder.

Every one of us has faced or will face terrible losses in our lives. Our dreams will shatter, our loved ones will die, our bodies will slowly fall apart. The question for me is this: Can I allow my practice to take me right into the heart of this sorrow, to feel the pain and the grief, and by going through it open into something larger?

My first time out in the world after Sierra's delivery, I pushed my cart numbly through Whole Foods, shopping for dinner: salad greens, avocados, tomatoes.

I couldn't imagine cooking. I pushed the cart to the deli counter, figuring I'd pick up something premade: some poached salmon, maybe. A pasta salad.

Aurelio, the young man behind the counter, greeted me cheerfully. Throughout my pregnancy he'd been scooping me up mountains of pasta salad, piles of orzo, buckets of teriyaki chicken wings, never commenting on my voracious appetite and ever-changing cravings.

He glanced down at my now-flat belly, then at the empty top

basket of my shopping cart. "How's your baby?" he asked with a big grin.

I stared at him. This was the first time I'd gotten this question, which I would get countless times again. I couldn't think of anything polite to say. "She's dead."

We stared at each other for a moment.

"She died," I said again, and burst into tears. I walked away, leaving the cart where it was, the groceries still in it. I drove home, crying.

My husband ordered Chinese takeout for dinner.

Two days later, I went back to the store. I went to the counter. Aurelio eyed me warily.

"I'm so sorry for walking away like that," I told him. "It was just too much for me."

"I know." He looked at me over the glass case. "It happened to my wife too. Just a year ago. Our baby died when she was a week old."

"Oh—I'm so sorry."

"My wife didn't get out of bed for a month. She didn't leave the house for three months. I know exactly how you feel. It's the worst thing in the world."

"I'm so sorry," I said again. Then, "What was your baby's name?"

His eyes lit up. "Angelo." I could tell how good it felt to say the name, to have his son alive in the space between us, just for a moment.

"Angelo," I repeated. "It's a beautiful name. I'm sure he was a beautiful baby."

"Yes." He looked down at the deli case. "What can I get you today?"

A new baby, one for each of us. A mended heart. Hope for the future. "A pint of caprese salad."

He gave me the salad with a sad smile. "I hope your day goes okay. Hang in there."

"You too," I told him. "You too."

Everywhere I went I saw babies. But everywhere I went, too, I heard stories of death, of loss. On the news, refugee children starved by the hundreds, the thousands. As I drove over the winding road from my house to Muir Beach, I passed a roadside altar, covered with flowers, where some mother's teenage girl drove her car off the edge of a cliff.

I looked at the eyes of the people I met—the checkout clerk at CVS. The bank teller. What tragedies had they lived through? What stories of loss, of heartbreak, did they carry with them?

How did we human beings get up every morning, put on our shoes, and head out the door, when the world was in flames all around us?

Six weeks after Sierra died, we met with the doctor to discuss the results of her autopsy.

"Unfortunately, we don't have any answers for you," she told us. "The baby was completely normal. The cord was normal. The placenta was normal as well. In these cases, all we can assume is that there might have been what we call a cord accident. Somehow, she got into a position where her body cut off the flow of circulation through the umbilical cord."

There's a classic meditation in Buddhism where you're instructed to meditate on the thirty-seven parts of the body: head hair, body hair, nails, skin, teeth . . . It's supposed to bring about detachment. I looked down at the sheaf of papers she had handed me and flipped through it, wincing at the intimate, graphic account of my baby's body: her brain, her lungs, her liver, her colon, her genitals, her spine. All laid bare by the coroner's knife. All of them normal—or, in the words of the autopsy report, "grossly unremarkable."

We asked our doctor about our chances for another pregnancy.

"Having a stillbirth once does not increase your likelihood of having one again." She laid out all the things the doctors could do next time around to support a healthy pregnancy and delivery. The words flowed by me: "triple screen," "quadruple screen," "stress testing . . ."

"With an amniocentesis we can test for over fifteen hundred genetic and chromosomal disorders," she told me brightly.

If this was supposed to reassure me, it didn't work. On the screen of my mind were playing thousands of things that I hadn't known could go wrong. Things that hadn't gone wrong with Sierra—but might with a future baby.

That night my husband left for a business trip, and I was alone in the house. I felt sad that Sierra's ashes were all alone in her empty bedroom. I got the jar and brought it to bed with me. I held it in my arms, and kissed the lid, and cried. "I love you," I said to the jar. I thought: *You are truly flipping out. You are a crazy lady, alone in the house, talking to her dead baby's ashes.*

I got up and carried them out to the living room and set them on the mantle, next to my wedding bouquet of dried roses.

I walked back in to her empty bedroom and looked around. A thin film of dust had already settled over the floor.

I am going to turn this into a beautiful meditation room.

It is all I can do: turn everything that comes into love and awakening. I will be an alchemist, turning loss into awakening and love. I will make her little nursery into a shrine to love, to beauty, to the fragility and beauty of life. I will turn my heart into a beehive, making honey from all those dead flowers.

Three weeks after Sierra died, I did yoga on our patio again. Above my mat, two wren tits were pecking in the birdfeeder hung in the branches of our apple tree. A hummingbird darted in and out of the bottlebrush.

I made my way slowly through the poses, as if I were walking through an earthquake-damaged house, lovingly assessing the damage. Afterward I lay on my back in Corpse Pose, watching a blue jay spray a shower of seeds to the ground. Looking at the beauty around me, I felt as if I were picnicking on the edge of an abyss into which every now and then someone I loved would silently tumble.

Lying there, I saw that I had two possible responses to Sierra's death. One was to contract in terror, to try to cling more closely to what is precious, wrap my hand tight around it, never let it go. An ultimately futile gesture, since it would all inevitably slip away.

The other response would be to cherish what was precious, breath by breath, with an open hand, knowing it could be snatched away at any moment and that it would ultimately be gone forever. To cherish each moment, knowing that every day is a gift and a blessing, that it may be the last.

The yogis had it right: The world is impermanent. But the world is also a sacred blessing. To hold both of those truths in our hearts at the same time is the razor's edge of practice.

Yes, there is tremendous grief in Sierra's loss. I will never stop missing her; I will carry her in my heart for the rest of my life.

But despite all the sorrow, what I have ultimately been left with is a sense of joy, of the precious miracle of incarnation. Of the way love is not bound by time and space. Of how the value of a life has nothing to do with how long it lasts. And of how the rippling effect of one life goes on and on, long after a person is gone. Sierra is not with me in her physical form, and I am so sorry. I miss her deeply. But she is definitely still here.

She is here in the way her dad and I wrap our arms around each other in the night or the way one of us says "Drive carefully" as the other leaves on an errand. She is with me in the way my heart softens when I see someone suffer. I see her in everything delicate and precious: a baby quail, the broken shell of a snail, a hummingbird flitting through the spray of a garden hose.

And although I would give back all these lessons in a second to have Sierra with me in physical form again, I see that what she has left is a real and lasting legacy. And ultimately, it's the only way any of us live on: in the way the world is different for our having been here.

We did convert Sierra's nursery into a meditation room. In the corner I hung a mobile of paper cranes made by three of her cousins to commemorate her death. I set up a little altar covered in Indian silk, with the statue of Kuan Yin and an incense burner made from the urn we used to hold her ashes. On the altar, in a white frame painted with morning glories, I placed Sierra's tiny, delicate footprints: tracks in purple ink on a piece of paper, already starting to fade.

And so, on that bright summer day, we scattered Sierra's ashes. We carried her little urn down to the base of the waterfall, to the spot where the stream poured into the lake. Her dad reminded me of what one Zen master said when he was asked about reincarnation: "First the stream, then the waterfall, then the stream again."

There were wildflowers all around. We sat in the grass with her urn between us and cried as we said goodbye to her, and we told her how sorry we were that she couldn't stay with us. We told her how beautiful it was in this place, with the flowers and the water and the snow-tipped mountains and the thunderclouds just starting to gather, and a whole forest full of animals so she wouldn't be lonely.

The ashes were different than I had thought they would be. I thought they would be gray and gritty, like fireplace sweepings. But they were like a little bag of broken shells, creamy white and pale yellow, with recognizable bits of bone, including a tiny little femur head the size of my fingertip. They rattled against one another when we scooped our hands into the plastic bag. I thought the stream would carry them off right away, but they sank to the bottom and were swept up against a rock. They lay there in a little white heap on the black granite, with the water rushing over them. They were still there when we left.

Now when I think of Sierra, sometimes I remember her as a squirming, kicking presence in my bulging belly; and sometimes as a beautiful dark-haired baby, lying still in my arms with her eyes closed; and sometimes as a little pile of white bones at the bottom of a stream.

The night after we scattered her ashes, the Perseid meteor showers came. I stepped out of our cabin into the windy night and looked up—flashes of light coming out of nowhere, streaking across a sky full of stars, and vanishing into the infinite darkness.

SUTRA 3

Buddha's Birthday

· · · · ·

WE HAD JUST finished watching the latest episode of *Survivor*, and it was time for the ritual we'd decided to do. I was thirty-nine weeks pregnant with our second baby—one week before my official due date—and my husband and I were going to invite him to be born.

We were in the downstairs den of the house we'd moved into together just after our wedding, when I was six months pregnant with our first child, Sierra. Now, the remains of dinner were still on the coffee table in front of the TV: greasy plates of salmon bones, potato skins, scraps of heirloom tomatoes. If I'd had things my way, we would have lit candles and amber incense and sat cross-legged on zafus in front of an altar. But my husband said, "You know I'm allergic to rituals. The less formal we make it, the better." Besides, I'd already dismantled the meditation room so it could be turned back into a nursery, if we were lucky enough to have a baby to rock there.

So instead we just sat on the couch and put our hands on my belly—once again, round and full and pulsating with life. *Thirty-nine weeks.* This was exactly how far along I had been when I had discovered that Sierra had died inside me.

My husband's palms were warm on my belly. The curve of the baby's bottom pressed up against my hands.

"We love you so much, and we'd love for you to come out soon, if you're ready," I said to the baby. "You can probably tell that I'm really scared. Don't worry—you're doing great. It's just that we loved your big sister very much too, and we lost her when she was just as old as you are now. So we're scared that we will lose you too. We just want you to know that if you want to come out and join us, the nest is all ready."

My husband leaned closer. "There are incredible things out here," he said. "Mommy's breasts, and computer games, and dogs, and movies to watch—you won't believe how much fun we're going to have."

Then the ritual was over.

My husband took the garbage cans down to the curb, then sat down at his computer to check his email.

I lumbered upstairs to finish packing my bag for the hospital. I filled my new toiletry kit with supplies: travel-sized soap and toothpaste, lip balm, contact lens solution, extra lenses—carefully checking each item off, as if I could guarantee that my baby would live by bringing an adequate supply of dental floss.

Then I crawled into bed and adjusted my props—two pillows behind me, two between my legs, two under my head, and my arms wrapped around another one like a giant teddy bear.

Every mother has a birth story. The classic myth of the birth of the Buddha—or rather, of the child named Siddhartha who would grow up to become the Buddha—goes like this: There was a beautiful woman named Maya who was the wife of King Suddhodana, the ruler of the Shakya clan of Kapilavastu in a region that now straddles the border between India and Nepal. Maya and King Suddhodana had been married for twenty years without having children. But one night the queen dreamed that a white elephant—a symbol of greatness in ancient India—appeared, circled around her three times, and entered her womb through her right side.

Queen Maya carried her baby inside her for ten lunar months, and then—as was the custom—set out to return to her mother's home to give birth. Along the way, she stopped in a grove of sal trees and—delighted by their beauty—decided to give birth there, standing up and holding on to a branch. According to the story, the baby prince emerged from her right side, took seven steps, and proclaimed, "I am the world-honored one." A few days later, her mission accomplished, Queen Maya died.

To me, this sounds like the version of the myth told by a man who has never given birth. The male baby is the hero of the story, not the mother who gave him life from her body. The woman is the passive vessel for a man's awakening journey, not a heroine embarked on her own grueling quest to become fully alive. It's a story stripped of longing, passion, pain, the mess and tangle of human hearts and human relationships, just as surely as it is stripped of sweat and vaginal juices, of amniotic fluid and blood and tears.

How might the story have gone if it had been passed down from grandmother to grandchild over the generations, along with the secrets of grinding spices and gathering dung for cooking fires? I imagine a tale that begins something like this:

Year after year, the king couldn't quicken the queen's womb with a baby. So many times she hoped for a child, only to see the blood staining her clothes once again! There were the four who came far too early, just clots of flesh and sorrow to be burned and never spoken of again. And then there was the one who was born perfect, but never cried, whom the king's physicians weighted with stones and cast to the bottom of the river unburned, as was the custom with saints and lepers.

Then one year, on a visit home to her mother's house, the wise midwife who attended all the family births gave the queen four bags of herbs to brew into tea. "Drink this one with the start of each monthly blood," she told her. "Give this to your husband, mixed in his wine, when the moon is new. Then visit the stables at night, give this one to the charioteer, and lie down with him in the straw. And drink this next one every morning after your first missed blood."

Her tea gave her dreams and visions. Her drugged husband fell into a deep sleep, and the charioteer came at her with the ferocity of a wild elephant, his trunk never resting. Her monthly blood stopped, and she began to grow larger.

Why imagine a fable that begins like this, riddled with disappointment, death, confusion, secrets, lust, lies? Because it says to us all, *You too. Out of your broken, screwed-up, incontrovertibly human life—not the imaginary, divinely royal life of your neighbor—something vast and beautiful can be born.*

Our doctor had told us that we needed to wait at least three months after Sierra's birth to start trying to get pregnant. Our midwife, Johanna, told me that it might be quite a bit longer than that before I even started menstruating again.

But four weeks after Sierra's delivery, my menstrual cycle started up, with its usual clockwork regularity. Johanna looked baffled when I told her. "This is how your mother had seven children," she said.

So two cycles later, as soon as we scattered Sierra's ashes, we began trying to conceive. I knew it was probably too soon. Our hearts were still ripped into tatters, my body still weak. But I had already been waiting for nine months to hold a baby in my arms. To wait another year seemed impossible. Baby making became my new obsession.

Last time around, our pregnancy had arrived unplanned, after a carefree, passionate, still-unmarried romp at the beach house where we'd gone for my family reunion. Now, I planned for conception as if organizing the invasion of a small country. Planning gave me something to do so I didn't feel so helpless and victimized. I wanted Sierra back. But since I couldn't have her, I wanted a replacement, and I wanted it now. At thirty-six, I was terrified that I would not be able to get pregnant again. ("I'm so sorry about your loss," an acquaintance said to me tearfully, holding my hands, when she ran into me at an event. And then, in the next breath, "And how old are you?")

So I read every baby-making book I could get my hands on, all bearing cheery, determined titles such as *Taking Charge of Your Fertility*. I xeroxed multiple copies of a fertility chart and began recording my vital signs—cervical fluid, cervical position, basal body temperature—with the precision of a NASA scientist planning a moon launch.

I compulsively surfed the web, visiting sites with names such as "What Are My Odds of Getting Pregnant?" (Answer: 1 in 4, in any given cycle, if I am having sex an average of three times per week; 1 in 2.7, if I have sex each of the four fertile days preceding ovulation; 1 in 3.6, if I have sex just once, two to three days before ovulation; slightly increased if I have an orgasm within 45 seconds of my partner's ejaculation; 1 in 10, if I am over thirty-five, no matter how often or in what position I have sex.)

I haunted newsgroups that used acronyms like BD (Baby Dance) for having sex and DH (Designated Hitter) for the person that you are BD'ing with. I bookmarked web pages comparing the sensitivity of various ovulation predictor kits and home pregnancy tests; detailing the appropriate levels of hCg (the "pregnancy hormone") at various dpo (days past ovulation); selling fertility-enhancing herbs and visualization tapes; giving advice on "keeping BD fun" (well, stop calling it BD, for one thing).

My life revolved around the thickness and quality of my cervical mucus. On the Trying to Conceive discussion board, there were tips: Use actual egg whites to supplement the cervical mucus. Take vitamin A. Dose yourself with evening primrose oil.

I did it all—as if, by checking every box, I would be able to bring Sierra back.

As the DH, my husband was on duty at ovulation time and for several days before, producing sperm. His job also required him to be romantic and tender, so that the night that our new baby was conceived would be both sacred and sexy.

So, predictably, we argued. We argued about when to make love, and how, and whether he was being romantic enough, and whether he had rubbed my back long enough before unhooking my bra. The fights always ended with me crying and him checking his email. But then we had to have sex anyway, because I couldn't bear to miss a night of egg-white cervical mucus.

In the back of my mind, the ghost of my yogini self begged me to relax. *Surrender to spirit,* she whispered. *Wait for the child who is meant to be yours, who is waiting to incarnate.*

But I was in no mood to hear her. Trusting, opening, surrounding, flowing—look where that had gotten me! I wanted the foolproof methods of science. Natural conception seemed shockingly archaic, random, and uncontrolled. *Just plant some seeds and wait for them to sprout? There must be a better method than that!*

My husband was doing research into cloning for his budding biotech company, and I found myself wishing that we had saved Sierra's cord blood. Maybe someday we could replace her, *exactly.*

But would it be her? Or a dim copy? Sierra was more than her genes. She was our bright hopes and our passion. She was our innocence. She was the sand in the sheets as we kissed. She was us dancing at our wedding, my burgundy wedding dress swirling over my round belly. She was us moving into our first house.

There was no replacing her.

When the first month passed without conception, I was crushed.

I began doing a headstand next to my bed immediately after we made love, to help the sperm on their journey.

My husband lay silent, watching, worried.

Nine months before our spontaneous ritual in front of the TV, my husband had scheduled a business trip to Texas A&M to meet with scientists about a research project.

I looked at the calendar. "That's exactly when I'm going to be ovulating. You can't go then."

"Well, why don't you come with me?"

So, a week later, I flew to Texas. We checked into a hotel overlooking the stone walls of the Alamo.

"You know what our slogan will be if this is where we conceive?" I asked him, laughing. "Remember the Alamo!"

The pregnancy test stick displayed its pink plus sign three days before my husband's birthday. I managed to hold in the news until his birthday morning, when I told him I wanted a video of me giving him his birthday present. I trained the camera on him and handed him a card: *Happy birthday, Daddy! I can't wait to meet you! Love, Bean.*

He put down the card and started to cry and laugh at the same time. "When you got the camera out, I didn't know what you were going to give me. I thought maybe it would be a puppy."

We all want guarantees, in our life, in our practice, that everything is going to work out. We want to guard our hearts and say *I will only love if my heart will not be broken.*

But there's plenty of proof that there are no guarantees. Life is a free fall through an abyss in which everything and everyone we love is eventually guaranteed to disappear.

In opening again to carrying a child inside me, I chose to step forward into this abyss. I chose to participate in bringing life into the world, knowing that every life is, in the words of the *Diamond Sutra*, "a star at dawn, a bubble in a stream, a flash of lightning in a summer cloud, a flickering lamp, a phantom, and a dream." Knowing that one day it was not just possible but certain that I and the child I treasure will be separated by death.

And that the only protection I would have is that my love would be large enough to hold even death in its arms.

Imagine the Buddha's mother's story continuing:

The queen longed to be home with her mother as her long-awaited child grew large inside her. But the monsoon rains that year were fierce, and they delayed her trip. When she was finally able to leave, the journey was plagued by disaster: rivers too swollen to ford, a damaged axle on the chariot that the young charioteer, distracted by the queen's beauty, didn't notice until it snapped and had to be replaced with a makeshift stick. So instead of being safe in her mother's house as her time came near, the queen was traveling the jungle.

The chariot jolted raggedly over the lumps and puddles, each lurch swaying her huge belly and sending jolts of pain searing through her back and down her legs. Sweat glued her sari to her back, matted her hair, trickled down the back of her neck. As night fell, she heard the coughing roar of a tiger and smelled the chariot driver's metallic fear. Her sister-in-law Prajapati stroked her forehead as it rested in her lap. "Almost there," she repeated over and over, till the words lost their meaning, became like the mantras chanted by the brahmin priests over their fires, prayers that hold the universe together. "Almost there."

My pregnancy with Sierra had been full of other activities—a writer's residency, a wedding, a move to a new home.

With this new baby, all I wanted to do was to grow a baby and deliver it alive. Everything else was in the way.

I canceled teaching engagements that might require me to fly, including an invitation to teach at a yoga conference when I would be eight months pregnant. I turned down a contract to write a yoga coffee-table book. Instead, I read everything I could about pregnancy and birth.

I opted out of pregnancy classes. Other pregnant women seemed unbelievably naive in their confidence that their future was laid out before them exactly as outlined in the What to Expect series of pregnancy books. They planned baby showers and listed the gifts they wanted on baby store websites. In the sixth month of pregnancy, they put their unborn children on preschool wait-lists.

All I could think about were the thousands of things that could go wrong at every step of the way.

Bean was a quieter baby than Sierra, more subdued, not as interactive with his kicks. He hiccupped a lot—a steady, rhythmic shaking different from anything Sierra had done. I had felt as if I had known Sierra from the beginning—her exuberance, her playfulness. Bean was more opaque to me. Was it because he was a boy? Was he more of an introvert? Or was it just because I was more guarded myself, more afraid to love? We chose a name for him, but I didn't dare call him that, even in my mind.

Whenever I woke up in the night and the baby was not moving, I'd poke my belly. I'd get up and shake my hips. I'd go down the hall to the refrigerator, chug a glass of orange juice, and stand there in my bare feet in the dark until I felt the baby wake up in response to the sugar.

I worried about what it was like for my new baby, incarnating into a womb where so recently another baby had died. My husband's mother, Joan, told me a story: A year before my husband's older sister was born, Joan had given birth to a stillborn child with a malformed head. A few years later, when my husband's big sister was a baby, a stranger had stopped Joan on the street. Joan told me, "He put his hand on my daughter's head and said, 'This baby has a double soul.'"

"Will Beanie have a double soul?" I asked my husband.

He put his arms around me. "He will have one soul," he promised. "One wonderful, magnificent soul."

"We are almost to Lumbini," Prajapati told her. "There is a guest house there where you will be safe."

Queen Maya moaned again. "Please, stop the chariot in the shade of these trees."

She got out, staggered toward a tree, and caught one of its branches to keep from falling as another wave of pain crashed. "My child will be born here. I can't go any farther."

We had no fantasies about doing a home birth this time around. My mother-in-law actually suggested that I move into the hospital for the whole last month of my pregnancy for round-the-clock monitoring.

Instead, I spent my third trimester going to the hospital twice a week for sonograms and nonstress tests. I listened to my baby's heartbeat boom over wall-mounted speakers while a ticker tape recorded every fibrillation. The technician held a buzzer to my belly that emitted a sharp, high-pitched sound that woke Bean up. He thrashed and kicked, and the technician measured the response of the baby's heartbeats to his own movements.

Waking up Bean several times a week with a loud noise—this couldn't be good for him, I thought. But the alternative was unthinkable. To get me through the time between appointments, I rented a Doppler and brought it home to listen to the baby's heartbeat there.

We did not plan a baby shower.

We did not buy any clothes for a baby boy.

We did not set up the crib, or pull the bassinet out of the basement, where it was stashed in a corner, wrapped in plastic bags.

As my thirty-ninth week of pregnancy began, my anxiety crescendoed. At thirty-eight weeks, a baby is considered full term. Forty weeks is the standard due date. With Sierra at thirty-nine weeks, I had been blissfully sure that everything would be fine—as I sailed into the home stretch, the biggest decision I thought I was facing was what kind of music to play during the birth. This time, with Bean, it seemed astonishing that anyone ever got born, given the number of things I now knew could go wrong. My doctors had assured me that there was no indication of any potential problem— but what did they know? There'd been no indication last time either.

I went to the doctor for a checkup.

"Your cervix is still shut tight. No dilation at all," he told me. "You're not having any contractions yet."

"He's full term, right? Isn't there anything I can do to get him out?"

"Well, given your situation, we could induce labor. But since there's no indication that anything is wrong, inducing labor actually increases the chances of a negative outcome."

I went home and lay down on my side on my yoga mat, struggling with impossible odds. I could feel my baby rolling under my hands, as perfect and complete as Sierra had been the night before she died. I could take him out, right now, and hold him in my arms by tomorrow! What if I didn't do that and something went terribly, terribly wrong again? What if I woke up tomorrow and he was lying lifeless inside me?

But what if I induced labor and ended up creating a complication that wasn't there before?

When my husband got home, I grabbed him by the hand and pulled him onto the couch. "We need to talk to Bean. We need to tell him that it's time for him to come out."

So, seated in front of our television, with the remnants of our dinner scattered before us, we spoke to him—clearly, urgently. It was all we could think of to do.

She pushed for hours, and no child came out.

She forgot that she was the wife of a great chief, the queen of the Shakya clan. She screamed and wept. She could not bear another child lost.

Fearing he would be blamed for the death of the queen, the charioteer fled, leaving his sword for the women to protect themselves as best they could.

The queen's sister-in-law whispered in her ear, "The gates of your womb are open. But it is not a child's head, but a foot that is emerging."

Maya tried to smile. "Trying to walk before he is born!"

But Prajapati did not smile in return. "The baby is trapped between two worlds. He cannot live half in and half out. If he stays there, he will die—and likely, you will too."

"Is there nothing we can do?"

She gazed into the queen's eyes. "With the sword of the charioteer, I can slice open your side and release the child that way. And it can live."

"And I?"

Prajapati shook her head.

The queen did not hesitate. "Sister. Get the sword."

Fifteen minutes after our couch ritual, lying in my bed, surrounded and supported by pillows, I felt a sudden sharp movement—something butting up hard and low against the inside my cervix. Then a stabbing pain and a pop, like nothing I had ever felt before. I put my hand between my legs and felt for blood. Nothing.

But then some wetness, and as I sat bolt upright, a gush of liquid, flooding the sheets. My water had broken. I shouted for my husband, who thundered up the stairs. "Get our bags," I gasped. "We have to go to the hospital right away."

And then we were grabbing lists of phone numbers and tangerines and cell phones and bottles of Recharge, and I was clambering into the car with my pants soaking wet and amniotic fluid still pouring out of me. And all I wanted was to get to the hospital and get hooked up to a machine that would play me his heartbeat and let me know that he was still alive, that this time everything would be okay.

An hour later we were back in the same familiar birthing rooms at the hospital in San Francisco where we'd delivered Sierra.

Hooked up to the remote fetal monitor, I walked with my husband up and down the halls, pausing to lean on him and breathe as the contractions came in enormous waves. In the birthing room, a ticker tape was printing out my baby's heartbeat, registering every contraction. I breathed into each contraction as if it were a particularly intense yoga pose. By 5:00 a.m., I was five centimeters dilated, and I was beginning to think that perhaps giving birth would be no big deal after all.

But after four more hours of contractions—each one carrying me to the limit of pain I thought I could handle—I was only six centimeters dilated. Exhausted and discouraged, I lay down to take a rest. That was when Johanna blazed into the room—a bundle of power and intensity, a samurai warrior of labor and delivery.

"You are afraid of feeling more pain," she told me, as she studied my chart. "So you are stopping the labor. You want the baby to be born, but you don't want the pain to get any worse. But in order for the baby to be born, the pain will have to increase. You will have to go past what you think is your limit."

I nodded. But inside I was thinking, *I went past my limit over a year ago.*

Johanna and my husband peeled up my shirt and, one on each side of me, together began firmly twisting my nipples to encourage the release of oxytocin, the hormone that triggers labor. I was so far gone that this weirdly intimate activity didn't cause me the slightest embarrassment. Within minutes, it worked. Powerful contractions kicked in, and with them, pain on a level I had never imagined.

"Stop," I moaned.

Johanna looked at me sternly. "That is the last time you will use the word *stop*," she said.

"I've had too much pain," I sobbed, catching at her hand. I was flashing back to Sierra's birth—the epidural-dulled pushing, the dead baby girl who was placed in my arms. "I can't handle any more."

"The pain of birth is not the same as the pain of death," Johanna told me sharply. "Don't confuse them."

In tribal cultures around the world, men have performed painful and bloody rituals to mark the transition from boy to man. Women have these built into our own life cycle. Blood comes every month. Labor and delivery call upon strength and courage and willpower we didn't know we had. They demand that we surrender to a process that is fundamentally out of our control. They split us open, turn us inside out, yank off the ego masks that claim we are in control.

Labor and delivery are wild and messy and animal and angry and bloody and painful. The transcendent act of giving birth is made up of the earthiest of elements: bodily fluids, a hospital gown stained with blood and excrement, the bruises left on a partner's arm by the agonized grip of our fingers.

We may find ourselves howling like cats; throwing up on the rug; emptying our bowels on the bedsheets; hurling curses at our dearest friends. We may get up off the delivery table in the middle of labor and announce to the doctors that we're going home, that we've changed our minds and aren't going to have a baby after all.

And labor is just the beginning. These moments come again and again in every mother's life—the times when we are asked to walk straight into our pain and fear, and in doing so, open up to a love that is greater than anything we ever could have imagined. Our hearts expand to embrace everything: life as beauty and wonder, life as things can break and go wrong. As mothers, we discover that we love our children in whatever form they are in: a kicking bulge in our womb; a baby sucking at our breast; a toddler leaving playdough crumbs on the couch; a pierced and tattooed teenager blasting rap music at midnight. We love them when they're ill and when they're damaged. We love them long after they have died. And in discovering this, we open to a kind of love that transcends form and time. It's at the heart of our humanness, yet you could easily call it divine.

Again and again, motherhood demands that we break through our limitations, that we split our hearts open to make room for something that may be more than we thought we could bear. In that sense, the labor with which we give birth is simply a rehearsal for something we mothers must do over and over: turn ourselves inside out, and then let go.

This is something the men who tell this story will never include: Her baby was slippery with blood and vernix. He cried as they put him to the queen's breast. As he sucked at her nipple, she could feel the rush of her milk letting down to give him strength, even as she felt the strength drain from her own body.

The baby and the queen looked in each other's eyes.

In a moment, a lifetime of love can flow between two hearts. In the space of a breath, infinity can spread its wings.

"You are my world-honored one," the queen whispered, stroking his wet hair. And she closed her eyes.

An earthquake rolled through my uterus. Johanna leaned close. "Use your rage," she said, putting her hands on my heart.

I had chosen natural childbirth because I wanted to feel every moment of my child coming into the world, wanted his mind and my mind unclouded by drugs as we looked into each other's eyes for the first time. I had been a student of yoga and meditation for almost twenty years, and I thought there was no pain I couldn't breathe into. "Breathe and smile," Thich Nhat Hanh had always instructed. "Grin and bear it," my mother used to say. Yet there I was, cursing, thrashing, growling like an animal, hitting the side of my hospital bed. "Goddamn it," I screamed. "Get me the *fucking* epidural!"

But by then it was too late for an epidural. A sudden urge blazed through me, a wave, a convulsion, my whole body clamping down in an involuntary push. I felt a ring of fire open between my legs. My husband was beside himself with excitement: "Here he is, he's almost here!" But in that moment, I didn't even care that I was having a baby. I just wanted the pain to go away.

Someone moved my hand down so I could feel my baby's head. "Let it in," I thought. "Let it out."

And then there was a heave and a great release, and a baby was crying; and my hands were reaching down and pulling a slippery, slithery bundle onto my chest.

"Hello, Forest," said my husband.

And Forest, only seconds old, lifted his wobbly head off my chest and turned to look, with bleary, unfocused eyes, in the direction of his father's voice.

Notes from a
Three-Month Baby Retreat

· · · · ·

IN THE ANCIENT scriptures of yoga and Buddhism, you won't find any accounts of a woman beginning her spiritual journey by nursing a newborn baby.

Babies are born, of course. The goddess Parvati—the consort of Shiva, the god of the yogis and master of death—gives birth to their elephant-headed son, the god Ganesh. The young Queen Maya gives birth to her son, Siddhartha, someday to become the Buddha.

But in stories like these, the women are not the protagonists. It is the baby who is marked for future greatness, enlightenment, transformation. After Siddhartha's mother dies giving birth to him, the infant prince is taken back to the palace and raised by his aunt, Prajapati. If her heart cracks open into enlightenment as she rocks him through the hot Indian nights, this is something the Buddhist sutras do not tell us. And how could they? The Buddha had a disciple with a prodigious memory, Ananda, who followed him everywhere and helped preserve his insights. No one did the same for Prajapati.

The first few months of my son's life—whenever I could grab a few moments to myself—I wrote in my journal. When I sent my notes off to the man who was then my agent, he was discouraging about the possibility of turning them into a book. "It all sounds pretty ordinary to me," he said.

It took me years to insist—yes, and that's part of my point.

DAY 2

It's the second day after my son's birth. I'm sitting on my living room couch with Forest in my lap, clumsily wrapped in a flannel blanket. Mustard-yellow poop is leaking out the side of his cloth diaper cover onto the blue-striped ticking of the "My Breast Friend" nursing cushion, which is strapped around my waist like an enormous doughnut. Too excited and happy and anxious to sleep since he was born, I'm stunned with exhaustion.

All afternoon I've been holding him. He looks so tiny when I set him in his bassinet—so far away, even if it's only two feet from me. When Forest was inside me, kicking and squirming under my heart, I longed for the moment he'd be out and safe in my arms. Now that he's out, it's hitting me that that he isn't safe anywhere. My husband frets: "I remember when I was about ten years old, I tripped and fell into a basket of newborn kittens that was on the floor by the fireplace. Two of them got squashed."

I love Forest so fiercely my heart hurts. I can't forget what had happened to the first baby I loved this much.

Last night, just home from the hospital, I lay in bed with my husband sleeping next to me and Forest on my chest, his heart against mine, his head tucked into the hollow of my neck. I was afraid to fall asleep, because I might roll over on him; afraid to lay him down next to me, because he might smother under my pillow or down comforter; afraid to set him down in the bassinet attached to the side of our king-size bed, because without my heart beating against his chest, his own heart might stop.

So I just lay there, listening to the shallow, arrhythmic flutter of his breath, willing it to continue.

A few hours before dawn, Forest spit up and began to gag, half-digested breast milk running out of his nose. In a panic, I sat up in bed, turned on the overhead lights, and sent my husband running to the medicine cabinet for the bulb syringe that the hospital sent us home with. We sat in the tangle of indigo flannel sheets, my husband holding Forest upright by his underarms, as I tried to suction the spit-up out of his mouth and nostrils.

"Don't do that! You're hurting him!" My husband looked at me, incredulously, as I jabbed the tip of the syringe up Forest's tiny nostrils.

"But look! He's choking!"

"Anne, I think spitting up is normal. You're making it worse. Just let it be."

Forest looked at us, eyes scrunched miserably against the light. His worry and concern felt palpable. *Do these people have the faintest idea what they're doing?* he seemed to be thinking. *Are they even remotely qualified to take care of me?*

When I finally fell into a fitful sleep with him still on my chest, I dreamed a terrible dream:

I am standing at the changing table in Forest's room, changing his diaper. I look down and see Sierra's body lying on top of the white bag filled with complimentary baby supplies that I brought home from the hospital. Sierra is wearing a diaper, and I think that I should change it, or perhaps just take it off and give it to Forest. But when I begin to change her diaper the horror hits me—she is dead. I can't understand why they sent us home from the hospital with her dead body as well as with Forest's living one.

I woke up with a jolt, panicked—where was Forest? As if in response, he started to wail. As I sat up and awkwardly put him to my swollen breast—which had begun to drip and spurt on its own at the sound of his cry—I knew that it was true: We brought Sierra home with Forest. She was there in the way that fear danced cheek to cheek with love in my heart; the way I desperately wanted to do everything right, as if Forest's life depended on whether I could keep him from crying. Sierra was there in the way I lay awake and listened for every breath, willing him to stay alive.

DAY 8

Motherhood has smashed over me like crashing surf. For years I've been dreaming of swimming in this ocean. But now all I can do is flail in the waves, trying to keep my head above water, coughing salt water up through my nose.

Until last week, my days revolved around an orderly rhythm worked out over almost two decades of spiritual practice. Every morning I'd wake up, write down my dreams, meditate, and do an hour of yoga; then I'd have a silent breakfast and get straight to my computer to write. I tried not to speak to anyone before noon; I didn't even turn on the telephone until my morning work was done. At night, I was always in bed by 11:00, shutting out the world with earplugs and an eye mask. My life was stitched together with countless small rituals, spiritual sutures to keep my psyche from splitting at the seams.

Now all that has been torn away. I sleep when Forest sleeps, wake when he wakes—which is usually after less than two hours. I pace the floor with him wailing in my arms, hour after hour. He screams whenever I set him down, so I make peanut-butter sandwiches one-handed with him tucked under my arm and use the toilet with him in my lap.

He only sleeps if he can hear my heartbeat. From midnight to dawn he lies on my chest, his head tucked into the hollow of my throat, awakening every two hours to nurse. In the day, he naps in my arms as I rock. If I dare to set him in his bassinet, he wakes up with a roar of outrage, red-faced and flailing.

"Babies at this age are very portable," my pediatrician assured me blithely when I called her last week to make our first appointment. "You can take him anywhere!"

Sure, I thought. *Portable, like a ticking bomb!*

"You won't always feel like you love him," my midwife, Johanna, told me when she came for his checkup yesterday. "You just have to act as if you do."

I feel staggeringly incompetent. I don't know the right way to pick him up, or put him down, or wipe his behind. He has worn the same shirt for three days straight because I can't figure out how to change it without making him scream. I haven't given him a bath because I'm afraid I'll drop him in the tub. My life is awash with alien gear: I wrestle with the straps on the car seat, the buckles on the BabyBjörn frontpack, the tubes of the breast pump, the Velcro on the nursing pillow, the slits on the front of my nursing shirts.

I know how to navigate even the most challenging yoga vinyasa flow. I can meditate for hours in silence without wriggling, facing down knee pain, back pain, demons of anger and fear.

But the practice of taking care of a newborn is an initiation like no other. And in the annals of spiritual practice written by men, I've rarely seen it praised or elevated.

I know young women who have been warned by their dharma teachers that if they have a baby, their spiritual practice will grind to a halt. Only one of my meditation teachers has a child. She once told me that after her baby was born, her own teacher told her, "You better not have another one or you will never teach again."

DAY 13

I've assembled an arsenal of holistically oriented childrearing manuals. They drift in a small avalanche across my couch; I flip through them as I nurse Forest for hours.

My favorite is a little book called *The Continuum Concept*, written by a woman anthropologist—herself childless—who claims she spent years in the jungles of South America studying the child-rearing practices of rainforest tribes. The book assures me that if I simply hold Forest in my arms all the time, skin to skin, day and night, he won't cry, won't get colic, won't die in his sleep. He won't become a teenager who deals drugs or a young man who sleeps with women and never calls them again. For God's sake, he won't even spit up.

Before Forest was born, I had ordered a cloth baby sling and—in the absence of tribal role models—an instructional video about how to use it. I planned to wear him everywhere in my Over-the-Shoulder-Baby-Holder sling while I went about my daily life harvesting corn and answering the phone and drawing water from the well and checking my email, in the manner of the ancient Maya.

It all sounded fabulous. The only problem is, none of it has worked.

Forest still cries a lot, and loudly. He cries every time I set him down. He cries if he has been awake more than fifteen minutes. He cries if I put him in a stroller or car seat. He cries whenever I change his diaper. He cries at the sound of his rattle. He cries if the lights are too bright.

And most of all, he cries if I try to put him in the sling, which he despises with a passion. He likes having his arms and legs extended and free, not coiled into a cozy fetal pose. When I try to cram him into the sling, he roars, kicking his legs against the fabric, his face contorted with fury, staring into my eyes with a desperate intensity. *What makes you think*, say his eyes, *that just because you are thirty-seven years old, and I am only ten days old, you have the right to tell me what to do?*

He seems wracked with frustration, like an old soul trapped in a helpless body. When a friend came over last week to bring me a lasagna, we stood by his bassinet together and watched him grunt and flail: *So many things to say and do, if only I could get control of my goddamned neck muscles!* "It's as if in his last life he died in the middle of all his projects, and he can't wait to get back to them," she commented.

In desperation, this morning I called my mother on the East Coast. "How did you manage with seven children?" I wailed.

"I worked harder with the first baby than I did with all the rest put together," she told me. "And after the first three or four, it's easy! The older ones just play with the younger ones!"

This did not sound to me like a short-term solution. I asked if she had any more immediately practical advice. She did: "Always make sure all your clothes are the color of peanut butter and jelly."

Unlike my own mother, my husband's mother lives right around the corner. But at seventy-eight, Grandma Joan is an unreliable narrator. In her memory, her babies never had leaky diapers, they never cried in the middle of the night, and they woke up cooing every morning. When she first saw my Over-the-Shoulder-Baby-Holder, she asked, "If carrying your baby in a sling is so great, how come they're all killing each other in Rwanda?"

"Mom, people are killing each other all over the world," my husband said.

She snorted, "Not with machetes!"

DAY 18

Last night, I woke up suddenly in the middle of the night. Forest was asleep, belly down, on my chest. His breath was shallow and fluttering. Was he breathing all right? I turned on the light to be sure. In response, Forest began to wail.

The more he screamed, the more anxious I got. His face grew red, his body stiffened, and he seemed in excruciating pain. I carried him downstairs to get my husband, who was pulling an all-nighter in his home office, preparing for a business presentation the next morning. Together we took turns rocking Forest, walking with him, bouncing him. Nothing worked. He screamed until he ran out of breath, choked, sputtered, began to scream again. I began to cry myself.

Finally, my husband called the hospital emergency room. "We have a two-week-old baby, and we're worried. We think there's something wrong with him."

He described the symptoms, then nodded as he listened to the response. "Mmm, hmm. Mmm, hmm. Great. Thank you."

He got off the phone and turned to me. "She says it sounds like gas. She says that sometimes that makes babies uncomfortable."

Uncomfortable? "I ate black bean tacos for dinner last night," I said uncertainly. "Maybe that's what did it?"

Forest cried until dawn, when he passed out in exhaustion in my arms. I collapsed on the couch, afraid to put him down, and tried to doze. As the sun came up, my husband talked on the phone with one of his best friends from high school—now a psychic healer, nutritionist, mother of four, and unofficial adviser to half the mothers in the SoCal town of Ventura.

After he hung up, he handed me a list. "She says you should stop eating dairy, wheat, yeast, soy, corn, legumes, garlic, onions, tomatoes, sugar, peppers, broccoli, and citrus fruit. You should also consider dropping fish, mushrooms, and eggs."

As if on cue, Forest woke up and began to cry again. My husband went downstairs to sleep a few hours before his meeting. I sat on the couch in my bathrobe and nursed Forest, eating cold oatmeal out of a mug with my left hand, and spilling it on his hair.

Just after Forest finally fell asleep, the doorbell rang. I got up in slow motion, baby still tucked in my arms, and moonwalked to the door to greet a FedEx deliveryman with some papers for my husband's presentation.

"Shhhh," I hissed, reaching for the envelope with one hand, jerking my head toward Forest. "He's sleeping."

The man nodded, his eyes averted. "Just sign right here," he said, staring studiously at my doormat.

I signed, wondering why he wasn't looking at me. The man took the paper and scurried off.

On my way back to the mirror, I glanced in the bathroom mirror and froze. I had forgotten to close the milk bar. One breast was hanging out through the slit in my nursing pajamas like an Amazon warrior's. A streak of spit-up ran down my shoulder, with a few crumbs of oatmeal lodged in it. Below my breast was a yellow poop stain. My unbrushed hair stood on end. My eyes were red-rimmed and glassy.

Who have I become?

Spiritual practitioners have costumes that communicate the dignity and value of their practice: the elaborate robes of the Zen monk, the form-fitting leggings of the yoga babe. What does my unkempt attire signify? Meditation practice is supposed to crack the facade of the construct of self, so something more real shows through. Is that what's happening here? Or am I just losing it?

DAY 19

Forest has consented to be in the sling around my neck as I write this. He is snoozing away, making little snorts and grunts, his brow furrowed as if he's pondering the big questions: *Poop, breasts, milk, the connection between them, the way the world disappears and recreates itself when I go to sleep and wake up, the way my purple and green rattle floats in front of me, vanishes. Where does it go?*

I'm realizing I could have paid a lot of money and traveled a long way to study with a guru like this—a demented Zen master or Tibetan crazy wisdom teacher, who might put a glossy ad in *Yoga Journal* promising to help you "cut through the rational mind."

On a long meditation retreat, there's this moment when you realize—There's Nothing Else to Look Forward To. This Is It. At first, you're sitting in meditation waiting for the bell to ring so you can get up. And then the bell rings and you get up and do walking meditation, slowly back and forth, waiting for the bell to ring so you can sit. Then you sit again, and your back hurts and your leg hurts and you're bored and you're waiting for the bell to ring so you can walk. And then the bell rings . . . After four or five cycles like this you begin looking forward to lunch, and then you stand in line looking forward to seeing what's on the buffet table; then you eat while looking forward to each next bite (you try to bring your mind back to the present bite but the next one promises to be so much better!). As you eat, you wonder if there will be second helpings available; there are, and as you eat them, you look forward to your nap after lunch. After your nap, as you do your "work practice" in the kitchen, you look forward to being done chopping vegetables so you go back and meditate again.

And so, you sit and walk, and sit and walk, and sit and walk, always leaning into the next moment. And after several days of this, something cracks deep in your mind and you understand on a deeper level, for a moment, what you previously knew only conceptually—that life itself only unfolds right now. Body sensations, thoughts, emotions, sights, and sounds arise and pass away, always in the present moment. And for a moment you really get this, and you are in bliss. And then the bliss passes, and you start looking forward to it coming back. And the whole cycle starts up again.

That's what this period of time is like—an endless meditation retreat. It has all the elements: the long hours of silent sitting; the walking back and forth, going nowhere; the grueling schedule and sleep deprivation; the hypnotic, enigmatic chants (". . . and if that looking glass gets broke / Mama's gonna buy you a billy goat . . .").

And at the center of it, of course, is the crazy wisdom teacher in diapers, who assigns more demanding practices than I ever encountered in all my travels in India: "Tonight you will circumambulate the living room for two hours with the master in your arms, doing a deep-knee bend at every other step, and chanting, 'dooty-dooty-doot-doot-doo, dooty-dooty-doot-doot-doo.'" Or, "At midnight you will carry the sleeping master with you to the bathroom, and answer this koan: How do you lower your pajama bottoms without using your hands?"

Like all great spiritual practices, these have been exquisitely designed to rattle the cage of my ego. They smash through my concepts about how things should be: myself rocking in the garden swing by the lavender bush, watching the hummingbirds, while my newborn sleeps in a bassinet by my feet. They pry open my heart to the way things actually are: myself standing by the diaper table, flexing one tiny knee after another into Forest's colicky tummy, and cheering when a mustard-yellow fountain erupts from his bottom, as his dad applauds, "Hurray! You're the Prince of Poop! You're the Pope of Poop!"

And I've finally realized: This is it. Nursing, diapering, rocking the crying baby, looking forward to nap, nap being over. The flashes of pure joy as he looks up at me and smiles. The next poop, the next pounce on my nipple. The waves of bliss and love. The waves of utter exhaustion and frustration.

The essential practice is just to be here for now. And now. And now. And with every breath of my "baby retreat," I am offered the opportunity to cradle my child in my arms, to feel my heart crack open, and to be present for a mystery unfolding.

DAY 23

Forest's moods change so fast. When he sleeps, his emotions flicker across his face as if he is rehearsing every expression he will need all the way through adolescence to old age: Rolling his eyes in exasperation, sneering, smiling, rounding his lips in an *ooo* of amazement, arching his eyebrows in disbelief, opening wide as if laughing in glee. Then the look of sudden horror: *Oh God, not the poop coming again! I thought I took care of that already, please mommy make it stop!* The wail of outrage, the red-faced grunts . . . then the expression of deep peace when it's all over.

Watching his face is a meditation in itself. It's like watching the human mind-body in its purest state, raw and unfiltered. Watching his face, I understand my own heart better.

In Buddhist practice, "nonattachment" is often elevated—a disentanglement from the world personified by the ideal of a celibate monk.

But parenting is explicitly about forming secure attachments— the bonds of intimacy that allow a child to thrive. This kind of attachment is an expression of love.

I feel plugged into the world now in a way that I never have been before. As I feed my child out of my own body, I see how I am fed by the body of the earth. I feel how I am crocheted to a chain of mothers before me, and a chain of unborn children who will inherit a world that I can't even imagine. I want Forest's grandchildren to be able to swim in the Pacific, and hike the granite ridges of the Sierra, and gasp at a blue heron standing on one leg in Bolinas Lagoon.

Is this "attachment"? Or connectedness?

In the legends of the Buddha's life, the young prince Siddhartha grows up in a palace, sheltered his whole life from the harsh realities of the world. His awakening doesn't begin until, as a young man, he slips past the palace walls and sees what are known as the four messengers, all of them also men: an old man, wrinkled and withering; a sick man, coughing and wheezing and leaking pus; a dead man being carried to a funeral pyre; an ochre-robed holy man, who has cast off the world of sickness, old age, and death to seek what is eternal.

Those four messengers are what set off his spiritual quest. Siddhartha leaves the palace in the middle of the night to look for enlightenment, without waking his sleeping wife and son, Rahula, his "fetter."

But what if the son were not a fetter, but another messenger? One who pointed the way to a different kind of awakening, the path that the Buddha didn't travel but his wife did?

DAY 25

Last night, Forest was writhing and grunting much of the night, even though I'd eaten nothing but baked potatoes and a salad for dinner. Around dawn I fell asleep and dreamed: *I hear about some people who claim they can stop your baby from crying "in just two minutes." I go to see them because I am desperate. I try to ignore the dead babies lying all over the place and hand Forest over. Then as I am walking away, listening to him wail, I see that there are more dead babies everywhere. I suddenly realize that they are going to kill him. That his last moments will be knowing I have betrayed him. I start to run back, thinking, he's so wonderful, how could I have done that, what if I am too late, has it been two minutes yet . . .*

When I wake up—what a joy to have him here in my bed, snoring next to me! "Cry all you want," I told him, and covered his head with kisses, inhaling deep to drink in the smell of his hair.

I think of what a Zen teacher told a friend of mine who was fretting about what career path to take: "Just being alive is enough. Anything else is extra." Right now, that feels true—for me as well as for Forest.

DAY 31

Forest is one month old. His baby hair is starting to fall out, so he has a sort of mohawk left on the top, and a fringe around the edge of his hairline, the rest of it disappearing. His face is getting rounder, so he looks like a fat, bald, middle-aged man. When he woke up this morning he was cross, his bowels giving him trouble again, and he looked at me suspiciously like a bank manager who was about to turn me down for a loan.

But a small miracle: he fell asleep for a while in his infant seat. So I spread out my mat and did yoga next to him—one eye always on him, one part of my attention always there.

At first, as I practiced, I felt the urgency to do as many poses as I could—I should get my body back into the shape it was before the birth! I should strengthen my abs! Tighten my butt! Release my upper back from the strain of nursing!

And then I realized—the challenge now is to do one pose, just one. But to do it well. Which means not to do it correctly, anatomically, but to do it fully, completely, feeling the magic of just this breath coming in, just this breath coming out. Legs like tree roots connecting with the earth. Spirit emanating out of my body like mist rising off a swamp.

I could feel my back muscles releasing into a wide-legged forward bend—my heart yielding, my head dropping down. In this shape, I bowed to the magic of this moment: my baby, one month old, sleeping by my feet in his infant seat, his little snores wheezing in and out of a tiny nose, the mystery of breath keeping him alive too. His mouth a pouting flower, his T-shirt riding up around his shoulders, stained with drops of balsamic vinegar from the salad I ate last night with him in my lap. His fingers curled loose, poised to reach out and grasp the world.

I must do this pose, fully. Then maybe one more. Then maybe one more. Until he starts to grunt, and get red in the face, and strain, and then burst into a wail—and it is time to pick him up, put him to my breast, and do the poses of motherhood again, a breath and a breast at a time.

DAY 35

I said to my husband, "Forest has so much personality that sometimes I forget he is a baby. Then he does something baby-like and surprises me."

"You mean, like he poops his pants?"

"Well, yes, there's that. But that doesn't surprise me—he's just a guy who does that sometimes. What really catches me off guard is when I sense how much he needs me."

How small he is, how completely vulnerable! He needs me desperately and knows it—so when he wakes up in bed when I've gone to the bathroom, and finds me not there, oh, the intensity of his wail! And the palpable relief when I immediately appear again and take him in my arms! It's so different when he wakes up in the night and I am there—my belly warm under his, my breath on his face—and he sighs a little and sinks back under.

I'd like to be able to hold myself, in my yoga and meditation practice, in the same way that I hold him. To feel my own warm presence there, so I don't have to be anxious or on guard or obsessed with achieving a particular pose or level of fitness.

My body has channeled a whole new life into the world. Does it care whether it has tight buns? It needs to be nurtured, cherished, supported so that a new strength can well up naturally from within—the strength of love pouring through bones and blood and muscle and milk, as naturally as my breast milk lets down when I hear Forest cry, or even a few moments before.

While he snoozed in his bassinet just now, I folded into a seated forward bend, releasing my heart toward the ground. I could feel that my body would never be the same as it was before pregnancy and birth—but then, nothing ever is the same as it was. Clearly what's called for is not to try to shape or control my body or try to beat it into the shape of someone else's. Instead I must let it unfold naturally into its next form.

This is my job in mothering too: to accept, to nurture, to create an atmosphere in which my child can unfold. Not to try to impose a shape on him from the outside but to trust his natural impulses, to water the seeds of what is best in him and let him blossom.

DAY 40

I'm scheduled to direct a conference on yoga and Buddhism that is coming up on the East Coast in a couple of months. My husband and Forest are going to come with me—plus, in a panic, I've just asked two of my East Coast sisters to meet me there as babysitters. When I planned this, Forest wasn't even born, and it seemed plausible that I would teach the whole thing with him cooing in that sling around my neck. Now it's clear that that will not be remotely possible.

Plus, I am having a major attack of insecurity about my keynote speech. What will I say? I'm not a yoga master or a dharma teacher! These days all I am is a mom!

I haven't done any formal sitting meditation since Forest was born, just sitting and nursing him; my walking meditation is the slow *kinhin* out of the room when I've put him down for a nap, praying that a creaking floorboard won't wake him, or the hours of pacing back and forth with him fretting and moaning on my shoulder. And as for yoga—well, I've come up with a new way of doing asanas: I lay him on his back on his sheepskin, wind up his mobile, and hold a pose for as long as the mobile music box lasts; then I wind it up again and do another pose. I can sometimes get fifteen whole minutes of yoga done that way before he starts to fuss! And the only problem is that I do it all to the tinkling ice-cream-truck tune of "Hush, Little Baby, Don't Say a Word."

DAY 42

Forest is asleep next to me in our king-size bed, looking so tiny in the tangle of down comforter, pillows huge next to him. I know he is sleeping so deeply because the bed smells of my skin and sweat and breath and milk.

I have been mastering "the ten-minute yoga practice." It's a way to release the physical strains of motherhood—the ache in the shoulders and neck from rocking and nursing, the tweak in the low back where hormone-loosened ligaments let go their grip on the bones. Even more important, it's a way to bring myself back to my center and align myself with my intention to be present. Even if I've just eaten, I seize the opportunity to do a few poses when he snoozes—a few handstands, an elbow balance. Then, when he notices I am gone and demands me back, I see if I can maintain my stream of mindfulness.

My challenge is to accept that this particular baby, right now, wants to be held all the time. To accept that what he needs in order to thrive—to grow to his maximum potential—is to constantly be in someone's arms, in someone's lap. This might be more than—or different from—what some other babies his age might need, and this is okay. It doesn't mean that he will be a needy person, a disagreeable, demanding child. This is simply who he is now.

Here's what I realized in my last mini-yoga and meditation sessions: you don't need to go to India to visit the birthplace of the Buddha, the "awakened one." The Buddha—as in, the capacity of the human heart to be awake—can be born anywhere, every moment. Born in failures and disappointments and broken hearts and failed relationships and shattered dreams, as much as in triumphs and successes. Born in my tight muscles, my cramped neck, the poses I try to do and fail, the ones I used to be able to do and can't anymore.

When I reject my body—because it is imperfect, impermanent—I reject my life; and as I embrace my body, I embrace my life. This fleeting, impermanent, glorious, imperfect life that is not turning out at all as I expected.

As I write that, next to me Forest opens his eyes, studies me for a while with his serious blue-gray eyes, makes an astonished, thoughtful O with his lips, then goes back to sleep.

DAY 77

Forest's eyes are almond-shaped, enormous, glowing. He watches everything with this intense absorption, his lips parted in amazement. Sometimes it is all so intense that he just has to suck on his fist. What other response could there be?

My favorite moment of the day with him is first thing in the morning. He still wakes up every hour or two throughout the night—but then I just nurse him in the dark, half-asleep. But at daybreak, I lift him, still grunting and struggling, into my lap and smile at him and say, "Good morning, Forest!" And he stops grunting and looks straight at me and breaks into a smile so big his eyes crinkle up and practically disappear and his ears start to wiggle. His whole body squirms with delight, like he's so happy to see me he's about to explode with joy. And even if he keeps grunting (because that darn poop! it's just so stubborn!), he's smiling at the same time. He opens his eyes wide and looks at me again, and grins again, this big toothless happy grin, so wide I can see the streaks on the roof of his mouth.

That's the best moment.

But along about 4:00 p.m., I am sometimes so tired of being Mom. When my neck is hurting because I slept half the night before sitting up with him in my lap. When all I have done all day is nurse and change diapers and walk around the house showing him things he points at: *This is squash! This is the refrigerator! There, out the window, there are the deer who are rutting in our yard, literally chasing each other around the lawn doing battle, because your dad and I keep forgetting to close our gate, and there's no more garden left to protect anymore anyway, because we've let it slide back into wilderness and neither of us has a moment to weed or water or mow!*

Tonight as I was nursing him to sleep—which took two hours, playing the same CD of classical music over and over, nursing and rocking and putting him down oh-so-carefully, but then he'd wake up when his head hit the lambskin, and I'd have to start all over again—I was thinking, *what if I just surrendered to just doing this, without trying to do anything else? What if I let go of being a teacher, being a writer? What if I dropped into this role the way I might drop into my life as a monk at a monastery—taking on the new dharma name of "Mom" that erases my previous identity as surely as the Japanese dharma names assigned by a roshi?*

Suppose I just let myself be nobody but Mom, for a while?

Forest is asleep now, in his co-sleeper, and I am huddled on the bed, shielding the light from my computer screen with a pillow, hunching over to see under the pillow to tap the keys. Trying to write about him. It sounds like he's waking up . . . I have to stop writing now. Can being Mom be enough? How about being nobody?

DAY 87

Forest had his first trip to the beach the other day. It was sunny at our house, but foggy and a little chilly at Muir Beach. I put him in the frontpack with a jacket and hat on (the hat kept creeping down over his eyes, but he didn't seem to mind) and draped him with blankets. My husband and I walked up and down the beach, pointing out: Ocean. Dogs. Big kids (one-year-olds and two-year-olds). He was moderately interested, but apparently didn't think it compared to shopping at Whole Foods. He had this slightly critical look on his face, like, *I'm a baby who's been around the block a few times. I know a thing or two. What do you want to show me now? Well, not bad, not bad . . .*

I have been trying to get him used to drinking from a bottle, so his dad or a babysitter can feed him and I can be gone for the length of a yoga class. But he is not cooperating. I pump a little breast milk in the morning, and then my husband offers it to him in a bottle later in the day. He drinks maybe half an ounce, sputtering and spitting out the nipple every few sucks, then breaks down and cries. Afterward, he talks about it for a long time, indignantly. It's as if he's a wine connoisseur who's gone to a fancy restaurant and been served a glass of cheap jug wine—the fact that it's got alcohol in it doesn't make up for the delivery method. Even after the bottle has been taken away, he keeps talking about it: *The nerve! Can you believe it? At the prices they charge? Hey, you guys, did you hear what they did to me?*

DAY 99

Forest is three months old, and what everyone said would happen is happening: It is getting easier. He is sunny, smiling—my little lover, gazing at me adoringly, laughing at my jokes, melting my heart. We bought a mountain stroller, so now I can head to Tennessee Valley, Mount Tam, or wherever else I might want to hike—and instead of screaming throughout the whole walk, he is peering around at the world with a goofy, wide-eyed grin.

Of course, I loved him from the start. But now I find myself lying in *savasana* at the end of yoga class thinking about his smile, wanting to get up and run home to kiss him. Last night he was sleeping in the co-sleeper while I was in the living room, working on my laptop. I heard him start to toss and grumble, and he didn't seem to be resettling, so I tiptoed into the room and lay down on the bed next to him. The room was dark, but I reached out my arm and felt around until I touched the little blanketed bundle of his body. In the darkness I felt a tiny little hand reach out of nowhere, come down on top of mine, and grab my finger. He sighed and went back to sleep.

My identity is breaking open the way my pelvis broke open to let him into the world. My psyche is dilating like my cervix, making room for something new. I am becoming Anne-with-Forest.

There's a classic Zen koan in which one monk asks another, "How does the bodhisattva Kuan Yin use her many hands and eyes?" The second monk responds, "It is like someone in the middle of the night reaching behind her head for the pillow." The answer evokes the naturalness with which compassion wells from the awakened heart.

Maybe motherhood can release the heart as surely as monastic practice. Or to say it another way—maybe with years of practice, a monk could be like a mother in the middle of the night, reaching for her baby's hand.

I'm thinking about the talk I'm going to give at the yoga and Buddhism conference next month. I'm going to ask: Can suctioning the snot from a sick baby's nose have the simplicity and purity of a nun's prostrations? Can wiping out a diaper pail lead to "the awakening of the Buddha and the ancestors"?

On one level, maybe these questions seem absurd. Nothing could be further from the regimented march of a formal retreat than the disheveled dance of motherhood. The books on my bedside table used to be about pursuing awakening in the Himalayas. Now they are about preventing awakening in the middle of the night. There's a diaper-changing table where my altar used to be; my zafus and zabutons have been repurposed to cushion Forest's play area.

Forget about chewing a single raisin for ten minutes and admonitions to "when you eat, just eat." I'm on the phone with Forest on my hip, ordering baby-proof covers for the electrical outlets as I eat cold veggie pot stickers with my fingers straight from the cardboard box and rub fresh spit-up into the floor with one socked foot. It's hard to find the moment even to tell myself that this is a spiritual path—I'm too busy looking for Forest's other bootie.

And yet. Last week I had tea with Fu, the Zen priest from Green Gulch Zen Center who was one of the officiants at our wedding and at Sierra's cremation. Seven years ago, she and her partner adopted Sabrina, an HIV-positive baby born to a crack-addicted mother. I asked Fu how becoming a mother had affected her practice. "I became a human being," she told me. "And that's what Buddhist practice is all about—becoming a human. Through meditation I had gotten very good at putting a little bubble around me. My love for this child was a crowbar that ripped open my heart."

I know that a traditional meditation retreat offers opportunities that the daily life of a mother can't—for example, the chance to cultivate in silence, undistracted, the skills of mindfulness, insight, and one-pointed concentration.

But for me, mothering has been the deepest practice I've ever taken on. It's a constant assault on my ingrained selfishness—a wake-up call to the snoozing bodhisattva within. I've let go of props I thought were indispensable—a decent night's sleep, my morning ritual of yoga and meditation. I've been offered the opportunity to study my mind as it changes as quickly as my baby goes from giggles to squalls. When I wake up to the sound of a cry at midnight, I can resent Forest for breaking into my dreams. Or I can rock him in the dark, milk pouring out of me, and let myself soak in the intimacy of a moment so precious and fleeting it breaks my heart wide open.

Could there be any better way to get my nose rubbed in the truth of impermanence than to love a child in a jagged, careless world? Napping with Forest—his head on my breast, my nose pressed against the dark silk of his hair—I watch the heartbeat fluttering in the soft spot on his skull. Forget about freeways, and plutonium, and stealth bombers—I've been warned that even a teddy bear could suffocate him in his crib. At night, when he's been silent a couple of hours, I creep into the bedroom and stand beside him until I hear him sigh.

And even if everything goes absolutely perfectly, I know that this particular Forest—the one who warbles and passionately sucks on the bill of his rubber duck as he splashes with me in the tub—is going to dissolve like bubble bath. Yesterday he was a kicking bulge in my belly as I swam laps in the July sun; tomorrow he'll be a middle-aged man, scattering my ashes in a mountain lake. Watching Forest drool and gnaw on a frozen teething ring, my husband says, "It's so beautiful that it hurts."

I know these insights aren't the pristine diamond of samadhi. They are a sloppier, stickier kind of realization, covered in drool and Cheerios crumbs. But maybe this is the gift of mothering as practice—a kind of inclusiveness that embraces chaos and grit and imperfection. The journey of motherhood is a cascade of the extraordinary disguised as the unremarkable, of the universal mysteries manifesting as mundane details. Motherhood practice is not based on control or keeping things tidy. It makes room in its heart for an electric train—or a preteen slumber party—in the middle of the living room floor. It doesn't slip away in the middle of the night to search for enlightenment. It stays home with Rahula, the fetter, and finds it there.

As mothers, what can we make of that story of the Buddha leaving his family? I asked Fu.

"Oh, but he wasn't the Buddha when he left his child. He was a young prince, in terrible pain," she answered. "If you're awake, you don't leave your child. Where would you go?"

Butterfly Kiss for the Buddha

. . . . .

I'M SPEEDING DOWN Sir Francis Drake Boulevard on a glorious fall day, running through yellow lights, completely stressed out, trying to get to the meditation hall on time.

I'm teaching the daily yoga classes at a women's meditation retreat at Spirit Rock, a Buddhist retreat center in a rural valley north of San Francisco. But my beloved babysitter, Megan—a twenty-something Zen student with beads and tiny electronic parts woven into her turquoise-and-blonde dreadlocks—had gotten caught in a traffic jam and arrived at my house an hour late. Then I got stuck in the same freeway snarl myself. As I barrel down the winding country road, I imagine a cop pulling me over: "But, officer, it's a dharma emergency! A hundred women in deep meditation are waiting for me!" I burn rubber into the Spirit Rock parking lot, walk up the hill to the meditation hall as fast as possible while still appearing mindful and serene, and get to the yoga room with seconds to spare, just as the bell is ringing to end the last sitting period.

It's two days into the seven-day retreat and I'm already exhausted. I would have loved to have participated in the entire schedule of this silent meditation intensive, "Reclaiming the Sacred Feminine," a title that hinted that it might explore some territory that wasn't exactly mainstream Buddhist orthodoxy. But as the mother of a two-year-old, sitting a full retreat isn't possible. So I'm flip-flopping identities each day: a mom all night and morning, a yogini all afternoon and evening.

Unfortunately, Forest has been cutting two molars this week. Last night, he woke me up six times between 11:00 p.m. and 4:00 a.m., at which point I finally brought him into bed with me—where he thrashed around for another two hours, whimpering and talking in his sleep. At one point he cried out in delight, "What's that down there? It's . . . it's the gas pedal!" Then he half woke up and began rooting at my chest, mumbling, "More gas pedal! More gas pedal!" in what appeared to be an archetypal male conflation of car and breast.

By day, he has been in classic two-year-old mode, exploring the limits of autonomy and personal power. All is harmonious as long as I let him indulge his current olfactory obsession: opening and sniffing every jar in my spice drawer, identifying each by scent. That morning, we'd sat and smelled them together for over an hour—"Nutmeg! Cardamom! Rosemary! Turmeric!"—until my nose hummed and tingled in what felt like a practice dreamed up by a Zen master on LSD.

But when I tried to take him to meet some friends at a nearby park, all hell broke loose. Forest didn't want to leave the car; he just wanted to sit in his car seat listening to Al Green's "Love and Happiness" nineteen times in a row, while taking periodic hits off his bottle of cinnamon, which he had insisted on bringing with him. Exhausted and starved for adult conversation—even if it was just comparing teething notes with another mom—I did not handle the situation quite as tactfully as I might have. The outing ended in a fiasco, with the absurd spectacle of me grimly hauling a screaming, flailing child toward a playground, in a shower of tears and cinnamon, while he shrieked as if I were carrying him off to the electric chair: "No slide! No swing! More 'Yuv and Happiness!'" I finally surrendered and took him back to the car. As I started the engine to drive home, the tears turned off like a faucet and were replaced with beams. "I just want you to cooperate," he told me cheerfully—then chugged a juice box and passed out.

So as I drive off to the retreat that afternoon, let's just say I don't exactly feel like the Divine Mother. But arriving at Spirit Rock feels like diving into a pool of peace. The center is tucked in a valley of burnt-gold hills; the autumn air is a musky, minty blend of sage and pennyroyal. After teaching two gentle yoga classes, I sit the rest of the afternoon in the domed meditation hall, dipping thirstily into a vast well of silence.

In two years of motherhood, my body has forgotten what a meditation retreat is like. It's astonishing to find myself, even for a few hours, in the midst of a hundred silent women, all of them moving slowly, as if underwater—sometimes smiling, sometimes weeping as they stop and sit down in the middle of their hundred individual lives, each as intense and vivid and complicated as my own. I sink into the luxury of having nothing to do but feel my body and heart, breath by breath. For a few hours I stop skimming along the surface of my life and swim into the depths.

As I walk from my silent dinner toward the meditation hall that night—pausing to savor the crimson sunset and the wild turkeys rustling through the long grass—I find myself asking my perennial question: How can I make my life feel more like a meditation retreat? How do I bridge the apparent gap between yogini and mom?

In a dharma talk that evening, the *vipassana* teacher and psychotherapist Debra Chamberlin-Taylor—a mentor of mine for over a decade—offers a few hints. The *sacred feminine*, she explains, is a psychological term for an archetypal spiritual dimension that exists in both men and women. It is nonlinear and receptive. It's about being, rather than doing; integrating, rather than analyzing. It moves in spirals and circles, rather than lines and angles. It intuitively perceives all of life as an interconnected whole (which, of course, is also one of Buddhism's central teachings). It values the world, the body, the emotions, relationships, the connections of the heart. But in our daily lives—and even in our spiritual practice—it is often paved over by the more masculine attributes of action, analysis, and achievement.

In Buddhist practice, this powerful energy is symbolically represented by images such as Kuan Yin, a female manifestation of an awakened being who "hears the cries of the world" and responds to them. In Tibetan practice, there's the compassionate goddess Tara in her myriad forms and colors. In other spiritual traditions, it takes the form of a Divine Mother, such as Mother Mary, or a consort, such as Parvati. Invoking such images, says Debra, can help us relax and expand our meditation practice to embrace with compassion the chaos of our daily lives, rather than trying to escape it or push it away.

Debra emphasizes that both men and women can benefit from connecting with the image of a Kuan Yin or Tara. It's not about trying to project "feminine" and "masculine" qualities onto actual women and men. However, she says that for her, there's been something especially powerful about leading all-women retreats.

Whether shaped by biology or by culture, women's deep involvement with relationships, family, children, and home has traditionally been viewed in most religions as an impediment to spiritual practice. "On a women's retreat with women teachers, they will come into dharma interviews talking about their divorces, their hot flashes, the pain of leaving their children for the first time to go on retreat—things they say they have never dared to talk about on a meditation retreat before," Debra says. She is sitting on the dais flanked by two statues: a traditional male Buddha, and a slender, busty female deity called Prajnaparamita, the mother of all Buddhas. "And when these experiences are seen as sacred, as part of the spiritual journey—rather than as something to be discounted and passed over en route to something more 'spiritual'—the whole field of awareness opens up, and women can go deeper into their meditative practice than they have ever gone before."

That night, Forest is restless again, waking up and calling me over and over. He doesn't want to come to my bed, but he also doesn't want to be alone in his crib in his bedroom next door. Finally, at three o'clock in the morning, I lie down on the floor of his bedroom, wrapped in a quilt, to keep him company as he falls asleep.

The floor is hard; I can't sleep. So I lie there and meditate, feeling my breath go in and out. I am trying to rest with exactly what is: exhaustion, the aching bones, a vast loneliness wrapped around my heart.

Yet I find myself also opening my heart to the joy of that moment: My child lying in his crib, clutching his blue blankie and his stuffed lion. The room filling up with his earthy, yeasty smell, like a cross between lawn clippings and baking bread. The intimate textures of my daily life, filled with "Love and Happiness" and the smells of cinnamon, nutmeg, cardamom, and ginger.

And in that moment, I am on retreat, present in the moment—as much as if I'd been in a cloister at Spirit Rock.

Kuan Yin, I remind myself, does not hide from the world. She sees it all and embraces it, like a mother holding a child. She finds the sacred right here, amid the smells of the spices, the tantrums, and laughter. She finds it in the relationship struggles, the teething, the pain and joy and mundane tasks of everyday life. She reminds us that rebirth is possible in every moment and, indeed, is only possible in this moment.

The next morning, running around the house in his pajamas, Forest stops and points to the beautiful sandalwood Buddha statue on my mantelpiece. "There's the Buddha!"

I get the statue down and hand it to him. "Eskimo kiss for the Buddha!" he says, and he rubs his nose against the Buddha's. "And now a butterfly kiss for the Buddha!" And he flutters his eyelashes, intimately, against the Buddha's cheek.

The Terrible Twos
(Or, More Yuv and Happiness)

. . . . .

THIS IS A story I couldn't bring myself to tell until years after it was over.

It is a tale of tantrums. Of tears in the middle in the night and howls of rage. Of someone standing on the back patio, smashing plates on the ground and wailing, because they didn't get what they wanted.

Oh, wait. Did you think I was talking about Forest?

AUGUST
"DO YOU WANT TO BUY SOMETHING???"

I open my eyes blearily. In the pale glow of the streetlight through the closed curtains I can see Forest, who turned two last month, sitting bolt upright in bed next to me, clutching his stuffed lion. I'd carried him into bed with me at 3:30 a.m. from his crib in the next room, when he wouldn't go back to sleep after I nursed him. He has tossed and turned next to me for a couple of hours, muttering in his sleep. Now he has jolted wide awake, seized by an idea that is just too good to keep to himself.

"Do you want to go to the store and buy something???" he shouts again.

I know it isn't really a question. At two, he reverses his pronouns, mirroring the way other people speak to him. For example, "Do you want some juice?" means that he's thirsty. When he tells me, "I won't do that," he means that he doesn't want me to do something, and he's hoping that's what I'll say.

"It's too early, sweetie." I roll toward him, away from the empty pillow on the other half of my king-size bed. I always leave that side of the bed open, even though no one but me has slept there for months. "The stores aren't open yet."

"Do you want to go in the *car*! Do you want to drive? Do you want music! Music, *music*!"

I snuggle my arms around him. "You are my sunshine, my only sunshine . . ." I sing sleepily. "You make me happy, when skies are gray . . ."

He pushes me away with a contemptuous shriek. "Do you want music on a CD!"

"We could put a CD on the stereo," I suggest.

"A CD in the *car*!"

"Forest, it's still dark. The stores are closed. This is really, really not an option." I look at the other side of the bed—the pillows stacked, the comforter pulled neatly up, waiting for a mate who's not there.

A few months earlier, when Forest was nineteen months old, my husband moved out.

I'm not going to give you the details of how our marriage unraveled. I'm not going to tell you what things could not be undone, what words could not be unsaid.

I'll just share with you this one terrible image: I am screaming at my husband as he puts on his coat. I am crying and grabbing his arm. When he twists it away, I hit him on his shoulder. And when he walks out the door and closes it behind him, I turn and see Forest kneeling on the floor of the living room, crying. He is banging his forehead against the floor, over and over.

With a few deep breaths, I try to switch from melting-down woman to *Mommy*. I scoop up my son and hold him close.

From the outside, my life as a poster-mama for "mindful mothering" appears to be going great. I have begun publishing regular essays about mothering as meditation practice. I just directed a conference on "spiritual parenting" for the Kripalu Center for Yoga and Health. I've become the West Coast editor for *Tricycle: The Buddhist Review*—a job I can do part-time from my home office. And

I teach a regular Friday morning yoga and meditation class at Spirit Rock Meditation Center.

But here's what my readers and students don't see: I am living alone with Forest, who still doesn't sleep through the night despite several failed attempts at "sleep training." Following the advice of my "attachment parenting" books, I'm still breastfeeding him on demand whenever he asks for "nummy," although he has been eating solid food for more than a year. And since "demand" doesn't end with nightfall, I haven't slept more than three straight hours since he was born. Exhaustion is wearing me into a bundle of shredded nerves. After he falls asleep, around seven o'clock each evening, I don't light a candle and meditate, as I always tell myself I will. Instead, I turn on the TV my husband had left behind and watch *Dr. Phil* and a rerun of *Friends* while I eat my solo dinner. Then I pass out on the couch, my dirty dishes parked on the carpet beside me, until Forest wakes me up to nurse again a couple of hours later.

Compounding my pain is a sense of spiritual failure. I am a yoga and meditation teacher. I teach and write about serenity, calm, peace, clarity, connection. How can my life be such a mess? I am so ashamed of the problems in my marriage that I haven't even told my friends and family that my husband and I are separated. This, of course, makes it hard to reach out for support. In my fitful sleep, I regularly dream that the characters from *Friends* have dropped by my house to keep me company. When I wake up, I feel bereft.

Now, outside the bedroom window, the sky is streaked with rose and orange. Forest nurses until he calms down and forgets about CDs and cars. I am half-asleep when I hear him begin to murmur a word under his breath over and over, so softly I can't make it out. This is something that he does when a thing is so wonderful and out of reach—and he wants it so badly—that he can't let himself say it out loud until I say it for him. Looking down, I see he is smiling.

Awake now, finally, I guess the word: "*Teabag*?"

"Teabag!" he exclaims ecstatically. "Do you want a teabag? Do you want some tea? Is it ready?"

I kiss the top of his head, inhale the smell of his hair. "Sure."

He slides out of bed. "It has to steep. Forest will steep it!"

He runs joyfully down the hall in his footsie pajamas. I slip on my robe and follow him, thinking of all the things that I long for that seem so impossible I don't dare say them aloud.

SEPTEMBER

"Before we begin," says the couples therapist cheerfully, leaning back in her chair, "I have one very important question."

My husband and I sit side by side on the therapist's soft, cream-colored couch. There is a floor-to-ceiling mirror on the wall behind my husband, so I can't look at him without seeing myself. *Is this some kind of metaphor?* I wonder. The therapist's pit bull is sleeping beside her, casually blocking the exit. On a side table, a lit candle shaped like the head of a Buddha is slowly melting.

"My question is this," she continues. "Are you coming to therapy to put your marriage back together? Or to consciously take it all the way apart?"

My husband and I look at each other. I catch a glimpse of my worried face in the mirror behind him. The dog shifts and whines in its sleep, its legs twitching as it chases an imaginary intruder.

Finally, one of us says, "We don't know."

When I come home from therapy, Forest—who I left with his babysitter—is sitting on the kitchen floor next to my old boom box, hitting the repeat button on his favorite Bob Marley CD. As I walk in, he looks up at me with a big grin. "Every little thing! Gonna be all right!" he announces.

I pick him up and wrap him in my arms, hoping he is right.

My husband and I are determined not to let our fracturing marriage impact our coparenting of Forest. We are not going to use him as a weapon to hurt each other. We're going to make sure that whatever happens between us, he will have two parents who love him.

We've agreed that at just two years old—and still nursing—Forest still needs to live with me. Forest's dad will help support me to go on living in our home. Late most afternoons, Forest's dad comes over after he's done at his office. While I get in some yoga or get some writing done, he chases Forest around the living room, holding the stuffed lion and pretending to roar. Sometimes we take Forest for walks together, with him walking between us, each of us holding one of his hands. We all dance together and clap our hands to his favorite song by Al Green, "Love and Happiness." Forest shouts, "Do you want more 'Yuv and Happiness'?" And we play it again.

We are still a family. Except that after giving Forest his bath, his dad leaves, and I'm on my own again for another long, long night.

Forest is in the middle of what is often called the "terrible twos"—the age when toddlers claim their sense of their independent personhood by defying and testing their parents. He's a funny, precocious kid who hit all his milestones early—talking at ten months, walking at eleven. He's also what my parenting books call—tactfully—"high need." He demands constant interaction, negotiating every transaction like a little lawyer. He's especially good at this when I'm trying to slip out of the courtroom for a break. On yet one more night when I'm exhausted and Forest doesn't want to sleep, I drag myself into the dim light of his room in response to his call. Forest, standing in his crib, wide awake, greets me.

"How 'bout we make a deal?"

"Forest, we already made a deal. More nummy and then you get in your crib with no crying—that was the deal."

Long pause, then, hopefully, "More deal?"

Forest has eccentric obsessions and rituals—for example, he'll regularly turn down a trip to the park in favor of dragging me to the "weird gri-age" to eat a bowl of blueberries with him one at a time, while he ponders and kicks the mechanism by which the garage door opens and closes. While he sleeps, my journals fill with notes and anecdotes about this small, goofy person I'm living with.

As we were walking into the house yesterday, Forest pointed at a container of liquid soap for washing the car, which earlier I had stopped him from pouring on the ground.

"No wasting," he says.

"That's right," I say, "no wasting."

Pause. "Do you want to waste???" asked with great eagerness.

"No, I don't want to waste."

Chin puckering. "I really want to waste!!!"

"No, no wasting."

In despair: "Oh man! I really want to waste!!!"

I'm in love with him. And I'm exhausted.

For my Friday morning yoga and meditation class at Spirit Rock, I am leading a deep-dive series on *metta*, the quality of loving-kindness that Buddhism teaches is the natural state of the human heart and mind, once all the things that obscure it are removed. At this ragged stage in my life, claiming this as my natural state seems about as plausible as announcing that my natural home is on Pluto. But still, every week, I guide my students to melt the armor around their hearts through gentle backbends and twists—to do their poses with kindness, greeting each part of the body with compassion. After yoga, I lead guided meditations in which we recite the classic metta phrases over and over while broadcasting healing energy in all directions: "May all beings everywhere be happy. May all beings be healthy. May all beings be safe. May all beings live with ease and well-being."

One Thursday afternoon, in the middle of the metta series, I get in a fight with Forest's dad when he arrives to take Forest for a walk to the park. After they leave, I go into my yoga room and kick the wall next to my meditation cushions so hard that I leave a big dent next to the altar, right behind my little bronze statue of Kuan Yin, the goddess of compassion.

The next morning my foot hurts so badly that I can't do standing poses in class. I revise my sequence so it's all reclining, restorative positions. "Radiate kindness in all directions," I instruct my students in my most soothing voice, as they drape back over their bolsters.

"Metta is a purification practice. It brings things to the surface," my mentor, Anna Douglas, tells me. "And sometimes what it brings to the surface is all the things that are getting in the way of your access to metta. So often, when you do metta, you feel the opposite."

Great news! The practice seems to be working.

OCTOBER

Forest has a new obsession: smelling the tiny bottles of essential oils I keep on the window ledge in my bathroom. He can identify each with a sniff: lavender, clove, ylang-ylang, cedar, mint, pine. Whereas he used to wake up in the morning and say, "Do you want to listen to Al Green?" now he wakes up and asks, "Do you want to go smell the bergamot?"

He has also developed a craving for the cherry-flavored Infant Tylenol I give him when he has a fever. Between demands to "go smell the essential oils," he demands hits of "red medicine" and wails when I refuse. Sometimes I compromise and take him to Whole Foods for a red smoothie instead. "Now we're cooperating," he tells me cheerfully as he sucks it up through his straw.

"He's a total stoner kid!" I tell my sister on the phone. "It's like, 'Hey man, let's drop some red medicine, put on some Al Green, and smell the essential oils.' Is this my punishment for a misspent youth?"

My sister reassures me that this is totally normal two-year-old behavior. But I'm starting to wonder. One night, while his Grandma Joan is visiting from down the street, Forest screams so long and loud for red medicine that she leaves in a huff—her children had never screamed like this, she berates me, *not once*. After she leaves, Forest keeps screaming. I am so tired, lonely, and at the end of my rope that I scream back—a long, wordless shriek that stops him in his tracks, his face convulsed with horror. Then I collapse on the sofa, crying.

"Mommy! Mommy!" he wails in distress, then suggests, "Some nummy will help Mommy feel better!"

And then, with anxious determination: "Mommy's happy! Mommy's happy!"

I sob, "I'm sad."

But then I pull myself together, put on my Mother mask, and say, "But you do make me happy. I'm happy now. Is Forest happy?"

He briefly—and horribly—makes his face into a caricature, a grimace, of a happy smile. Then he drops the mask and goes back to crying.

"Metta—loving-kindness—is not about producing a particular feeling," I once heard Ajahn Sumedho, a Buddhist monk, say. "It's about the attitude of the mind and heart with which you meet everything—even the rage and hatred. It's not about pasting on a happy face. It's about being with the tears with kindness."

Can my metta practice include this moment too? Can its healing energy touch even the parts of me—and my family—that are the most broken? Can it help me reknit my unraveling heart?

I know I'm not the only meditation practitioner—or teacher, for that matter—to crash on the submerged rocks in the sea of human relationships. As a journalist chronicling the world of yoga and Buddhism, I've told their stories: The alcoholic, married Zen master who had affairs with his senior students. The Indian guru who encouraged his devotees to lifetimes of celibacy—with the exception of secret trysts with him.

But I still believe that somehow, if I had just done my practice right, my life would look different. My husband and I would be living happily together. My two-year-old would snuggle sweetly in his grandmother's lap at every visit, giggling as she read "Sarah Cynthia Sylvia Stout / Would not take the garbage out!" On the rare occasions when he pitched a tantrum, I would follow the advice in the parenting books: *Set firm boundaries. Respond, don't react.* And he would be happy again.

Instead of thinking of the collapse of my marriage as a failure, a disaster, can I hold it in my heart as my koan, my doorway into the deepest wounds of my psyche that need healing? Can it be the knot that I must penetrate with loving awareness so I can dissolve into the big heart of my true nature? Can my broken heart teach me to cherish my connection with all the other aching beings in this imperfect world?

I rock Forest as he cries. "May you be happy," I tell him silently. "May you be peaceful. May you be safe. May you live with ease and well-being."

I try to hold myself with the same kindness.

NOVEMBER

I snap at Forest when he won't stop banging his cup on the sliding glass door to the patio. His chin starts to quiver, so I hug him and say, "I'm sorry I snapped at you. Mommy's just feeling sad."

He studies my face. "Mommy is sad and pretty."

"Oh, thank you, sweetie!" Now I feel even worse about snapping at him.

He thinks for a minute and says, "E minor."

I know he's been learning to recognize the chords that his dad plays on the guitar, but I don't understand what he means. "What about E minor?" I ask.

"E minor is also sad and pretty."

My husband and I are both seeing other people—while still going to couples therapy with each other to try to figure out what form our relationship is going to take.

I never ask him who he's seeing. She's just the phone, ringing unanswered in his pocket as we push Forest's stroller down the sandy path to Muir Beach. She's simply the reason I get his voicemail when I call him at midnight, worried because Forest has a fever.

He doesn't ask me about the man I'm seeing either—a carpenter and massage therapist I've been friends with for years. My acupuncturist has listened to my pulses and told me that I need to "eat more meat and have more fun." So my lover cooks me steak, unclogs my kitchen drain, massages me with lavender-scented almond oil in front of the woodstove in my living room, scatters rose petals on my bed before we lie down together. He always leaves before Forest wakes up to nurse.

Meanwhile, my husband and I drive together to couples therapy every other week, trading stories about Forest on the drive up and back. In the therapist's office, we try on various visions—maybe we will stay married but also see other people and live in separate houses! Maybe we will build another house on our property, right up the hill from the main one, and one of us will live in it! Maybe we could try an approach we'd read about called "bird-nesting," where there is one house that the kid lives in, and the divorced parents take turns visiting instead of having the kid come back and forth!

A part of me knows none of these arrangements will ever work. But when Forest gets sick, his dad is the only one who worries as much as I do. When Forest says something hilarious, my husband is the first person I want to tell about it. Forest is *ours*. After one difficult night, when Forest had kept me awake from 2:30 to 5:00 a.m., his dad greets him the next evening by asking, "Did you have a difficult night?"

Forest answers, "You did. And so did Mommy."

"Good empathy!" his dad says, encouragingly. And when Forest looks puzzled, "That means, good *feeling*."

Forest's face lights up with comprehension. "Just like the feeling when the poop's about to come out!"

And his dad and I burst out laughing together.

I keep trying to find my way to a kind of love that can hold this whole strange, painful situation. I think of something I heard Thich Nhat Hanh say when someone asked him the difference between lay practice and monastic practice. "They're exactly the same practice," he said. "But monastic practice is easier."

There's one way of doing yoga that's about perfection: polishing your postures until they sparkle like a magazine cover.

And then there's the yoga of the slipped disc, the blown-out knee, the bad-news blood test. The yoga that's about holding in your heart your broken and bumbling human body, even when—especially when—it's clearly falling apart.

It's this yoga that I'm turning to now—the yoga that teaches me that it is through my brokenness that I can touch my full humanity, the way I might touch the soft spot on the top of a baby's head and feel the heartbeat.

I remember years earlier, just out of college, I went to the post office to mail a package and the woman behind the counter was crying. She wept, silently, as she weighed my package, took my money, printed out the sticker, and affixed it to the box. Back then I didn't know what to do or say. I pretended she wasn't crying. I said a polite thank you and turned away.

Now, it amazes me that all of us aren't regularly bursting into tears as we go through our days. Now, I know what I'd do: I'd meet her eyes across the post office counter. I'd say, "I'm so sorry you're hurting. I know how you feel."

I'd send her metta.

JANUARY

I dream that I am on a meditation retreat.

I can't make it to the meditation hall, though, because I am trying to clean up a child's play area, which is littered with plastic horses, pigs, and sheep. I am frustrated and anxious.

Suddenly my teacher, Thich Nhat Hanh, appears in front of me. I feel a powerful blast of his distinctive energy—firm, peaceful, and radiant, "a cross between a cloud and a bulldozer," as another Zen teacher once described him. I instantly feel at peace.

Lovingly and with utter certainty, Thich Nhat Hanh gives me a spiritual command: "Your practice is to take this one small area and make it beautiful."

Is this time of my life terrible? Or wonderful?

Here's one thing that I've learned for sure through my practice of yoga and meditation: Nothing is solid. Drop below the *idea* of things—my back, my shoulder, my child, my marriage—and what is revealed is a shimmering, ever-changing, shape-shifting river.

Life isn't painted in solid swipes of all one color, like a fence. It's as pixelated as an impressionist painting. It's made out of countless dots of moments—some ecstatic, some heartbreaking. And joy and sadness oscillate, breath by breath.

I might say something like *I have a bad back*. But my meditation practice tells me to look closer at what I call "bad," to name what I actually feel, moment by moment: Is there pressure? Tingling? Burning? Throbbing? Is the sensation continuous or does it move around? What I call pain may be made up of a thousand shimmering sensations—some of them unpleasant, some of them not.

And I can also turn my attention to somewhere in my body that isn't hurting—that may actually feel wonderful. Yes, my back hurts. But the cool taste of a peach from the farmers' market is still a sunburst of joy in my mouth.

It's like that with my life. My journal wails my hard times:

Last night, Forest woke up at 4:30 to nurse; then called me ten minutes later, wanting a diaper change; then again, five or ten minutes later, wanting another diaper change. When I called through the wall of his room "No! Wait until morning!" he sobbed, "You can't sleep with a pee-pee diaper, you don't want to sleep with a pee-pee diaper," over and over until I changed it. Then five minutes later he needed it changed again. After that, he wanted to nurse again. ("One more nummy, then sleep. Are you having a hard time sleeping?") Then he refused to get back in his crib. By this time, it was six o'clock, and I was so exhausted, and I knew it would be light soon. I shouted, "Go to sleep! Go to sleep!" He burst into tears and lay down, clutching his blue blankie, his breath hiccupping, sobbing "Forest's sleeping! Forest's sleeping!" So of course I picked him up and said I was sorry, nursed him (still hiccupping) till he calmed down. When I put him back in his crib, he fell asleep until 8:30. But I couldn't get back to sleep. I felt so awful, such a bad mommy, such a failure at my life. I wanted to call Forest's dad and rage into his voicemail, "Why aren't you here?"

But on the next page, it sings to my joy: how I curl with Forest on the couch and read *Jamberry* aloud to him. "One berry, two berry! Pick me a blueberry!" It describes the intoxicating smell of his neck, and his bright laughter, and the way he grabs his "rhythm sticks" from the basket of toys and begins to drum on the top of the coffee table, shouting "Feel the beat!" It tells of Forest nursing and suddenly beginning to breathe loudly through his nose. He looks up at me and says, "Forest's purring like the kitty!"

My practice has taught me to pay attention to these moments—to shift my attention to what isn't hurting; to feel the joy and connection, and rest in them.

The true yoga, I have to learn again and again, is not about fitting my body into the idealized shape of a perfect pose. It's about meeting my body and my heart just as they are—flawed, fragile, and glorious.

I can't reboot into a new metta-fied version of myself, always shiny and happy and serene.

But I can remind myself that my capacity for metta exists and incline my mind in its direction. I can meet even my failures to do so with kindness.

And when I do, metta helps me remember to not let the parts of my life that are hurting overwhelm the rest—so I don't miss the magic.

Yesterday, after we pulled into our driveway, Forest refused to get out of his car seat—he just wanted to sit there and hear "The Animal Song" over and over. "It's by Bob Dylan," he reminded me. So I cranked up the volume on the CD, got out of the car myself, and began to dance in the driveway. Eventually he got out too and began to dance with me, bending his tiny legs, bobbing up and down.

"*Man gave names to all the animals / in the beginning / long time ago . . .*" The *asphalt was warm under our bare feet, the breeze was cool, the crows fretted in the redwoods. The eucalyptus tree glowed in the setting sun.*

MARCH

Forest has been learning to use a training potty, which sits next to the big toilet in my bathroom. We have established a ritual: he poops in the little potty, then I dump the poop into the big potty, then he flushes it down.

One day I space out in the middle of this process—thinking about getting out the door in time for yoga—and flush the poop myself.

Forest insists that he has to poop *again*, so that he can flush it. He sits on the potty with tears pouring down his face, screaming, "Do you want to poop? There's no poop! Why is the poop not coming out? Mommy help you! Forest has to poop more and then Forest flush it down the toilet!"

Just then, my husband walks in for his afternoon visit.

"I'll take over," he says. "You can go to yoga."

But Forest howls, "No! Mommy help you! Do you want to poop *right now*??"

"We could flush something else down the toilet!" I suggest, inspired.

Forest gets an expression like maybe there's a tiny ray of light in the darkness. "Something else? Flush something else?"

"Like a piece of bread!"

Forest's face lights up. "Bread turns into poop," he says thoughtfully, just checking to make sure.

"That's right," I say. "Bread turns into poop when you eat it."

Forest looks suspicious. "Bread turns to poop when you flush it down the toilet!" He insists.

"That's right." I'm willing to agree to anything. "Bread turns to poop when you flush it down the toilet."

My husband gets a piece of bread from the kitchen and squeezes it into a pale brown log. He carries it into the bathroom on a napkin. He proclaims, "Here comes the poop! Don't touch the poop!"

Together, he and Forest toss it into the toilet. Forest flushes it. My husband and I are laughing so hard we are practically pooping our pants ourselves. My husband says, "This is the strangest ritual I have ever done."

But the bread doesn't go down! It comes bobbing back up! Forest looks terribly worried. "Maybe we'll have to weight it down with little rocks," I say, trying to keep a straight face.

But Forest flushes again and it goes down this time, and we all say, solemnly, "Bye-bye poop," and then Forest is happy again.

"But I have to say, it will feel a little weird next time I make toast," I tell my husband.

Love—I am learning through being a mother—isn't just an emotion. It is something you have to *do*.

Yes, you have those amazing moments when your heart cracks open and you just cannot believe the waves of bliss, your good fortune. But you don't always feel that way. Small children scream, they are difficult, they are shockingly immature, they do not leave you a moment to yourself.

"All children want," my mother once told me, "is 100 percent of your attention 100 percent of the time. If you give that to them, they are happy."

So you keep showing up. You keep showing up, and taking care of them, because love is not a state of being. Love is a verb.

And gradually you are transformed into somebody else. The little straitjackets you have pushed your love into begin to soften and fray.

That's when the real metta can start to flow.

MAY

We are visiting my friend Rachael, and Forest decides he wants to exit her house through the cat door in her kitchen.

Ever since a mutual friend introduced us earlier this year, Rachael—whose daughter Sonya is a year younger than Forest—has been a lifeline. Like me, she had a full career as an artist before becoming a mother—in her case, as an actor, director, and acting teacher. Like mine, her marriage has challenges. "Life's too short not to be real with each other," she says—and we tell each other about our loneliness, our frustration, our ambition, our exhaustion, as we watch our kids "parallel play" on her living room floor. She's one of the few people I've told that my husband doesn't live with me anymore.

Forest is definitely too big to go through her cat door.

He can put his head through the flap, but then his shoulders get stuck. He can put his legs through, but his butt won't go.

But he just won't believe that he is too big. He keeps trying and trying, getting more and more frustrated and exhausted. "Mommy help you!" he keeps crying. "Do it, please!"

"You're too big," I tell him again and again. "You need to go through the big boy door." When he won't let go of this obsession, I try to distract him with a cheerful, "It's time to go home and have a burrito!"

But he just stands there sobbing, his chin quivering. He says, "Okay, here's the deal. We go through the cat door. *Then* we go through the big boy door. *Then* we go home and have a burrito. Does that sound like a plan?"

Trying to get through a door you can't fit through is a futile task. But Forest's not the only one who's been trying to do that, I reflect as we drive home.

I've had this idea of our marriage as a door my husband and I need to fit through—a door of a certain shape and a certain size. The problem is, it's the wrong kind of door. And there's just no way we are going to fit through it.

About six months after the cat door incident, Forest's dad and I tell our therapist we are going to get a divorce. After the session we drive away together, tears streaming down our faces. "I love you," he says as he drops me off at what is now my house, not ours. "I wish I could be the one to come home with you, comfort you. I wish I could."

POSTSCRIPT

By the time Forest's dad and I actually signed our divorce papers, Forest would be five, and his dad and I would be friends again. After the notary witnessed our signature, we went out to lunch together. We toasted each other with sparkling water. We promised to coparent "till death do us part."

A few days later, in the car, Forest told me, "Some kids' parents live together and love each other. Some live together and don't love each other. Some don't live together and don't love each other. Others don't live together but love each other.

"That last kind is the kind that you and Daddy are."

It sometimes takes a long time for metta to transform a heart.

It's not like buying an airline ticket to a different city—a one-way ticket to metta, please!—and flying there nonstop. More often it's like a long backpacking trip through a desert. Every day you wake up, look around—same arid dry sand for miles. And you go on walking, earnestly checking your compass and the stars. After days you may find that you have been walking in circles and are back in the same place that you left from. You start out again.

And then one day, there are a few sprigs of grass in a meadow, and then more, and then a little stream. And one day—much, much later—you realize you are living in a green field, by a meadow and a stream, and you can't remember the last time you were thirsty. And you can't quite pin down the moment that the landscape changed. You just know that you are no longer where you were.

Here's something that I wish I had known, as I wept in that car with my husband that day after our therapy session: That many years later, I would be riding in a different car with Forest, age thirteen. Trying to change lanes through unrelenting traffic, I am stressed out by the time I will glide up the on-ramp onto the freeway.

"Phew," I say, as my shoulders relax. "That's a relief."

"You should send a message to your past self," Forest tells me. "Your self of a few minutes ago. Tell her it's all going to work out."

"What do you mean?"

"Well, time runs in two directions," he says confidently. "So when something stressful happens, and then it works out, I always send a message to my past self, letting me know that it's going to be okay. And when I'm feeling stressed out, I tune in to get the message from my future self—and that helps me relax."

So here's what I'd like to say to my past self: "You will be happy. You will be healthy. You will be safe. You will live with ease and well-being."

And off in some other dimension, I imagine my past self, believing me through her tears.

Beyond the Beyond

· · · · ·

FOREST WAS FOUR, and his preschool teacher was dying of lung cancer.

I'd known that she was fighting it a year earlier, when I first enrolled Forest in the Peaceable Kingdom, the wonderful little Montessori school that Toni ran on the bottom floor of her hillside home.

But month after month she continued to show up in her classroom every weekday morning—as she had for over thirty years—sitting at the head of a low table on a child-size chair, her spine ruler-straight and her gray hair cropped short, greeting each child with a warm smile and a firm instruction to "put on a smock and choose some work to do." Just after Christmas, though, after a particularly rough bout of chemotherapy, she left the classroom, went upstairs, and went to bed. She didn't come back down.

"Toni is resting," her assistant, Sarah, explained to the children.

But after she had been gone a few weeks, Forest came to me one evening in the kitchen as I was stir-frying tofu and broccoli. "Toni is never going to get better. She's never going to come back to school."

"Did Sarah tell you that?" I asked.

"No," he told me. "I just figured it out for myself."

"We don't know for sure that that's true," I told him, trying to choose my words carefully. "But she is very sick. Does that make you sad?"

He nodded. "It does."

Forest had come to the Peaceable Kingdom as a three-year-old refugee from a larger, more chaotic preschool, where he had spent his days sitting alone on a chair in the corner singing to himself and watching the other children squeal and play. By age three, he'd grown into a precocious, thoughtful, but eccentric child who could converse with adults about relativity but couldn't figure out how to play blocks with another little boy. Toni took him under her wing—as she did all the children—teaching him math and reading while training him step-by-step in the fundamental rules of social engagement: "Forest, go ask Baxter, 'Can you show me where to hang my coat?' Now say, 'Thank you, Baxter!'" A native Frenchwoman and strict disciple of the Montessori method, Toni had faith in the power of social conventions, and her rules quickly penetrated our own home too. Within a couple of weeks, Forest was watching me disapprovingly as I sneaked a piece of pasta with my fingers before placing our dinner plates on the table. "At the Peaceable Kingdom Montessori School," he reproved, "we aren't allowed to start eating until everyone is sitting down and a grown-up says 'Bon appétit.'"

Forest's first questions about death had started long before Toni got sick, as he encountered dead bugs, dead flowers, the half-eaten mouse our cat deposited on our doorstep, a crow we found in the garden with maggots crawling in its eye sockets. "Does everything die?" he asked as we buried under a lavender bush a hummingbird that had flown into our sunroom window and broken its neck. "Will I die too? Will you?"

I hadn't prepared any good answers in advance. As a California Buddhist mom, I didn't have a culturally agreed upon story to tell him, like the one I had learned as a child in Catholic school: when you die, your soul goes to heaven to live with Jesus. When it comes to discussions of the afterlife, Buddhism—at least the secular, intellectual brand I'd been studying here in the West—didn't really have any answers I thought would be reassuring to a three-year-old. ("Well, sweetie, it all has to do with the chain of interdependent co-origination . . .") Unlike some brands of Buddhism, the paths I'd studied didn't emphasize reincarnation, at least not in any literal sense, and I had trouble telling him a story I didn't believe myself. But I wanted to tell him something that would make him feel safe.

"Nothing really dies," I told him. "It just turns into something else. Everything is always changing form. Do you remember the pumpkin that rotted into the earth in your garden? Tomatoes sprouted where it used to be. This bird will go back to the earth and turn into lavender flowers and butterflies."

"When you die, will you turn into a flower?" he asked, looking a little worried. "Maybe," I said, patting the earth down over the hummingbird. He thought for a while, then asked, "But will the flower know that it used to be Mommy?"

He'd gone right to the heart of the central koan, the question of the persistence of individual consciousness. This was what had always bothered me too about New Agey stories that tried to gloss over the finality of death by professing an eternal identity. If you don't *remember* that you used to be a shepherd in medieval England or a princess in ancient Egypt, what difference does it make that you were?

Now, all I could say to Forest was what would come to be my mantra when it came to questions of the afterlife: "I don't know."

When Toni had been absent for over a month, Forest paused one evening as he was bouncing naked on my bed after his bath. "I'm going to assume that Toni's dead," he said.

"Oh, Forest-berry, she's not dead." I wrapped a towel around him and pulled him into my lap. "She's just very sick."

"But she's going to die."

I pressed my face against his damp hair. "She probably is."

"Will the worms eat her body?" he asked.

"Yes, they probably will." I wondered if I was a Bad Mommy. Maybe I should make up a nicer story than this: *No, no, sweetie, worms don't eat people. They just eat crows.* But Forest's dad and I had always prided ourselves on telling him the truth, as best we could.

"But she won't feel it," he said thoughtfully. "Because she will be dead. How long will it take her to go back to the earth and turn into something else?"

"Oh . . . about a month? Maybe a few months?" I felt myself getting into deeper and deeper waters. What kind of images was he creating in his head of his beloved teacher?

"Oh, that's way too long." He shook his head. "I think maybe . . . a day. And then she'll turn into a cat."

All on his own, it seemed, Forest was generating from scratch the theory of reincarnation, the story that—whether or not you literally believe it—captures an eternal truth: that nothing is separate from anything else, that all life is inextricably interwoven from generation to generation. He smiled at me. "So if I see a cat coming up to me and saying 'meow, meow,' I'll know it's Toni."

A few weeks later, Forest and I drove to Lake Tahoe so he could play in the snow for the first time. It was just the two of us, a special mommy-son solo adventure before I left to attend my first residential meditation retreat since before he was born. After a day of sledding, as we snuggled under a blanket by the fire, he asked me, "When children die, do their mommies die with them?"

The question took my breath away. Forest didn't know yet that he'd had an older sister. "Sometimes they do, but not always," I said. I stared at the flames, remembering Sierra's sweet round face, the fire of her cremation. A month after she died, I dreamed I went to visit her in a damp basement, where she was crying *"Mama! Mama!"*

Forest shook his head. "No, that's not right!" he said. "You're wrong about that! A mommy wouldn't let her kid be dead all by himself!"

"You could be right," I said. Certainly, some part of me had died with Sierra. Sometimes I am able to see her in the lavender bushes and the butterflies and Forest's plump lips and long fingers, so much like hers. Most days, that's not nearly enough to bring back that part of me that had gone with her.

"So if I die, you will die with me." Forest leaned his head against my shoulder. "So it will be okay. We won't be lonely. And we can talk to each other in dead language."

A few weeks later, we were sitting on the couch together, reading his current favorite bedtime story, *Will You Be My Friend?* It's a sweet story about a bunny and a bird who live in an old apple tree. The first time we'd read it, he had burst into tears in the middle, when the rain blew in and ruined Bird's nest. "What will she do?" he wailed, his face crumpling. But now that he knew it had a happy ending, he wanted to hear it over and over.

This time, when we finished, he said, "I wish I could live in an apple tree. Maybe I could die and turn into a bird!"

"Maybe you could just *pretend* to be a bird," I said, trying to steer the conversation away from death. But he wouldn't be deflected.

"Sometimes," he said, looking worried, "they take your body and burn you up. They don't even let you turn into something else."

"Who told you that?" I asked.

"Mary." Mary was his beloved babysitter, a Buddhist vegan belly dancer with a silver ring in her nose and deer tracks tattooed on her calf, who had taught him to bake bread, grow tomatoes, sing folk songs, and identify wildflowers. Mary is passionately devoted to the Whole Truth: She also told him, apparently, that eventually the sun would explode and burn up the planet Earth. ("But we don't have to worry," he reassured me. "It won't happen for a long time, until all the people on Earth have died out.")

"Well," I said now, "even if they burn your body, you still keep changing into something else. The ashes will change to something else. Remember the fireplace ashes we put in your garden? They'll be lettuce this summer."

He nodded. "So even if they burn me up, I'll still turn into animal, or maybe another boy, or something."

He sat for a while, obviously puzzling something out. "So . . ." he said. "Before I was a boy . . . before I was even a seed inside you . . . was I something else? Like an animal? Or another boy? Or was I just a boy right from the beginning?"

Possible answers flashed through my mind: *Before you were born, you were your father and mother, getting stoned to Brian Eno in a college dorm room twenty years ago and laughing till it hurt. You were your granny and grand-dad, dancing at an officers' hop in Georgia in the middle of World War II. You were a baby girl named Sierra, who your mommy and daddy loved so much they had to make a new one right away.* But before I could find any words, he went on.

"I think, probably, I was just a boy right from the beginning. That's what I think," he said. "That was a really good story. Is it time for bed yet, or do I have time to listen to 'Steal My Kisses' on iTunes?"

. . .

In early March, in the middle of the spring rains, Toni died.

When I told Forest, he looked worried but didn't cry. "How do you know?" he asked.

"Her daughter called and told me."

"But how do you really, really know for sure?"

I suggested to Forest that we could light a candle and some incense, and send love to Toni. He looked at me as if I was losing my marbles. "Mommy," he explained patiently, "Toni's dead."

"But we can still send love to her spirit," I said. "That's the part of her that lives in our hearts and will never die."

He nodded. "That's the part of her that will turn into something else," he said.

At school, each of the children had a different theory about where Toni had gone. Max said she had turned into a giraffe. Lulu said she was a star. Colin insisted that she had gone back to France.

Toni's husband was making a garden in their front yard, where he would scatter her ashes under a Japanese maple. The children would plant sunflowers and daffodils there.

It was spring, and the wild irises were blooming, just as they were six years ago when Sierra died. The baby quail were marching through our yard again, and the cat was stalking them. I couldn't give Forest any real answers about where Toni went. But I hoped he would always see her in the red maple leaves and the golden faces of the sunflowers. And I hoped that as he grew up in a world where nothing he loved could be held on to forever, that this way of seeing would be of some comfort to him.

On the Spectrum

. . . . .

THIS IS THE story about a diagnosis: *Your child's brain isn't normal.*

It's a story I didn't tell for many years because I was afraid that speaking it publicly would solidify it into truth. I could only tell it afterward, when the diagnosis—which seemed like a mountain—had turned into mist.

An old Chinese fable tells of a farmer whose horse runs away. When the neighbors commiserate, he simply says, "Bad luck? Good luck? Who knows?"

The farmer says the same thing when his stallion returns with a mare and a foal. And again, when his son is thrown while training the new colt and breaks a leg. And again, when the broken leg prevents his son from being drafted to fight a war.

Bad luck? Good luck? Who knows?

"I'm very concerned about Forest." My sister-in-law, a child psychologist, had pulled me over to a corner of the screened porch of our beach house.

Forest had just turned three, and we were finishing a weeklong family reunion on Sullivan's Island, just off the coast of Charleston. Every year, the whole Cushman clan chipped in to rent a few houses for our ever-growing tribe—which by then consisted of my parents, their seven children, their eighteen grandchildren, their two great-grandchildren, and an array of spouses and partners. The island had wide beaches with soft, fine sand; bathtub-warm waves where we spotted porpoises diving at dawn and swam in phosphorescence under the full moon.

But Forest wasn't particularly interested in splashing in the waves. Nor was he a fan of building sandcastles or digging moats. He preferred to carry a bottle of red Tylenol around the living room, or stare at the whirling ceiling fan trying to analyze the flicker of the blades, or sit in the sink turning the water on and off, on and off, over and over again. He had gradually stopped referring to himself as "you," but now he referred to everyone in the third person, including himself: "Mommy won't pat Forest on the head! It irritates him!"

"He's exhibiting rigid, repetitive behaviors," my sister-in-law continued, as we sat down on chairs gritty with sand, next to the abandoned bucket and shovel in which Forest had shown little interest. "He's ultra-sensitive to sounds and touch. And the way he scrambles his pronouns—that's very, very alarming. If that doesn't stop soon, I'd be very concerned."

I stared at her blankly. Repetitive behaviors, sensitive to sounds, idiosyncratic speech—wasn't that just normal toddler behavior? I didn't have anything to compare him to. "Concerned about what?"

"When you get home, take him in for observation and testing. I'll send you the name of a facility I've collaborated with in San Francisco. If they can't get you in, they'll be able to recommend someone."

"But—what would they be looking for? What do you think is wrong with him?"

She looked at me sadly. "I don't want to diagnose anything without testing. Oh, Anne—as a mother, and as a sister, my heart goes out to you."

Here's a strange thing, or maybe it's not so strange: When I go back, years later, and look at my journals from that time, I find almost nothing about the diagnosis. I just find stories of moments as they unfolded:

The other day Forest asked me, "Mommy? Do rocks have skin?"
"No."
"Why do rocks not have skin?"
"Well, because they're not exactly alive. Not the same way you and I are alive."
"Do they grow?"
"No, they don't grow."
"Why don't they grow?"
"Um . . . because they don't eat anything."

"Why don't they eat anything?" And then, as I'm pausing, trying to figure out why they don't eat: "I know why! Because they don't have mouths!"

Was I writing about a child who was brilliant, funny, adorable? Or a child who was weird, dysfunctional, doomed?

Two days after my conversation with my sister-in-law, I was back in California. At the end of a long day of travel home from the family reunion, it was almost midnight, and I was exhausted. After tucking Forest into bed, I couldn't wait until morning—I sat down at the computer and began to type phrases into Google. *Head banging. Tantrums. Doesn't play with toys. Doesn't play with other children. Says "you" when means "I."*

A flood of entries came up, all headlined with the same word: *Autism. Autism. Autism. Autism. Autism.* And a new word I'd never heard before: *Asperger's syndrome.*

Asperger's, I read, is "on the autism spectrum." It's a neurological disorder characterized by a "triad of impairments affecting social interaction, communication, and imagination, accompanied by a narrow, rigid, repetitive pattern of activities." People with Asperger's could be relatively high-functioning. But clearly the world didn't consider them "normal."

I read down a list of characteristics, all of them eerily familiar: Not playing with toys. Lack of interest in other children. (Forest at age two, pointing at a boy at the playground while shrieking in horror, "*What* is *dat*?") Unusual interests and repetitive behaviors. ("Do you want to smell the spices?") Fear or distress due to unexpected sounds or noisy, crowded places. (Carrying Forest out of his cousin's first birthday party as he shrieked in outrage and pain, after the kids began blowing on the noisemakers that were passed out as party favors.)

Even the things his dad and I bragged about to each other—his prodigious memory, his advanced vocabulary, his preference for conversing about wildflowers with adults at the playground rather than playing on the slide with other toddlers—all, apparently, were evidence of a crippling and incurable neurological disorder.

According to what I was reading, my child would never have friends the way "neurotypical" children would. He would not feel love or empathy or compassion. In social situations he would always be on the outside looking in—a robot in a litter of puppies.

And not only that—this was a genetic condition, which meant that it must be our fault. One of the theories floating around the Internet was that the increase in Asperger's and autism resulted from inbreeding fostered in elite universities and Silicon Valley tech culture: geeks marrying other geeks, producing dysfunctional super-geek spawn.

I had grown up as a "weird kid" and a bookworm. While other seventh-grade girls were putting on lip gloss and talking about boys, I was still galloping around the playground whinnying and jumping over bike racks, pretending to be the Black Stallion. I had married—and was now divorcing—an eccentric genius who had been kicked out of Princeton twice before graduating, and who had always been allergic to conventions such as a nine-to-five job. Apparently, we had crossbred our quirks.

I turned off the computer and dropped my forehead to the edge of my desk. In the past few years I'd survived the death of a baby, the collapse of a marriage, and now—my beloved son would have no friends?

Forest yesterday morning, after blowing his nose: "Mommy? Why is it that sometimes snot is a liquid and sometimes snot is a solid?"

The evening after my Google marathon, after Forest went to bed, I sat on the couch in my living room with Forest's dad. We were living separately now, on our way to a divorce, but I knew there was no one else in the world who loved Forest as much as I did.

I expected him to freak out when I told him what was going on. Instead, he looked thoughtful but not worried. "Well, we've always known that Forest is special. He's wired a little differently than other kids. I don't know that that's a bad thing."

"They say that the way he reverses pronouns is one of the signs of the disorder. He might never speak normally."

"We'll just explain it to him," he says confidently. "We've never really tried."

"They say he won't have friends. They say he won't know how to connect or exhibit empathy."

He shakes his head. "That just doesn't sound like the Forest I know."

"But what if—"

"Anne. We have to have faith in Forest," he said. "*I* have faith. No matter how far he goes inside a dark cave, I have faith that we'll be able to go in there and make contact with him."

Yesterday Forest was eating a big bowl of peas and ravioli. When he was done he looked at the empty bowl, somewhat wistfully, and asked, "Do peas and ravioli have a past tense?"

Does love have a past tense? Does marriage have a past tense? Does meditation have a past tense?

I arranged a consultation with a child psychologist. While we were waiting for our first appointment, I enrolled Forest at a cheerful, bustling preschool. I thought its focus on hands-on learning combined with a touch of academics would be a good fit—unlike the Waldorf school we visited, where Forest regarded the wooden toys and silky scarves with utter disinterest, like a college professor in a sandbox.

I watched as Forest bravely waved goodbye and took his seat in a little chair he pulled up just outside the "sharing circle" of twenty-six other children sitting cross-legged on the carpet. When I picked him up a few hours later, he was still sitting in the same chair, while the other children jostled for space around long, low tables covered with finger paints, crayons, and wooden blocks. "He didn't seem to be that interested in the materials," the teacher told me. "He didn't want to paint or draw. But he was very good! No trouble at all!"

"You did a good job at school," he informed me as I drove him home.

"Yes, you did!" I said. "And Forest says, 'I did a good job at school.'"

"*I* did a good job at school."

When I took him back the next day, though, he burst into tears. It turned out that he had thought that "going to school" was a one-time thing. He was devastated to learn that he was going to have to go every day (let alone another twelve or sixteen or twenty years).

Every day that week, I dropped him off and waved goodbye. Every day, when I picked him up a few hours later, he was still sitting in the same chair.

Early in the second week of school, I took him to the appointment with the child psychologist. She was a warm woman in her midforties, with short hair, enormous brown eyes, and a bright sunny office full of toys. I left him with her for a couple of hours of testing. A few days later, she went to his school and watched him for a morning.

"He's not a disciplinary issue," she told Forest's dad and me when we met with her to go over her conclusions. "And I don't think he's autistic. But I do think that he has Asperger's syndrome. He has a very sweet personality, which makes it easier. But I'm not going to sugarcoat it. He has a hard life ahead of him."

"Is there anything we can do?" I asked.

"There is no cure for Asperger's. But there are things you can do to handle the symptoms. I recommend you get a play therapist and enroll him in social skills training." She scribbled a phone number and name on a piece of paper and handed it to me. "I also recommend that you switch him to a smaller, quieter school where he can get more personal attention."

As we walked out the door, she called after us, "Good luck!"

Yesterday, the "play therapist" was here to coach Luca and Forest while I chat with Luca's mom, Lisa. Forest greets Luca enthusiastically, wants to play "chase" (the only game he knows). He chases Luca and accidentally knocks him down, Luca's stocking feet skidding out from under him on the hardwood living room floor. Luca wails and runs to Lisa, who keeps telling him, "It was an accident," while Forest asks me over and over, "Is he crying or laughing? Why does he not want to play chase anymore?"

"This," said the play therapist cheerfully, placing a plastic disk the size of a drink coaster on the coffee table in my living room, "is spaghetti!"

Forest, age three and a half, leaned over and examined the therapist's offering—a plastic disk about the size of his hand, molded in the shape of a pile of noodles, with a smear of red on top. "Why is that spaghetti?"

"It's *pretend* spaghetti," the play therapist explained. "Just like this"—she gestured at the green plastic sprig next to it—"is *pretend* broccoli. And this is a *pretend* banana. Do you want to have dinner?" She picked up the plastic banana and held it to her mouth. "Yum, yum! Do you want to try it?"

Forest looked at her as if she had lost her marbles. He picked up the broccoli and held it to his cheek. "Yum, yum," he repeated obligingly. His face was saying, "This is a weird, weird world. But if you want me to act as if these little bits of plastic are edible, I'll try to do it."

The therapist had begun coming to our house once a week for play coaching sessions. By that time, I'd transferred Forest to Peaceable Kingdom, Toni's tiny, orderly Montessori preschool in her downstairs living room. (I got the feeling that Toni was used to teaching "social skills" to American kids—she simply called it "manners.")

Forest's dad and I had made a decision: We were not going to use the term *Asperger's syndrome* to define our child, or even to describe him—not with him, not with each other, not with our friends, not even with his teachers. We would just look at the specifics of his challenges and gifts, and work with them.

Because here's something I already knew for sure from my yoga practice: As soon as you have the idea of a "yoga pose" in your mind—say, for example, Triangle Pose—the idea also arises in your mind of "doing it wrong" and "doing it right." You think that Triangle Pose is the way it's pictured in *Yoga Journal*—the muscles rippling in the abs of the guy with no shirt on, the perky breasts and lithe waist of the yoga bunny. The feet are this far apart. The hips flex at this angle. The ribs roll this way, the gaze that way. You hold the image in your mind, and then you try to mold your own body into it—wishing you could snip off the parts that don't fit, like the extra dough around the edges of a cookie cutter.

But what happens to your yoga if you stop trying to fit your body into the mold of a pose and instead let it find its own unique expression, from the inside out? Your body is tight in some areas—you help it open. It's weak in others—you encourage its strength.

You come to understand that your body will not look like the body in the photo in the yoga book—because that photo is not alive and it's not you.

And gradually you come to see—every human body is a collection of gifts and challenges that are intimately related. The flexible spine that enables a deep backbend has a tendency to be unstable. The strong hamstrings from decades of cross-country running impede the ability to bend forward.

Do you want to force your spine into a backbend that's picture-perfect? Or you do want to find the freedom, the ease, the joy, that is available within the spine that you actually have?

Forest: "If there is an earthquake will our house fall down?"
   Me: "You don't need to worry about our house. It's very solid."
   Forest (eyes getting big): "Are some people's houses liquid????"

I began taking Forest to a twice-weekly social skills group that met at 8:30 in the morning at Parents Place in San Francisco, a forty-five-minute drive from our house.

The first time at Parents Place, he disappeared into a playroom for a couple of hours while I traded stories with the other mothers in the waiting room: The freak-outs at birthday parties, the meltdowns at malls. One child wouldn't speak at all. Another was a biter. Another had been kicked out of kindergarten. I felt guiltily encouraged when their stories were worse than mine.

Then I opened my laptop and worked on the novel I was writing, disappearing into a fictional world that now seemed light-years from mine: a young woman traveling through India, with no child yet, no ex-husband, no neurological testing.

Afterward, Forest emerged cheerful. "What did you do?" I asked.

"We threw things at each other. Then we had cinnamon toast."

"What else?"

"Just throwing things and toast," he repeated, looking at me like, "Get a life of your own."

When I called the group leader to press her for more details, she told me she was teaching Forest to say "That's too loud. It's hurting my ears" when kids shouted. She was teaching him how to approach a group of children and ask, "Can I play?"

"He just needs a little help learning the rules," she told me optimistically. "Some kids figure it out more intuitively, from the bottom up. He has to learn it from his mind, from the top down. But once he practices it a little, it will become natural, and he won't have to think about it anymore."

When I got off the phone, I found myself thinking, *I want social skills coaching too!*

I want someone to teach me how to go to a party as a single mom and strike up a conversation with a single dad. How to put on eye shadow. How to order clothes that actually fit from a catalog and accessorize them with silk scarves and dangly earrings. How to have people over for dinner and talk to them without burning the soup and remember to offer them something to drink at the same time I am chopping veggies.

I was realizing that I too had always needed "a little extra help learning the rules"—but generally, that help had not been available. As a teenager at boarding school, I hadn't known that there were products that kept curly hair from frizzing, or who Fleetwood Mac or Pink Floyd were, or how to dance at a school dance, or that there was a difference between wide-wale straight-leg corduroys (the good kind) and narrow-wale bell-bottom corduroys (the kind I was wearing). In college, I hadn't known that when a drunk guy made out with me at a party, it didn't mean that he loved me and wanted to be my boyfriend. As an adult, I was only just figuring out what an individual retirement account is, and that if you got rid of the sheets stained with bong water that had been covering your futon since college, both your heart and your linen closet might have more space for something new.

Forest, I began to understand, was a mirror for me.

At the playground, Forest sits and watches the other children playing on the slide, like an anthropologist watching the activities of a tribe he finds intriguing but incomprehensible.

"Go down the slide," I urge him. "Show me that you know how to do it."

"I know how to do it!"

"Then show me."

He pauses. "Do you know how to go down the slide?" he asks, cannily.

"Yes, I know."

"Then why don't you show me?"

Shortly after Forest started social skills training, he and I were sitting on a grassy slope above a playground overlooking the San Francisco Bay—dotted with windsurfers, sailboats, and ferries carrying suburban commuters to and from their jobs in the financial district. Rollerbladers, bikers, and joggers flashed by on the wide, paved bike path behind us.

As he pulled his peanut-butter sandwich out of his backpack, another mom sat down beside us, watching her daughter on the swing set below.

"What are you having for lunch?" the mom asked Forest.

"Well," he said thoughtfully, "for solids, I am having a peanut-butter sandwich. For a liquid, I am going to have a juice box. Actually, of course, the box is solid. It's what's *inside* it that's liquid."

The woman looked over at me with a kind of recognition, like one member of a secret society meeting another. I almost expected her to offer me the secret handshake. "He reminds me of my son Jake at that age. That's just the kind of thing he would have said."

"Would your son go down the twisty tube slide?" I watched her daughter whirl down it, shouting with glee.

"Are you kidding? I'd have to force him. He'd be wailing, and I'd be there on the slide with him in my lap, saying 'This is fun!' as I tried to get through the tubes without smashing my head."

"Forest would rather categorize by species the flowers next to the swing than actually sit on the swing," I confessed.

"Jake liked to count the bricks in the wall by the sandbox. You know what worked better than anything else? Sensory integration training. You do it with an OT—an occupational therapist. It just seemed to get him inside his own skin."

"How's Jake doing now?"

She laughed. "Oh—he's fine. He's in first grade. He has a best friend. He's still way more into astronomy than T-ball, but who cares? Call Children's Therapy Services in San Rafael. Ask for

Teresa. She's amazing. I think she could get a robot to dance and fall in love."

"Mommy? Is that a bench or a swing?"

"It's a bench swing."

"That's not my right question. My question is, is it a bench OR a swing?"

"Well, if I had to choose, I'd say a swing."

"Why a swing?"

"Because it swings back and forth."

"Well, it looks like a bench. So I think it is a bench. But it moves back and forth. So I think it is called a 'momentum bench'!"

"That's a very good name for it."

"Do you want to go sit on the momentum bench with me?"

I took Forest for evaluation to Teresa. As we were talking in her office, a baby began to cry in a room down the hall. I went on talking, but Forest froze, his head pivoting in the direction of the sound.

"Do you see that?" Teresa said. "He has extra keen hearing. He can hear it from three rooms away. Most kids wouldn't even register it."

She took Forest into the next room for a battery of sensory testing. When she returned—leaving Forest playing with blocks with her assistant—she told me, "Forest has all the characteristics of what we call *sensory integration disorder*. He has extra keen hearing, for one thing. His ears are very sensitive, not just to sound but also to pitch. So sounds that might be too quiet for you or me to hear are very obvious to him. And he can hear sounds that are of a much higher and lower register than you or I can. That's what I suspected when I heard him register that baby crying three rooms away."

"Sometimes he complains that he can hear the electricity humming in the walls."

"Yes. Environments that may seem quiet to us can seem actually quite full of sound and stimulation to him. And noisy environments—like, for instance, a birthday party—can be excruciating."

"Ohhh."

"Also, his brain has difficulty screening out noises that are in the foreground from those that are in the background. For most people, that's pretty easy. You can sit in a café with music playing and a hum of conversation all around you and the barista grinding coffee beans on the other side of the room, and you can still focus on the story someone sitting across from you is telling you about their breakup. For someone with Forest's kind of brain, that's not possible. To his brain, it all appears to be happening at basically the same volume and same level of intensity. It's *all* in the foreground. That can make the world a pretty overwhelming place."

"Ohhh," I said again. I felt as if my child were coming into focus for me. I remembered him as a toddler, shrieking "Go home!" when we walked into a crowded room. I remembered him as an infant, waking up at the click of the car seat he was snoozing in being lifted out of its base, or the unsnapping of my frontpack as I tried to ease him out of it.

"And there's another issue, which may or may not be related. His sense of balance—which, of course, relates to the inner ear—is off."

She explained one of the tests she had done. She stood Forest on a disk and spun him around and around. Then she watched his eyes to see how quickly they returned to focus. "With most people, the eyes settle and you recover your balance within a few seconds. For him, it can take up to a minute."

"So that's why he doesn't like playing on slides or swings?"

"That's right. He's moving through a world where he's perpetually off balance, where everything is literally swirling around him much of the time." She looks at me. "I'm no psychologist, but I can imagine that that would affect the way you interact with people."

"And then I guess there's a feedback loop—if you're avoiding kids because you feel off balance, then you're not learning how to relate to them."

"That's right. And it's not just his ears that are sensitive. It's his whole body. He registers touch on the skin far more intensely than other people. Things such as scratchy shirts or tags might drive him crazy. The kind of touch that others might find soothing, he finds painful."

I flashed on infant Forest, tense as a board in my arms as I tried to swaddle him in blankets to calm him down. Even in the hospital, hours after his birth, a nurse had marveled that he was the first infant she had ever seen who had broken out of the swaddle she'd wrapped him in.

"Given this sensory overload, it would only be natural to disconnect from your body and live in the world of your head. The good news is, there's a lot we can do, especially at this age," she said. "The brain can be retrained very easily. It's highly neuroplastic. We can teach his brain to distinguish between foreground and background noise. We can teach his brain to find balance even when the inner ear is disturbed."

"How do we do that?"

She smiled. "Just bring him to me."

I started taking Forest to Teresa two mornings a week. Sometimes she put headphones on him, playing tones and sounds to teach his brain to sort out foreground and background noises. She wrapped him in yards of bright Lycra cloth and spun him in a trapeze-like swing, bouncing him from one place to another. She taught him to hop on one foot and to walk in a figure eight while calling out letters and numbers on cards she held up in his peripheral vision.

After one of the early sessions, she showed me a "self-portrait" he had drawn: himself with a tiny, sticklike body, an enormous head, and four brains. "This is how he experiences himself. He is disconnected from his body, and it's no wonder. His body is an overwhelming place to be."

She gave me a soft bristle brush. "I want you to brush him all over, from his head to his toes, a few times a day. The more often, the better—but at the very least, do it when he first gets up in the morning and just before he goes to bed at night."

"What does this do?"

"What I say to him is 'it gets the tickles out.' It's getting his nervous system used to stimulation so he can tolerate it better. More important, though, it's wiring his body up with his brain. It's giving him a kinesthetic sense of his body in space."

I wish someone would brush me from head to foot every night! I thought as I brushed Forest down that night.

I shared his sensitivities. I can't converse in a noisy restaurant or make dinner with a TV on in the background. My idea of a relaxing vacation is a silent meditation retreat. An astrologer once told me, "You are like a satellite dish tuned to receive signals from the farthest edges of the universe—that has been set down in the middle of New York City."

When I came to yoga, I too felt like a stick-figure body with four brains. I remember a moment when I was in boarding school, studying in my library carrel, surrounded by books: AP biology. AP American history. AP French. I was sixteen years old, had never had a boyfriend, had never kissed a boy or even held hands in a movie. I remember lifting my head from my books, gazing around the library and thinking, *I am nothing but a disembodied brain. I am not male or female. I am just a mind.*

For me, in my twenties, yoga had been the way I had slowly, slowly reinhabited my body. Moving and breathing at first had been like breaking concrete with a backhoe. I could barely feel anything below my neck—or if I did, it was broad strokes: Shoulder. Leg. I was looking in at my body from the outside. But gradually the concrete had broken up. My body had come alive and begun to sing.

Forest was coming home to his body a good twenty years earlier in his life than I had. I hoped it would spare him some of the suffering I had experienced.

Yesterday Forest wanted to play Rolie Polie Olie *on the computer. I said I would set him up and he could play while I was changing my clothes and getting ready to go. He said, "But I want you to keep me company. My mind works better when you are there."*

"Oh, that's interesting."

"And when you aren't there my belly feels all funny. It doesn't feel good in here." He puts his hand on his stomach. "And when you aren't there my mind changes. It feels different. And it doesn't feel good here." He puts his hand on his chest. "Here, in my belly!"

"This is yummy rice," three-year-old Sonya tells Forest, who is now almost five. They are sitting across from each other at a kid-sized table in her dining room, eating cheesy broccoli.

"That's not rice," Forest corrects her. "It's broccoli."

"No," she says smugly. "It's rice."

It's the summer after Forest finished preschool, and we've moved from the house I used to share with Forest's dad to a nearby town where two of my best friends live with their children. We've begun raising our kids together as a tribe, playing together as naturally as puppies tumbling in the grass.

But playing together involves a certain amount of conflict. Right now, Forest looks like his head is about explode. "No!" Tears start to run down his face as he expounds the logic: "Rice is brown, this is green! Rice is little grains. This is big pieces shaped like trees! It's broccoli."

"No," Sonya says with sweet finality. "It's rice."

As Forest freaks out, I take him aside. "What's important is that *you* know it's broccoli," I tell him, feeling as if I am offering a primer on relationships that many adults could benefit from. "You don't need to convince *her* that it's broccoli."

The older Forest gets, the easier these lessons and negotiations have become. For instance, I've been able to explain to him the difference, when listening to music, between "focused listening" and "casual listening." Focused listening is the kind he likes to do, where he sits at his computer listening to iTunes songs over and over while tracking the seconds that flicker at the top of the screen. ("Mom! The electric guitar starts at two minutes and thirty-three seconds!") Casual listening is the kind that it seems most other people enjoy, where music is on in the background but you still carry on conversations, eat dinner, or play Go Fish. Together, we work out a way to know whether—and when—we're doing casual or focused listening. We even have a time-out hand signal he can flash me so I don't interrupt at the wrong time.

One afternoon, I have to separate him and Sonya after she persists in repeatedly interrupting him while he is "focused listening" to music. I invite her to join me and her mom in the kitchen, making cookies. He stays in his playroom, listening to Depeche Mode and intently tracking the exact minute and second that the synthesizers transition to voice.

After ten minutes he rejoins us in the kitchen. "I'm sorry I got mad," he tells Sonya. "I do love you. I just needed a little time alone."

I think of all the times those simple words—from me, or from someone I was dating—could have transformed a relationship.

Maybe we *all* could have used a little more social skills training growing up.

Forest: "How do you spell the number eight?"
  Me: "E-I-G-H-T."
  Forest (long pause, before landing on the culprit he's heard is to blame for all that is wrong in the world): "Did George Bush decide that?"

Two weeks before Forest starts kindergarten at the local public school, Teresa runs a battery of tests and tells us that all his results have normalized—he no longer needs sensory integration training. He is able to sort out foreground and background sounds, she told us. His inner ear has stabilized. His sensory sensitivities are all within the normal range.

Forest also graduates from his social skills group. Instead, his kindergarten offers him an individualized education program that includes social skills training: a couple of times a week he meets with a group of other boys from his class and plays Chutes and Ladders or Candyland.

Wonderfully, reassuringly, no one seems to think his challenges are anything dire or insoluble. The school psychologist writes out goals in specific terms:

Annual Goal: Forest will use "eye gaze" to gain perspective of his communicative partners following a visual/verbal prompt with 80 percent accuracy in 4/5 trials. (My translation: He'll look at people when he talks to them.)

Annual Goal: Forest will demonstrate his ability to engage in a conversation using his skills of answering and asking questions related to the given topic with peers at 75 percent accuracy in 4/5 trials given minimal adult cues. (My translation: If everyone is talking about what's for dinner, he won't start lecturing us about who is currently the tallest person in the world.)

Forest makes a new friend in kindergarten, a little boy named Ethan, who is also passionate about music. At recess they sit in a corner of the playground and talk about space travel and their favorite songs instead of playing on the swings. When Halloween comes, Ethan dresses up as Sheryl Crow and Forest dresses up as a giant pumpkin. They go trick-or-treating together—and I realize with relief that Forest will be able to find his tribe wherever he goes.

Halfway through the year, the psychologist who had first diagnosed him with Asperger's visits his class to observe him. In her notes she describes his politeness, his eagerness to please, his prodigious memory and vocabulary, his musical abilities. She notes that when the "cleanup" music, a Mozart concerto, began to play, he stopped and stood in the middle of the carpet, transfixed.

"He has outgrown his diagnosis," she tells me when I meet with her. He no longer fits the criteria for Asperger's syndrome; instead, she now believes that he is simply "gifted."

"Gifted kids develop asynchronously," she tells me. "They are very advanced in some areas while lagging in others. I recommend you do some reading about the unique needs and challenges of raising a gifted child."

A new label, a new diagnosis, a new set of things to research and fret about. But he is still the same child. The system is just viewing him through a different lens.

Good news? Bad news? Who knows?

There are still challenging moments. For instance, the time I am driving home from the beach after a long day, and Forest starts screaming in the back seat because I take the Sir Frances Drake exit instead of the Central San Rafael exit for our route home, and so we don't get to drive past the Artworks Downtown banner that stretches over Fourth Street between C and D. He is shouting that we need to do the whole trip home over again—starting all the way back at Muir Beach, forty-five minutes away—so that he can see that banner. "Use your flexible brain," I say over and over again, the way the occupational therapist taught me. But Forest keeps shrieking until finally I lose it and shout back—"*No!* We are not going back to Muir Beach! It's bedtime!" Whereupon he looks stricken, bursts into tears and sobs, "You are supposed to be my *friend*."

But these episodes are farther and farther apart.

In the fall of second grade, one of my fellow moms tells me

about discipline problems the teacher has reported with her son. He's been sticking his leg into the aisles to trip people, stealing the cheese puffs out of other kids' lunches, peering under the doors of the bathroom stalls while other kids pee. "You're so lucky," she sighs. "Your boy is so *easy*."

Had Forest been misdiagnosed initially? Or had he just fundamentally changed as a result of the interventions he'd received?

One of the central teachings in Buddhism is *anatta*—generally translated as "no-self," or, more accurately, "not-self." It means that the *I* we perceive as fixed, solid, and permanent is an illusion. It is not an entity—*I* is simply a convenient term and construct for an ever-shifting phenomenon that emerges moment to moment as part of a complex web of what Buddhism terms *causes and conditions*—our ancestry, the weather, what we ate for breakfast, what time our parents made us go to bed when we were a child, the countless elements and experiences that make up a life.

As a parent, this can be liberating news: Our child's identity is not fixed. It's changing faster than their baby teeth fall out. Their bones and their minds are both growing, shaped by what they do, what they eat, what experiences they have.

They are fluid, like a river.

Every child is a bundle of gifts and weaknesses that are intimately entwined. Sensitive hearing makes a child scream and melt down at a preschooler's birthday party—and can be the gift that later helps that child compose a symphony. The wild child who won't sit still in class has the adventurous spirit that may send her deep into the Amazon to work with native healers and bring back their wisdom about plants.

The journey to growing up is not a freeway going from Los Angeles to San Francisco by the fastest route. It's more like following a meandering back road up the coast, where maybe you're stuck for miles behind a hippie van painted with flowers and vines. Maybe you decide there's no hurry after all, and you pull over to picnic on a beach where you pluck wild huckleberries, sweet and tart at the same time.

I do know that at times it is hard to remember the gifts that lie nestled inside our human brokenness, just waiting to be loved awake. But I also know that they are there.

Near the end of second grade, we take Forest to be tested at a school for gifted children. It's a tiny school—just forty kids from kindergarten through eighth grade. Students are grouped in multi-age homerooms where they can socialize with their age peers but work at their own pace: if a kindergartener is ready to tackle the eighth-grade math book, the teacher helps the child do it.

"Being gifted is not the same as being academically successful," one of the founders tells Forest's dad and me. "Gifted kids often do poorly in school because they are bored or lack social skills." So this school emphasizes collaborative skills and project-based learning, and the teachers understand that different kids develop different parts of their brains at different paces.

Forest's dad and I watch from the back of the room as the head of the school puts Forest through a battery of tests. She recites a series of numbers to him and asks him to repeat them back in reverse order. (Trying to do it along with him, his dad and I find that our ability stops at about six numbers; Forest effortlessly remembers ten or more.) She reads stories aloud to him and asks him to tell them back in his own words—he recounts them back almost verbatim. They teach him a new symbolic alphabet and ask him to read and write short stories in it, which he does with ease, on the spot.

A week later, they invite in his dad and me to give us the results: a grad-school-level capability of cognitive reasoning, near-verbatim ability to recount stories from memory, a stratospheric IQ. "He is profoundly gifted," says the school founder.

Good news? Bad news? Who knows? A few years earlier, the verdict was that our son's differences meant that he was probably never going to have friends, might not even be able to live on his own. Now they apparently mean that he is probably going to invent a time machine or save the planet from global warming.

Was our son gifted? Or was he damaged? How about me? How about his dad? Was it good news or bad news that we had gotten married, and then divorced? Are we failing at our lives or succeeding?

Through our journey on the spectrum I was learning that life is far too complicated to fit into the tidy diagnoses we give it.

Here are some of the things I didn't know as Forest started third grade:

Forest will thrive in his new school. He will fall in love with his teacher, who will wrap him in an acceptance as warm and maternal as her embrace. He will make a new best friend, who will become like a brother to him. Vaughan will come with us on camping trips, ski trips, outings to the beach. They'll have sleepovers at each other's houses, with pancake breakfasts in the morning. They will invent their own role-playing game, called Epic Hamster Wars, and spend hours illustrating a card deck for a Pokémon-style game they dub Creature Cubes. Forest will write novels and self-publish them through CreateSpace. He'll demonstrate Fibonacci's sequence for a Pi Day celebration. He'll play Puck in *A Midsummer Night's Dream.* He'll get a black belt in mixed martial arts.

His childhood diagnosis—"on the spectrum"—will slip to the back of our minds and melt away.

As he grows up into a warm, kind, and sociable middle-schooler, I'll forget that I ever imagined it would go any other way. I won't hug myself in delight to see him playing in a mountain creek with his best friend, or marvel when he starts playing guitar in a rock band. When he hits high school, it won't surprise me when he gets his first girlfriend, or is elected class representative to the student council, or writes and directs a one-act play.

I'll just watch him growing like a plant, or a yoga pose—from the inside out.

And one day when Forest is about eleven, we will sit at our kitchen table looking back on who and how we used to be.

He will say to me, "Some kids are born already understanding what's going on, what the basic rules are of this planet and this whole game of being a human. I wasn't like that. It took me a long time to figure it out."

"Same with me, Forest," I will tell him. "Same with me."

The Big Questions

· · · · ·

"DID THAT CHICKEN want to die?" Forest asks me. He's five years old. We're sitting at our kitchen table, and I'm gnawing on a rotisserie chicken drumstick I bought at Good Earth. He's eating cheese ravioli.

"I don't think anyone gave it a choice," I confess.

"What did it think when it saw the farmer coming to kill it? Did it run away?"

"It probably tried to."

Forest looks at me thoughtfully. "Was its mother *sad*?"

Forest was three when, waiting in line at the meat department at Whole Foods, he became a vegetarian.

His qualms about flesh eating had started a few days before, when he learned that while soy burgers were made from soybeans, salmon burgers were not, in fact, made from salmon beans. "Not a fish that swims in the sea!" he had laughed in disbelief when I explained what the source material really was. And then, concerned: "How do they get it to stop swimming in the sea and be a burger?"

On our next grocery run, he perched in the basket of a heaped shopping cart, gnawing on a sesame-seed bagel and surveying the items arrayed behind the glass at the meat counter.

"I'd like a pound of ground turkey," I told the white-aproned clerk. Forest spun around in his seat. The week before we had admired wild turkeys waddling through the tall grass at Spirit Rock Meditation Center—their red wattles, their curved beaks, their drooping tail feathers. "Turkey? Where??" he asked.

"Um . . . right there." I gestured, reluctantly, at the heap of shredded raw meat. He leaned over and stared at it, then looked at me suspiciously. "What do you mean, *ground*???" he asked.

These days I cook mainly vegetarian food at home, and until recently Forest has been gracious about my occasional carnivorous moments. But lately he's been getting in my face about it. Now he presses me for details about how the chicken died.

"Somebody probably cut off its head," I tell him.

"Didn't that hurt the chicken's feelings?" he asks.

I've explained to him that life endlessly devours life, that eating usually involves killing another living thing, and that the important thing is to do it with gratitude and respect. I tell him that different people make different decisions about what kind of living creatures they're willing to eat. Even Buddhists have differing opinions on how to interpret the nonkilling precept, with sincere practitioners, including monks, running the gamut from vegans to omnivores.

"You can eat the fruit of a tree without killing it," he argues.

Am I going to have a little Jain in my home, living on fruit and nuts and wearing a white mask so he doesn't inhale any insects?

Even baking bread raises tough questions when he learns that yeast is a living organism that gets killed in the oven. "Does yeast know it exists?" he asks, frowning. "Does it think, *I'm yeast! And I don't want to die!*?"

On vacation, he melts down when he sees me smash a giant cockroach with my flip-flop in the bedroom of our beach house. "That cockroach wanted to live!" he sobs. "And now they're going to put you in prison."

"Sweetie, they don't put people in prison for killing cockroaches," I explain.

"But they put the man who shot John Lennon in prison!"

I clarify that John Lennon was a Beatle, not a cockroach, and that people usually do try to get rid of cockroaches in their homes because they carry germs and could make people sick.

"Does *get rid of* mean '*squish*'?" he asks.

"Sometimes," I admit (although I remember that once on a retreat I met a Thai monk who persuaded ants to leave my tent by chanting the *Heart Sutra*). After thinking for a while, Forest asks, "What does *get rid of George Bush* mean?"

When it comes to unanswerable questions, chickens and yeast and George Bush are just the beginning. Learning to read and write, Forest insists that we google a question he laboriously types into the computer himself, with me helping him sound out the words: "Why do people kill other people?"

I tell him you can't find answers to that question on the Internet (although our search does bring up a slew of articles on gun control). In the following months, we revisit the topic of war and violence again and again. We talk about ignorance, and pain, and starvation. We talk about battles to control resources such as food and water. We talk about people who believe that if you're hurt, hurting someone else will make you feel better; and people whose mommies and daddies weren't able to teach them that it's always better to use your words.

But every answer leads to more questions. Why didn't their mommies teach them? Why don't we send them food instead of fighting them? "It's mainly *guys* who kill people," he says over dinner one night.

"Why do you think that?" I ask.

"Because when I see the newspaper and there are pictures of wars, it's almost always men. Why do men fight wars and women don't?"

And then there are the questions that cut right to the heart of the mystery of existence itself. Scraping up the last of the ice cream out of his bowl one evening, he asks me cheerfully, "When I'm dead, will I remember *me*???"

Those megaquestions tend to come at bedtime. "Where did the earth come from?" he asks as we snuggle under his comforter and look up at the glow-in-the-dark constellations on his ceiling. "Where did the very first people come from? Will people still be here to watch the earth when it dies?"

I offer a two-minute summary of evolution and the big bang. "But why did apes start turning into people?" he persists. "And where did all the stuff that was in the big bang come from?" And then a few minutes later: "That explosion—what was it called? The big bang? Is that what made San Rafael?" (This nearby city, though relatively small at sixty thousand people, clearly feels galactic in scope to him.)

When he hears about Forest's existential queries, my eighty-three-year-old father—a Catholic, retired Army general—sends me an email: "Why not just tell Forest that some people say that God made all things, visible and invisible, and leave it at that? Then he can work out the rest as he goes along."

Just refer the inquiries up the chain of command to the ultimate Commander in Chief? I resist the idea. But as the questions keep coming, I have to admit defeat. I swim in a sea of mysteries. Every few minutes Forest confronts me with my own ignorance. I do not know how plastic is made. I do not know if the earth always had a moon. I do not know how computers print or how film is developed or whether yeast poops. Many of the things I used to know I no longer remember—how to solve quadratic equations, the reasons for the War of 1812, the difference between mitosis and meiosis. And many of the black-and-white things I used to be sure of—what good people are supposed to eat and not eat, why Forest's daddy and I are no longer married—have now dissolved into shades of gray.

For some answers, Forest and I can turn to the dictionary, the encyclopedia, or the Internet. I buy him a beautiful book about the origins of the universe called *Born with a Bang,* which tells him that every particle of his body is made from stardust formed in a mother star that exploded billions of years ago. Curled on the couch by the fire with him in my lap, I read it aloud to him, and we marvel together.

But ultimately, I want for him what I want for myself—to be able to live in the mystery itself and trust its creative unfolding. I want him to wrestle with the challenge of how to live with peace and integrity in a complex and sometimes violent world. I want him to learn, as the poet Rainer Maria Rilke writes in *Letters to a Young Poet,* to "try to love the questions themselves, like locked rooms and like books written in a foreign tongue." I don't want the illusion of definitive answers to form a tough skin on his tender heart, which still vibrates with equal sympathy for yeast, soldiers, cockroaches, John Lennon.

Forest still thinks that I can give him answers. But the truth is that he is the one who is teaching me. His endless questions remind me again and again of the joy and heartbreak and unsolvable koans that surround us at every moment. And they remind me to be grateful for the chance to be alive in the middle of this vast unknown.

Every night before dinner, Forest and I hold hands and he offers an improvised blessing. One evening, as the relentless spring rains beat down on our roof, he takes my hand, looks at our baked tofu, rice, and salad, and says, "Thank you to the earth for making all this food. Thank you to the rain for helping to grow it. Thank you to all the great people we love. And thank you to the big bang for making it all happen."

It's the first time I've ever said "thank you" to the big bang. But I have a feeling that it won't be the last.

Astronomy Lessons

. . . . .

ON A CLEAR spring evening when Forest is six years old, we drive to the Chabot Space and Science Center in the Berkeley hills to look at Saturn through a twenty-eight-foot telescope.

Outer space is Forest's latest passion. He pores over jumbles of books with titles such as *100 Things You Should Know about Space*. He has a deck of cards bearing images from the Hubble Space Telescope on one side and space trivia on the other: "How is a supernova formed?" "How can scientists tell which direction a galaxy rotates?" Space has never been something I've thought much about, so Forest's books, which he likes me to read aloud to him after dinner, regularly blow my mind. "'Dark matter' is what scientists call all the stuff in the universe that they know is there but can't find!" one book has informed us cheerfully. It goes on: "Scientists can guess how much matter is in the universe by measuring how galaxies move. This shows them that stars and planets only make up a small part of the universe. The rest is invisible!" I'd thought about that one all week, astounded that astronomers aren't all raving mystics, prostrating in abject awe before their telescopes.

"What's outside the universe?" we read in the same book a few nights later. "Scientists are still trying to guess, by using clues left behind from the birth of our universe. They are pretty sure there would be no time, distance, or things there." That last sentence sounded like a chant that should be intoned in a Zen temple to the beat of an enormous drum. But instead I was reading it at my kitchen table while Forest nibbled on a pink, egg-shaped cookie that he believed was hidden in our house on Easter morning by a giant magical rabbit. And who could blame him? In a world of big bangs and wormholes to other galaxies, I could almost believe in the Easter Bunny myself.

Forest and I go to the Chabot observatory with one of Forest's best friends, Nick, a bright-eyed, dimpled kindergartener three months younger than Forest, who shares Forest's passion for science. Nick is fascinated by microbiology—his favorite toys are his stuffed microbes (cuddly renditions of germs ranging from influenza to anthrax). One Halloween he went trick-or-treating costumed as "athlete's foot." Forest and Nick have been friends since before they could walk, when Nick's mother, May, and I used to stroll to the neighborhood park with the boys in frontpacks over our hearts. On one of those walks, May and I discovered that we shared the same birthday, and we've celebrated together ever since.

When Forest needed social skills therapy when he was three for what was being called an autism spectrum disorder, it was Nick I called over to be his playmate in coached games in our living room. And it was May, herself a special-education teacher, who was most vocal in reassuring me that he was going to be just fine: "Your child is bigger than his diagnosis."

A few months later, Nick's preschool teacher noted that he was behind on his physical milestones and recommended a checkup with his pediatrician. "It's probably nothing," I reassured her. "Kids develop at different paces." But the following week, May called me, sobbing, and told me that Nick had just been diagnosed with Duchenne muscular dystrophy, a genetic disease that causes severe muscular degeneration. "Most kids who have it die by their early twenties," she told me. My heart aching, I told her Forest and I would always be there in whatever way we could.

At six, Nick is now undergoing experimental genetic therapy that, over the next decade, could mean the difference between life and death for him. He can't run as fast as other children, and he has a hard time climbing stairs. But in the presence of his bubbling laugh, it's often hard to remember his illness. It's hard to remember that left unchecked, the disease will claim his legs, and he won't be able to walk. Eventually, it could stop his heart.

Of course, over the course of their friendship, Forest has had his own set of developmental challenges, although none life-threatening. Over the years, this friendship with Nick has often been a refuge for them both, a safe place to celebrate each other in all their gifts and difficulties. They've shared their mutual passions for things most of their peers just don't get, such as making an elaborate map of the IOI freeway with crayons and construction paper. They've created their own code language, which involves things such as naming a favorite dessert made of ice cream and cookies "peach flavored bunny rabbit." Once they organized their own protest march in Nick's kitchen, objecting to the fact that they couldn't play upstairs in his dad's home office. Carrying hand-lettered signs, they stomped back and forth through the kitchen, bellowing out faux-hippie freedom chants about their right to access the upper reaches of the house.

Before our visit to the space center, Forest and I meet up with Nick and his mother on the outdoor patio of a Thai restaurant. "Boosey-duck!" the boys greet each other in their private nonsense language. Then they discuss—over spring rolls and pumpkin curry—the size and speed of the asteroid that smashed into the earth sixty-five million years ago, rendering the dinosaurs extinct. Nick says the erupting lava burned the dinosaurs to a crisp; Forest argues that the cloud of dust and ash blocked out the sun, causing them to freeze and starve. They punctuate their scientific debate by blowing through straws into their water until it sprays all over the patio and then stomping in the puddles. While May and I finish eating, they dance to the country-western band playing in a near-by courtyard—waving their arms over their heads, rolling on the ground, and leapfrogging over each other.

We arrive at Chabot just as the sky is darkening over the dome-shaped observatory, which houses the largest telescope in the United States open to the public. As we wait in line, Nick and Forest regale us with Saturn trivia: Its rings are actually made of chunks of ice and rock. It's almost 800 times the size of the earth, but it's so light that if you put it in a giant ocean, it would float. Forest chats with the woman behind us—a fellow space geek in her midthirties—about Jupiter's 62 moons and about Proxima Centauri, our sun's nearest star, which is four light-years away. "Do you know how far that is in miles?" the woman asks. Forest frowns thoughtfully. "To calculate that," he said, "you'd have to multiply 186,000 miles per second, times 60 seconds per minute, times 60 minutes per hour, times 24 hours per day, times 365 days per year, times 4 years. I can't do it in my head. There are too many zeroes."

When it's our turn, we climb up a stepladder one at a time to peer through the telescope's eyepiece. "Mom, you've got to see this!" Forest gasps. I climb up for my turn and press my eye to the viewfinder. There, nine hundred million miles away, is Saturn—bright yellow, ringed, and as shiny as candy. It looks just like the plastic Saturn suspended by string and putty from Forest's ceiling. Dotted around it are the five shiny specks of its largest moons.

On the deck outside the observatory, more space buffs are gathering. Many of them have brought telescopes of their own—a kind of astronomer's potluck—and they are training them on different celestial objects for anyone to see. Forest and Nick race giddily from telescope to telescope, checking out Venus and craters on the moon, shouting out "I newt you, newt you, newt you!"—another mysterious game that only they understand.

"Nick, come see this red giant!" shouts Forest, peering at a distant star named Betelgeuse. A red giant, I know from Forest's space books, is an ancient, immensely swollen star on its way to blowing up or fading out. Some astronomers predict that Betelgeuse will go supernova in the next thousand years or so, in a massive explosion that will be as brightly visible as the moon in our night sky—a smaller scale version of the ancient exploding star that created every element in our solar system. But that night, even through the telescope, Betelgeuse is still just a blurry reddish speck, five hundred light-years away.

The moonlight is so bright tonight you can almost read by it. Forest and Nick, momentarily satiated on outer space, practice their cartwheels. May and I sit on a low cement wall and watch them: two boys as mysterious and impermanent as spinning planets, their bodies made from stardust forged in the belly of an ancient sun. I imagine the awe of the first astronomer to point a telescope at the sky and see Saturn's rings—when for millennia humans had only been able to see a dot in the sky, a deity whose movements they believed could plunge their own lives into chaos.

Years earlier I had asked May how she managed to stay so cheerful as she worked to keep Nick healthy—researching treatments, taking him to doctors, keeping him strong with supplements, and praying for science to come up with a cure. She'd said, "No one knows how long they're going have with their child. I just try to enjoy every day."

As I watch the boys turn cartwheels under the moon, a Zen chant runs through my head: "Within light there is darkness, but do not try to understand that darkness. Within darkness there is light, but do not look for that light."

No one knows what gravity is, Forest's space books have informed me. It's just a convenient name we give to the attraction that keeps the moon wheeling around the earth and the earth around the sun—that keeps the different pieces of the universe yearning toward each other, instead of ricocheting off into space.

With human beings, maybe that job is done by love.

Watching Forest and Nick turn cartwheels, I remember Sierra kicking inside me. And I ache with my longing to keep both Forest and Nick happy and safe in a world of car wrecks and viruses and guns and bullies and malfunctioning genes. It is a wish so huge I can't even calculate its size; there are too many zeroes.

All I can do is be present with them both—feeling the tug on my heart of everything in the universe I know is there but can't see, peering through telescopes at stars dying and being reborn, light-years away.

A Passage Back to India

. . . . .

TWO DAYS INTO my trip through India, I realize just how much has changed since I last backpacked through here a dozen years earlier, as a footloose young traveler researching an ashram guidebook.

This revelation arises as I check my email in the Vishnu Internet Café in Bodh Gaya, a pilgrimage town in rural northeastern India, down the street from the temple marking the spot where the Buddha is said to have attained enlightenment almost 2,600 years ago. Last time I'd been to what was then the sleepy little town of Bodh Gaya, there were no Internet cafés for travelers in India—in fact, I'd only recently gotten an email address myself for the computer I'd left behind in California—and I'd felt as if I'd time-traveled to the land of the ancient rishis. Now, outside the window, a pony pulls a cart emblazoned with an Airtel ad past a group of Tibetan monks shopping for Nikes. Inside, at a public computer topped by a garlanded shrine to Ganesha, the Hindu god of new beginnings, I pore over pictures of Forest—now almost seven years old— currently snorkeling with his dad in Hawaii.

Hijacked by homesickness, I log off and try to call them, but the rural phone lines won't let the call through. *Letting go of personal ties is part of the spiritual path*, I remind myself as I struggle with my disappointment. *The Buddha himself left a young son behind so he could meditate in Bodh Gaya.* "No problem, madame," the phone wallah interrupts my musings—and hands me his personal cell phone. I tap in Forest's dad's number—and as I hear it ring, I feel the wireless bonds of family that connect us around the world.

I've come on this trip to do some last-minute site research for the novel I'm just finishing—*Enlightenment for Idiots*, the tale of a young American wannabe yoga teacher looking for awakening while floundering through her increasingly disastrous love life. I'd begun writing the novel when Forest was just two years old, as an attempt to synthesize wildly different transformative experiences from my personal life—traveling through India, becoming a mother, going through a divorce. In its first incarnation, it had been written in the form of letters back and forth between two best friends who had planned to go to India together, until one of them gets pregnant through an affair with her yoga teacher and has to stay behind. But six months into the writing, someone in my writing group told me that she was having a hard time telling apart the voices of the two characters. That's when it had hit me—*What if they're actually the same person?*

Now the novel is almost finished—in a month I'll be handing it over to my editor at Random House. But first I want to update my impressions of places I'd visited over a decade ago, while looking at them through the eyes of my novel's twenty-nine-year-old protagonist, Amanda. Rishikesh, the Himalayan town where Amanda goes to find a yoga master and get over her breakup with the cheating boyfriend she's vowed never to see again. Varanasi, the city of Shiva, where devout Hindus come to die and be cremated in open fires along the banks of the Ganges, and where Amanda learns that her ex has followed her to India to try to win her back. Bodh Gaya, where he and Amanda quarrel outside the cave where the Buddha used to meditate, and she gives him the unwelcome news that her spiritual journey is now going to include a baby.

I didn't want to travel in India alone, the way I had a decade earlier. So I managed to convince the Indian Tourism Office in Los Angeles to give me not one but two free tickets in exchange for the great PR my novel would provide to Indian tourism. My dear friend Janice, a fellow yoga teacher and mom whose daughter is two years younger than Forest, would be going with me. She is part of the sisterhood that supported me after my marriage fell apart, when I'd moved to the tiny hippie town in West Marin where she lived. We've raised our kids like brother and sister. Neither one of us has ever been away from them for more than a few days. As we'd stuffed our carry-on backpacks into the overhead racks and sat down in our Air India seats, we looked at each other in amazement.

"It feels fantastic," Janice said. "But it also kind of feels as if I've forgotten to bring one of my arms."

I had first come to India when I was roughly my character Amanda's age, on a guided tour of Buddhist sites led by an Indian friend I'd met on a meditation retreat. Admittedly, I'd been distracted from my spiritual quest by the fact that I had developed a major crush on my tour guide. I spent most of my meditation under the Bodhi Tree—a fourth-generation descendent of the actual tree that sheltered the Buddha while he eradicated all desire—wondering if it would be possible to lure him into a romantic evening in the baths of the Japanese resort in Rajgir. (Alas, it wasn't.)

My crush melted away as soon as I got on the plane home. But my love affair with India didn't. A year later, I'd gone back, armed with a book contract, a travel-weight yoga mat, and a laptop computer (which I abandoned in favor of a spiral notebook after I blew an ashram's electrical circuits).

Over the next couple of years, I spent almost eight months in India, trekking from guru to guru. I'd sweated through backbreaking yoga classes, meditated with Tibetan lamas, bowed before orange-robed swamis with names as long and curly as their beards. I'd careened in decrepit buses down roads jammed with cows and elephants and fume-belching trucks, their windshields decked with streamers and images of blue gods. I'd learned to tie a sari, to go without toilet paper, to eat rice and dal with my hands, and to ask at least three people before assuming that I was on the right train. Hiking toward the source of the Ganges River, I'd gotten caught in a Himalayan blizzard and spent the night in a cave with a sadhu, one of the wandering renunciate mystics who have been part of the fabric of Indian society since long before the time of the Buddha.

Then I went home to California—and as the years went by my memories of India had dissolved like incense smoke. I'd gotten married in a Zen temple, given birth to a beautiful daughter, wished that I could have died in her place. I'd given birth to a healthy son and learned that green shoots of joy can sprout from the scorched earth of despair. My marriage had unraveled, and I'd wept and smashed wedding china on the deck behind our house. I'd divorced and moved to a mountaintop home, where I had watched hawks circling on the currents of wind below my windows. My son had started kindergarten, lost his first tooth, and had his first piano recital. His dad and I had sat side by side in the audience and cheered.

And shortly after I turned forty, a character had walked into my mind and begun to insist that I tell her story: a young woman looking for love—and enlightenment—in all the wrong places.

While Forest was two and three and four, I'd worked on *Enlightenment for Idiots* just a half hour a day—stealing time for my characters while caring for him, teaching yoga, and working part-time from home as a *Tricycle* editor. When Forest was five and a half, I'd gotten the book contract, which enabled me to drop my other work and just write while he went to kindergarten and first grade.

And a month before my novel's manuscript was due, Janice and I stepped off a plane in Calcutta.

In Calcutta, a glittering glass-and-steel office complex called Technopolis looms over the festering slums and dusty, cratered roads. On a freeway billboard, an Indian woman in a skimpy leotard lounges seductively on a giant tub of "India's first probiotic ice cream." Floating down the Ganges in Varanasi in a rowboat just after dawn, I see a sadhu in an orange loincloth step out of his tent to answer his cell phone, which rings to the tune of a sacred chant in praise of the god Ram. In a gem shop in Rishikesh, an Indian salesman in a Western business suit dangles a giant amethyst in front of three American women in saris; they all close their eyes and chant *om* together. I walk past them through a sea of plateglass storefronts, looking for the simple little town I remember. It's like studying my own face in the mirror—as I don my Indian *salwar kameez*—and trying to find the youthful, fresh-skinned traveler I used to be.

But the magic of India that had first enchanted me is still here. Golden light still filters through a haze of dust, suffusing everything in its soft, dreamlike glow. The smell is still a ripe perfume of burning cow dung, exhaust fumes, incense, and rotting garbage. Corpses still burn to ashes in pyres lit from a flame that's been kept alive for thousands of years. On the train from Calcutta to Gaya, I rattle and sway through rice fields plowed by oxen and men in white loincloths guiding wooden plowshares whose design hasn't changed for centuries.

Past and present still overlap in a rich collage, creating the sense that anything—anything!—could happen at any moment. And when I plug in my PalmPilot to charge the battery, my electrical adaptor fries with a familiar, almost comforting sizzle.

A decade earlier, my entire travel budget had come to about $150 a month—about half what it now costs to stay overnight in a business hotel near the Delhi airport. In those days I never took taxis, even for long rides—instead, I jolted everywhere in three-wheeled autorickshaws, holding my shawl across my nose and mouth to keep out the choking fumes. I slept on bug-infested mattresses, the bare floors of ashram dormitories, the wooden benches of sleeper trains, the rutted earth of caves. My backpack held just three sets of socks and underwear, one change of *salwar kameez*, a baggie of grimy earplugs, and a fluctuating assortment of spiritual literature, which I mailed home periodically to my growing research library.

In the new India, I can now afford to travel in a bubble of comfort that didn't even exist a decade ago. Some things haven't changed, though. I get violently ill the afternoon we arrive in Khajuraho, a dusty little town in central India whose tenth-century tantric temples are covered with exquisite carvings that are among the world's most famous erotica. I spend one wretched night throwing up in the bathroom of the grubby backpacker joint that my character Amanda would have chosen. Pigeons nest in the bathroom ventilator fan, their droppings coating the bathtub. The smell of the sewer wafts up through the toilet bowl. Through the floor the soundtrack of a Hindi TV show blares, featuring lots of explosions and car crashes. I'm only dimly comforted by the thought: *These are great details. I'll put them in my novel when I get home.*

The next morning, still sick, I beg Janice to call a cab—and we head to the Taj Hotel, where a flutist is playing by the fountain in the crystal-chandeliered lobby, and a bellhop hoists my backpack and asks me, solicitously, if I want him to adjust my neck. As we pull into Rishikesh a day or so later, Janice asks if we should stay in an ashram. I'm only half-joking when I answer, "This time around, I'm not into service work. I'm into room service."

But I've changed in more important ways as well. The last time I came to India, like Amanda, I'd wandered for months, tethered to my past life by the slimmest of links: a few postcards surrendered to the Indian postal service with no guarantee of delivery; the occasional blurry fax; one or two pricey long-distance phone calls over hissing, echoing lines. This time, two weeks is the longest I can bear to be away from my six-year-old son. In an Internet café in Varanasi, with an orange-robed sadhu asleep by a motorcycle on the steps outside, I download a song that he and his dad have recorded for me. I tear up as Forest's high-pitched voice sings, "Sending you love on incense smoke / so much love that we practically choke . . ."

These days my heart is anchored to my life back home with roots that Amanda could only dream of. My spiritual seeking has less to do with exotic adventures and more to do with honoring the daily rhythms of ordinary life. And this anchoring helps me appreciate India in a deeper way. Sitting under the papery-white bark branches of the Bodhi Tree, I watch pilgrims from around the world chant, prostrate, and meditate—saffron-robed Cambodian monks, maroon-robed Tibetan nuns, black-robed Japanese priests. *Everything changes,* the Buddha taught; *nothing we love can be held on to forever.* After more than a decade of love and heartbreak, I understand the power of those teachings from the inside out in a way I hadn't when I sat under that tree twelve years before.

As I sit, I close my eyes. This spot is where Amanda will see her ex-boyfriend after months apart. She has news to tell him—she is going to be a mother. *Oh, Amanda,* I think. *You have no idea what you're in for.*

By the end of our itinerary, Janice and I are both ready to head home. We take a rickshaw from the yoga Disneyland of Rishikesh to Hardwar and haul our backpacks onto the train—only to find an Indian couple occupying what we believe to be our seats. After some brandishing of train tickets, we realize—we have the wrong day! We'd been so eager to get home to our kids that we had misread the dates on our tickets. We return to Rishikesh for one last blast of India.

It's Holi, the festival of colors, and the streets are filled with revelers tossing colored powder on each other. We're chased through the streets by two drunk guys who spatter us in purple and green before we make it back to our hotel. There, sipping chai in the courtyard, we meet a Canadian man in his fifties with brilliant blue eyes, who is returning for the first time to the mountain pilgrimage town where he'd lived as a rare Western sadhu thirty-five years ago—this time bringing with him his wife, a red-haired woman in a *salwar kameez* who has never been to India before. He takes us all out to the streets again, promising to keep the revelers at bay.

As we sit with him and his wife on boulders by the Ganges in the blazing sun, cooling our feet in the icy green waters, he points to the cave in the hills across the river where he had lived. He tells us how he had turned in his passport at the Canadian embassy and headed barefoot into the mountains wearing nothing but a loincloth. He had lived for years on handouts from village people as he walked from guru to guru, looking for enlightenment. Eventually, one of his yoga masters told him that he had gone as far as he could on his spiritual journey as a renunciate. To go deeper, he needed to go back to the world and grow up. So he'd gone back to Canada, married, and raised five children. He'd founded a successful company that sold decking materials.

As we talk, he stares out across the waters, as if he might be able to spot the young man he had once been, waving at him from the cave he used to live in. Just downstream from us, a sadhu plunges into the water to receive the blessing of the goddess Ganga, as sadhus have done in this spot for over a thousand years.

I think of the person I had been when I came to this town before, and of the imaginary character I am dreaming into existence in my novel. I think of my son, waiting for me in California. I feel the past bleeding through into the present and the present bleeding toward the unknown future, like ink through thin paper.

SUTRA 12

Adventures in Dharma Dating

· · · · ·

THE IDEA FIRST comes up when Forest is almost five, as a joke between me and my editor at *Tricycle*. As a newly single Buddhist mom, why don't I post my profile on a couple of the new online "dharma dating" sites and write about my experiences?

I find the notion both intriguing and horrifying. After my marriage went down in flames, finding a new romance by dating strangers was the last thing on my mind. (Perhaps this had something to do with the fact that I was still wearing nursing bras.) For years, I'd mocked the idea of shopping for a mate the way you'd shop for a book on Amazon. ("Add This Man to My Cart!") Once, while browsing for a used couch on Craigslist, I'd popped over to the Men Seeking Women section for a look, and the ads all ran together in my mind: *6-foot divorced sofa, 45, brown hair/blue eyes, overstuffed cushions, slightly cat-clawed, wants to spank you . . .*

But lately, several of my friends have actually met partners online; several others have had fun just going out for dinners, movies, and hikes with people they'd never have met without the Internet. According to the *New York Times*, almost 5 percent of the US population is now listed on Match.com. Arranging dates through Buddhist sites promises something novel: a wide assortment of potential friends, all of them single and interested in connection, and all sharing a primary interest in spiritual practice. As a mating strategy, it probably beats cruising a vipassana retreat.

Although I don't admit it to my editor, I'm lonely. I've broken up with the lover who helped keep me afloat during the heartsick months after my son's dad and I separated. We loved each other, but he was a passionate, free-spirited, childless guy whose spiritual practice centered on all-night peyote ceremonies, while I was still trying to get my child to sleep through the night. By the time we had finalized our divorce, my ex-husband and I were good enough friends that we went out to lunch together right after we signed the paperwork. But I miss having someone to share my life—and my bed—with.

Plus, at almost forty-two, I want another baby. I grew up as the youngest of a pack of seven, where a common question at the dinner table—designed to ascertain, for example, whether we could each have one meatball or two on our spaghetti—was "What's the ration?" It doesn't feel right to have just me and Forest at the dinner table, helping ourselves from a bowl full of enough mac and cheese for seconds, or thirds, or fourths if we want it. And I'm still acutely aware of the empty seat where, in my imagination, Sierra should be sitting.

My biological clock is ticking. Online dating seems as if it could be the fastest, most efficient way to order up the life I dream of: me, a husband, and a couple of kids sitting around the table, trading stories about our day over a meal we've cooked together.

The only problem is, I've never really *dated*.

In my midthirties, I married my college sweetheart, with whom I'd been an off-and-on couple since I was seventeen. In my twenties and early thirties, during the long periods when he and I weren't together, I had explored a series of relationships with some wonderfully offbeat men: A Brazilian massage therapist who was paying for his master's in somatic psychology by programming computers for a 900-line in Las Vegas. A French Zen student who baked a *tarte aux pommes* for my birthday and offered me bouquets of homegrown chard. A yogi who invited me to a clothing-optional "love and intimacy" workshop at his Santa Cruz home that culminated in a talent show where a seventy-three-year-old woman belly danced wearing nothing but a denim apron.

None of the connections, however, involved anything that you might call *dating*. We met while adjusting each other in Downward Dog or squabbling over unwashed dishes in the kitchen of a collective house. We migrated easily back and forth across the boundary between friendship and romance. I'm still friends with virtually everyone I've paired up with in the past twenty years.

Despite a couple of decades of therapy, I don't have a lot of faith in my ability to make wise choices in the romance department. I've analyzed my tendencies to the point that I could write a doctoral dissertation about them: I felt abandoned when my father spent four of the first seven years of my life in Vietnam—so I choose strong, charismatic men who are always on their way out the door. I grew up in a Catholic household where sex was never mentioned— so I choose sensual, passionate, wild, creative lovers who embody all the parts of myself I was not allowed to feel or even express. I am trying to prove to myself—and to the world—that I am no longer the tomboy geek with the big glasses she had chosen because they looked just like her brother's, who spent the junior high school dance standing in the corner with her best friend, watching the other kids do "the Bump." And as proof, I offer my lineup of sexy polyamorous boyfriends.

But any way you analyze it, I'm not sure I will recognize a suitable partner even if he's exactly what I've advertised for.

And at this point, I've been around long enough to know that a romantic partner is not a guaranteed ticket to a suffering-free life. Love, it seems to me, is a combination of serendipity and hard work. Wouldn't I be better off using my time and energy rooting out the cause of suffering—which my dharma practice tells me is craving—at its source? Instead of dating, shouldn't I volunteer at a soup kitchen? Shouldn't I focus on contemplating emptiness and interdependence to the point where I'd get just as much joy from an evening alone sorting socks as from a night making passionate love to Indian sitar music in front of a roaring fire?

Oh, who am I kidding? "Sure," I tell my editor. "I'll check it out."

WEEK 1

I get paralyzed in huge bargain-basement stores. Given fifteen aisles of shoes to choose from, I'm likely to give up on the whole project and go home barefoot. So I pass on the megasites and sign up for the two that sound explicitly Buddhist: dharmaMatch.com and DharmaDate.com.

Despite its name, dharmaMatch turns out to be a fairly general site, aimed at singles of all religious persuasions "who hold their beliefs, values, and spirituality as an important part of their life." Its homepage features a lovely young couple locked in an embrace, surrounded by giant soap bubbles—as if to remind us of the impermanent nature of romantic love, even as we pursue it.

DharmaDate is more narrowly targeted toward Buddhists: "We want it to be an informal sangha meeting place where you can be yourself. Or be your *non-self.*" The sign-up process includes a series of in-depth questions about practice and beliefs that are explicitly designed to screen out non-Buddhists (who, presumably, would otherwise be flocking there in droves, drawn by the legendary licentiousness and raw animal magnetism of dharma practitioners).

The first thing I must do, on both sites, is choose a screen name. I try for Yogini, but it has already been taken. Dakini? Same deal. I rule out Bikini as unwise and settle instead on Tahini, which also happens to be the name of my cat.

Although photos are not required, they're strongly encouraged, as the bait on the hook in the online sea. So I scramble through my files, trying to find a recent picture that doesn't lop off my head to focus on Forest. Sign-up questionnaires ask me to evaluate every aspect of myself: physical appearance, lifestyle, personality, dietary preferences. And, of course, spirituality. ("What happens after the body dies?" is a question I've never seen before in a multiple-choice format.)

In the last few weeks I've been contemplating putting my house on the market. The analogies to the dating process are unavoidable: clearly, before holding any open houses I should consider some major renovations—and perhaps a professional stager—to increase my curb appeal.

But without time or money for remodeling, I post myself "as is." Within hours of posting my profile, an email arrives in my inbox. "Great news!" it crows. "You've received a smile on dharmamatch. com from Siddhartha Gautama!"

Hmm. . . . Is the not-yet-enlightened prince who will eventually become the Buddha really the sort of guy I want to be flirting with this time around? True, Siddhartha was handsome, well educated, and rich. But didn't he run out on his wife and child to wander around with a bunch of celibate homeless people?

I click "Send a smile back" nonetheless . . . and now I am officially a dharma dater.

WEEKS 2-3

As the introductory smiles continue to arrive—". . . *from Manly-Meditator!*" "*. . . from DharmaDude!*"—the first thing I discover is this: there are apparently a lot of thoughtful, attractive, spiritual singles out there. Sure, there are some scary ones: the guy who rants that he likes trees better than people; the guy who suggests in his opening email that we live together on a ranch in Wyoming, where we will castrate our own goats. But for the most part, the smiles are linked to intriguing profiles: an Argentinean jazz musician in New York City who studies Tibetan Buddhism and hatha yoga and has a nine-year-old son; a burly poet in Ohio, who shares custody of an eleven-year-old daughter; a Zen priest in Southern California, whose online photo features his shaved head and black robes.

Wait a minute . . . a *Zen priest*? Shouldn't he be beyond all this? I picture him chanting in the zendo: *Desires are inexhaustible, I vow to end them*—right after I check dharmaMatch for any new hotties . . .

It just goes to show, as human beings, we're hardwired for connection. Of course, our practice helps us dissolve the illusion of a separate self and know that we are supported in every breath by the whole universe. But at the same time, it's also good to feel supported by a real live person who actually cares that we had a bad day, that the kids were brats, that the boss was a tyrant, that the computer kept crashing, that we failed to solve our koan.

I had recently read in the *New York Times* that 40 percent of the US population is single, up from 28 percent in 1970. And an increasing percentage of those singles are forty years and older. Many of the profiles I read, like mine, have ghosts hovering in the margins: ex-lovers, ex-spouses, shared children. Sifting through them, I envision us all bobbing around in the ocean after a great cultural shipwreck. We tighten our life preservers, clutch our bits of driftwood, and wave at one another across the water.

As Tahini, I begin exchanging dharmaMatch messages with the people who have contacted me. The jazz musician sends flirtatious messages at midnight, signing his name with a sprinkling of kiss emoticons. The poet sends poems he has written and photos of his cabin and sailboat on a silver lake. The getting-to-know-you questions pelt me through the ether. "What's the most fun thing you've done this week?" "What spiritual teacher has influenced you the most?" "What do you think true freedom is?" A resident of a Tibetan retreat center in Canada writes, "I smiled at you, but I have no idea what a smile means. Does this mean we're engaged?"

As a writer, I already spend a good portion of my days staring at my computer screen; I quickly discover that I don't want to conduct my social life there. The dharma-dating emails drown in the flood of messages from my real-world life: requests for article submissions, work appointments, family sagas, baby announcements, friends inviting me to potluck suppers. Untethered to the world of blood and bones, the candidates for my affection drift out of my mind like balloons on a windy day. I forget what I've said to the Zen priest, to the jazz musician. I forget whether the photographer in Massachusetts has grown-up kids, or whether that's the software designer in Palo Alto. I repeatedly forget my dating-site password. I'm tempted to copy and paste from one of my answers into another, just to save time—but surely that's tacky? Increasingly, I don't get around to returning the emails.

This, of course, has its own pitfalls. When I inadvertently fail to return a smile, I receive my first "flame": "Is this the way enlightened people behave? Well, if it is I might just as well go to the local bar and become an alcoholic. Smoke cigarettes and associate with big furry women who grunt when they talk. And what do you think might be the karmic consequences of being responsible for my demise?"

I decide to perform some geographical triage. I will politely decline correspondence with anyone who doesn't live within easy driving distance of me. Those who live nearby I will steer as quickly as possible toward face-to-face meetings.

WEEKS 4–5

I consult *Online Dating for Dummies*, which recommends that the first meetings be brief, for coffee or tea, and that they be held in a busy public place. So I meet my first date at a bookstore café that's bustling enough that I won't feel conspicuous. I wonder how many of the couples I see at the tables around me are meeting for the first time, exchanging chitchat while surreptitiously checking each other out to see if they can imagine spending the rest of their lives together.

My date, whose screen name refers to a legendary Scottish warrior, is a small, serious man with a British accent and a longtime vipassana practice. We look at each other awkwardly, clutching our mugs of herbal tea. I break the ice with what seems like an innocuous question: "So what do you do?" He gazes at me as if this were the weirdest question anyone had ever asked him and repeats, incredulously, "*Do???*"

I decide to do more prescreening next time. After a few intriguing email exchanges, I chat on the phone with a yoga practitioner who teaches world religions at a prep school near San Jose. We converse easily about our children (he has two preschool-age sons), our spiritual practice (we've studied with some of the same teachers), our academic interests.

Having children, I'm discovering, makes dating more complicated. I'm not just interviewing for a potential mate—I'm interviewing for the stepfather of my child. And his kids are part of his package as well. The fantasy can't just be about us entwined in bed on Sunday morning while our kids are at the homes of our respective exes. It has to also include us driving each other's kids to preschool or staying home with them when they have the flu, holding their heads while they puke into a bucket.

When I arrive at the bookstore café, my yoga date is not there yet. I browse through the paperbacks, discreetly eyeing each arriving customer. Across the aisle, a stocky, dark-haired man is doing the same thing. We exchange glances, then look away—clearly we are not the people we're waiting for. It takes a good ten minutes before we approach each other and discover that we are.

We order tea and begin to talk, trying to get used to each other's nonvirtual presence. Although I hadn't been aware of having any clear expectations, I feel slightly let down. This guy is every bit as thoughtful and pleasant as our conversation had led me to believe. But the man I had imagined was taller, with a commanding physical presence due to his twenty years of intensive Iyengar yoga. I find myself glancing toward the door, still waiting for that man to show up. I imagine that my date is probably waiting for a different version of me as well—perhaps one in retouched black-and-white, like my publicity photo.

Stirring my tea, I realize that this is one of the many strange things about online dating. Normally, when you meet someone, you encounter them first in the flesh, so whatever story you begin to spin in your mind centers around a character who vaguely resembles who they actually are. But when you meet someone online, the mind—in a textbook illustration of what Buddhism calls *papancha*, or "proliferation of thoughts"—fleshes out an entire image based on a tiny photo and a few lines of text, and then begins generating plots in which this imaginary figure plays a leading role. When you actually meet the person, they bear no resemblance to the person you'd imagined—how could they?—so you feel a wave of disappointment. It's like seeing a movie based on a favorite novel: *That's not Rhett Butler!* (Although, in that case, at least, Rhett is played by Clark Gable.)

WEEKS 6–10

I don't take the prep school teacher up on his offer to meet again—I'm moving to a new home, which will be a three-hour drive from where he lives. Distracted by the details of packing, I take a break from the dating assignment. My Internet connection goes down for a couple of weeks; I get back online to find a backlog of dharma-date emails in my inbox, along with a pile of tasks that need attending to. Dharma-dating feels like just one more assignment on which I'm falling behind.

I begin declining correspondence more often, saying truthfully that I'm just too busy right now. But I keep glancing at the profiles with idle curiosity, the way I sometimes stop in at garage sales. I'm fascinated to observe how quickly my mind rules people out—and on how little evidence. "The Great Way is not difficult for those who have no preferences," writes Seng-ts'an, the Third Chinese Patriarch. The same might be said for dharma dating. Free of the counterbalancing weight of actual human contact, I eliminate suitors for random, insignificant reasons: too short, too tall, too old, too young, too little hair, too *much* hair, spelling *vipassana* with the wrong number of *p*'s or *s*'s or *n*'s, claiming to be enlightened.

WEEKS 11–13

With another nudge from my editor, I decide to plunge back into the dating sea again. I meet up for dinner with a former devotee of the tantric guru Osho who now runs a car-rental business. I have tea with a music producer and vipassana student from Los Angeles, who regularly visits the Bay Area to record with a local musician. A professor of East Asian philosophy invites me to an "ecstatic trance dance" held at a Middle Eastern belly-dancing restaurant. A psychologist and mountain climber offer me a tour of his co-housing community.

What is the spark—chemistry, karma, neurosis?—that leads us to want to spend time with one person more than with another? Whatever it is, I don't feel it with any of my dates, although they are all likeable people. The very activity of dating feels fluffy and insubstantial compared with the weight and texture of my daily life, filled as it is with the countless domestic details of child-rearing, work, and friendships. Romance seemed easier to stumble into in the old days, when I didn't have so many . . . *appendages*. But, of course, these appendages are what make my life worth living.

I tell myself that I should probably persist past a first date. After all, haven't some of my best connections been with people I didn't immediately feel attracted to? But my life is already full of friends I don't have enough time to see. I resist the idea of carving out time for relative strangers. At the end of a long day, after I tuck my son into bed, I'm happier curling up with a good book than exchanging dharmaMatch emails with a sexy ex-monk.

Driving home from my co-housing tour, I reflect that this whole experience can perhaps be viewed as a kind of meditation practice. When you sit down to meditate, you never know what's going to come up. Some days you're hammered by relentless trivia; other days you're caught in storms of anger or grief or fear. What's important is just to keep coming back to the cushion, to keep opening the door to the possibility of peace and insight.

Perhaps dating is just a way to practice keeping the door of my heart open to intimacy—without attachment to results. In the process, I can notice the habits of contraction that keep me feeling separate from other people: judgments, expectations, fears, busyness, guilt, chronic feelings of insecurity or superiority.

Or is this theory just an attempt to spiritualize an essentially absurd activity, one riddled with consumerism and steeped in the double delusion that love is out there somewhere and that with persistence and a fast Internet connection we can track it down?

WEEKS 14–15

I go out to dinner with a computer programmer who used to be a Peace Corps volunteer in Nepal. Over Thai food, we talk for three hours, although I'd told the babysitter I'd be home in two. He tells me about the Tibetan teachers he's studied with and about the tantric sex workshops he used to attend.

Over the next two weeks he floods me with long, chatty emails. He tells me about books he's read, movies he's seen. He muses on artificial intelligence, the history of Supreme Court justices, his relationship with his nieces and nephew and sisters. I tell him that, as a writer, I don't enjoy socializing by email. He responds with a five-paragraph essay about a recent interview with Terry Gross on NPR.

I lose patience and send him a plea: "Ack! No! Stop! Send smoke signals! Beat on a talking drum! Skywrite messages in the blue! Throw tomatoes at my window! But no more emails!" I don't hear from him again.

I'm not cut out for cyber-dating, I decide.

It seems I am an anachronism. I'm just not interested in "getting to know someone" by typing words into a box on a screen. For me, connections unfold slowly, through repeated encounters in natural settings. I like to observe animals in the wild, not in the zoo—even if there seem to be fewer of them. Instead of exchanging pleasantries with strangers online, I'd rather go deeper into my life as it already is and celebrate the intimacy—with friends, family, and community—that is already nourishing me.

I've never been someone who spots love instantly. Overcoming my innate reserve usually takes days, weeks, even months spent sweating side by side on yoga mats or scrambling eggs in the kitchen of a shared house. At this stage of my life, I'm starting to believe that nothing will break through my busyness and melt my defenses but the rhythm of a project or activity shared over time, and that activity must be more meaningful than the shared project of looking for a date.

I don't want my *Tricycle* article to be one long advertisement for a mate. So I invent a tidy ending, in which I get back together with my most recent lover. Just so I won't be misleading my readers, I have one last fling with him.

We do love each other dearly, and we have great chemistry. And when we end our relationship again, at least it's not via email.

SEVERAL YEARS LATER

It's another four years before I find my mate. And I have to go through a few more failed attempts.

There's the single dad eight years younger than me and a two-hour drive north, who I'd met over a decade earlier on a Thich Nhat Hanh retreat and who looks me up after he reads my *Tricycle* story (undeterred, it seems, by the happy, coupled ending I'd invented—or perhaps understanding that such endings are often temporary). His son is kindergarten age, just one year younger than Forest.

After a couple of great dates, he comes to spend the weekend at my house with his boy. We tell our kids we are old friends and carefully censor any romantic vibes when we're in their presence. Despite a few awkward moments—such as when his son asks me, incredulously, "Aren't you too *old* to be a mom?"—we have a fabulous weekend of domestic bliss. We make pancakes together in the morning; go to the Scoop for ice cream cones in the hot afternoon; sit in the hot tub in our bathing suits while the boys bring us strawberries and mint they picked in my garden; tell a bedtime story together as we tuck the boys into side-by-side beds at night. At the end of the weekend our kids suggest we all move in together. But when I drive up the coast to Mendocino for a solo visit, our chemistry fizzles out. Apparently, what we were ready to launch a romance for was our fantasy of a blended family. Alone together, we can't make it off the launch pad.

Then there's the perpetual grad student of Sanskrit I meet at a yoga workshop, who spends nine months of every year in India working on an interminable dissertation. I find his unpublished translations of obscure yogic texts irresistible. From Varanasi, he writes me emails so funny and flirtatious that I'm convinced they are *even better* than being able to, say, meet for dinner on a regular basis. Over Skype, we talk for hours about meditation, yoga, and creativity until I'm buzzing with lust. He sends me compilation CDs of his favorite jazz. But when the conversation turns to a potential visit, he tells me that he is a renunciate at heart and committed to celibacy. He kindly lets me know that he has moved past the point, in his spiritual practice, where he needs a special connection with just one person—he wants to send metta to all beings equally.

Then there's the Italian filmmaker with four ex-wives on three continents, who I meet at a dance jam . . . You get the picture.

I take a long, long break from dating.

When people ask me, years later, how I met the man who became my life partner, I will often tell them that I met him in my hot tub.

The truth is that I had been hearing Teja's name for years and had even met him briefly one time when we were both eating lunch at a group picnic table under the oaks at the meditation center where he taught qigong and I taught yoga. Across the table, my eyes kept being drawn to his hands—long-fingered, both delicate and powerful, and somehow seeming more fully *inhabited* than any hands I'd ever seen. When I got home that night I'd immediately googled him and discovered two different online footprints, which at first I assumed must be two different people—one a professional guitarist who ran a recording studio called Samurai Sound, the other a Zen priest in the Hollow Bones order who was a sixth-degree black belt in aikido and a qigong master. But even after I discovered that these were the same guy, I didn't reach out to him. Musicians, I reminded myself, were terrible relationship bets—as were Zen priests, for that matter.

But a few months later, a dharma teacher friend called me and asked if she could bring a group of her fellow teachers over to my house for a hot tub after they finished the dharma talk at the retreat they were leading. (Yes, that *is* what your retreat teachers are doing after they chant about impermanence with you and send you off in silence to mindfully prepare for bed.) I didn't know that the Zen guitarist was on the teaching team, so I didn't have time to get nervous. As the group of us sat in the tub together under the branches of a live oak, listening to the coyotes howl in the hills, I was struck again by Teja's presence—his solidity, calm, and palpable quality of groundedness—as if his end of the hot tub were somehow heavier than the rest of it. Afterward, as we all lounged in my living room eating ice cream, he picked up my now eight-year-old son's guitar and began to play a Spanish classical piece. "You have extraordinary hands," I told him, watching them move across the strings.

"The left hand is very different from the right, because they're used differently," he told me. He held them out, fanned the fingers wide, and I placed my palms on his.

Later that night, after he'd left, I texted my dear friend Linda, a fellow writer. A decade earlier we used to carpool together to our jobs at *Yoga Journal*, talking about food and sex the whole way. I told her, "I've met the next guy I'm going to fall in love with."

After decades of tangled and turbulent romantic connections, I was astonished by the ease with which our lives came together over the weeks and months that followed.

It wasn't just the ease and intensity of our chemistry—it was the way I felt calmer whenever he put his hand on me, as if he were a grounding pole for the electricity that jangled my nervous system. When I got anxious, I'd lean against him and feel my breath release and slow down. His touch seemed to reach below my skin, melting the core of my bones, thawing something frozen deep in my belly.

Over the first months, every time we lay in bed together, I cried, as something deep inside me that had been longing to connect began to unwind. He never asked me to explain in words what was wrong. He just held me as long as it took for the tears to stop.

We were both refugees from shipwrecked marriages, finding late in life the kind of relationship we had always dreamed of being in. I knew that part of what had finally shifted for me was my ability to recognize something good when it came knocking. When I was a young woman, I would have pushed him away for any number of reasons: he put too much whipped cream on his pie, too much soy sauce on his rice, too much maple syrup on his pancakes. On the meals I prepared, I began leaving him notes about what was allowable: on a Mexican rice bowl, "This is not a soy sauce meal!" Amazingly, he did not break up with me over that. On one of our first dates, he showed up at the sushi restaurant straight from an afternoon of gardening, wearing a bandana wrapped around his head. "*A bandana!!*" I told my therapist, incredulous. "Like Willie Nelson! Can you believe it?" She's been married thirty years. She told me that her husband likes to wear a bandana too.

But this time around, I was able to notice my mind's habitual judgments and contractions for what they were—a misguided attempt to armor the vulnerability of my heart.

When I finally introduced him to Forest, I discovered an added bonus: Forest thought he was wonderful too. Now almost nine, Forest had been studying martial arts since he was four and had recently started learning guitar. He immediately recognized Teja's mastery in both areas. "You don't happen to have any ninja throwing stars, do you?" he asked at one of their early meetings, referring to the weaponry he'd heard about in samurai stories.

"Yes, as a matter of fact, I do," said Teja. And on his next visit, he brought them along and showed Forest how to throw them.

For our first Christmas together, Teja gave me a necklace with an om sign on one side of its medallion, a yin-yang on the other—a symbol of his qigong practice meeting my yoga. He gave Forest a beautifully illustrated role-playing book titled *Legend of the Five Rings*.

He also gave me a spacious, circular yoga mat—and as I spiraled and spun through my practice, I could feel the rectangular coffin-shaped box that I'd unconsciously been putting myself into start to dissolve.

Two years after we met, Teja moved in with us. He set up a man cave in my in-law unit, where he could hunker down with his sixteen guitars; his samurai swords; a keyboard and a music stand; microphones, amps, and recording paraphernalia; bookshelves of writings on qigong, dharma, and neuroscience; Chinese calligraphies; stacks of zafus and zabutons; a closet's worth of black Zen robes and crimson *rakasus*; wall hangings of Buddhas passed down from his great-aunt Leona, who had been a missionary in China in the early 1900s. It was a lair where he wouldn't keep me awake when he stayed up late rehearsing folk harmonies with his band Samurai Wolf; and where he could retreat when Forest and his fourth-grade friends were howling through our living room, testing from how far away they could leap into a giant beanbag chair.

And it was my favorite place to go on a date.

It's different finding a partner when so much of each of your lives is already behind you. I knew my ex-husband's history almost as well as I knew my own. My new love and I had to assimilate each other's pasts bit by bit.

Over the weeks and months, we swapped tales. I told him how I used to make hot bran mashes for my horse, Kentucky Lady, on Christmas morning. He told me how he'd bought his first guitar at age nine with money he'd earned from his newspaper route—a cheap instrument with strings so stiff they made his fingers bleed. I told him about how I'd started practicing Zen in college, after I signed up for a class in world religions only because it didn't meet too early in the morning. He told me how he'd grown up on stories of China from his great-aunt Leona—stories that inspired him to start training in martial arts at age fifteen.

As I heard his stories, they gradually sank into me as if I'd shared them—as if his past were being transplanted into me, through our bodies as much as our words.

Now, I imagine that I can see him with his brother in their teenage home in Des Moines. In the basement, they have set candles in wall sconces almost as high as the ceiling. They compete at taking running leaps into the air and kicking out the candle flames with their big toes—without knocking down the candles.

I see him in his twenties, during a year in a Christian monastery—his curly brown hair past his shoulders, a cross hanging around his neck. I see him in his thirties, tumbling across a rock-hard aikido mat in a dojo in Iwama, Japan. I see him playing guitar in his forties at the Palau de la Música Catalana concert hall in Barcelona.

Though I wasn't there with him for any of that, when we touch each other I feel as if I find *then* nestled in the heart of *now*.

His gray hair is shaved off now. I'm ten pounds heavier than I was before my son was born. I can't do a drop back into a backbend. He can't kick out a candle flame (though he can still snuff out the candles on a birthday cake with a flick of his wrist). We never knew each other as the young woman and young man we used to be.

But when we wrap our arms around each other, the energy that flows between us has no age. And I feel that all of my previous incarnations are kissing all of his.

The Best-Laid Plans

· · · · ·

FOREST IS NINE years old, with a 103-degree fever, and I'm having a spiritual breakthrough in our hotel room at the Dallas–Fort Worth International Airport.

Well, okay, so maybe it isn't exactly a breakthrough. Maybe it's more of a little crack in the prison walls through which a ray of moonlight can shine.

By *prison*, of course, I don't mean the hotel room. We actually had a very comfortable seventh-floor room with a panoramic view of the runway. That is, we had it until Forest threw up all over the rug, at which point we got switched to an identical fourth-floor room with a panoramic view of the parking garage.

No, by *prison* I mean those iron bars of thoughts and beliefs that . . . well, let me start the story a little earlier.

A few months earlier, I had begun planning a two-week trip to Guatemala with Forest to study Spanish and live with a Mayan family in a remote mountain village on the shores of Lake Atitlán.

I'd set up our trip through a nonprofit organization run by a young American couple who had made their home in Guatemala. The more they told me about our situation, the better it sounded. Our homestay family—Pedro, Gladis, and their three boys—could speak no English. We'd learn to make tortillas in Gladis's wood-fired stove. Forest would accompany the ten-year-old, Selvin, to the village school. Every morning, we'd take Spanish lessons while looking out at the three huge volcanoes that ringed the shimmering waters of what Aldous Huxley called "the most beautiful lake in the world."

What could be better? I booked our flights for Forest's February school vacation and began making plans.

· · ·

That's what I do: I plan stuff.

By the time I booked our flight that morning, I'd already planned a novel set in ancient Assam, a dinner of butternut squash and black bean tacos, a Skype conference with Forest's fifth-grade teacher, an online yoga workshop, and a trip to Walgreens to buy wart remover. And I hadn't even washed the breakfast dishes yet.

There's nothing wrong with planning, in and of itself—my plans have created some wonderful outcomes over the years (as well as, of course, some spectacular misfires). The problem is, my planning respects no boundaries. I plan while driving, while hiking, while washing my hair, while sitting on the toilet. I scribble my do-lists everywhere—crumpled napkins, torn-up envelopes, sticky notes, dream journals, the palm of my hand. I sit in meditation retreats planning to sit in future meditation retreats.

For decades after starting my Buddhist practice, my incessant planning—amazingly—remained largely invisible to me. Sitting in meditation, I noticed the ice storms of fear; the tsunamis of lust; the endless reruns of disastrous love affairs and childhood disappointments. But my planning mind was a constant background hum I took for granted, like NPR on my car radio.

But a few years before our Guatemala expedition, I'd actually begun to catch myself planning during my yoga practice. I'd always thought of my yoga as a sanctuary from the din of my thoughts—a sensual, intuitive, intimate realm I explore with no GPS. But then there I'd be, deep in a forward bend, swimming through a wordless flow of sensation and emotion—when I'd notice my own voice-over, preparing instructions to an invisible future yoga class about how to swim through a wordless flow of sensation and emotion. Or I'd be blissfully doing sun salutations under a tree on my deck when I'd catch myself planning a "yoga in nature" retreat, where I could do yoga under a tree on a deck.

Suddenly it was as if a blacklight had been turned on in my inner world—and all my invisible-ink planning was glowingly apparent, scrawled like graffiti over every available mental surface. I realized how often I slaughtered my actual life—the smell of bay laurels in the rain, the creamy surrender of an avocado to my spoon—on an altar to a ghostlike future. I saw how regularly I sat outside the wide-open gates of heaven, trying to order the keys online.

I was horrified. All those decades of meditation and yoga, and things were still this bad? Surely there must be something I could do about it. There must be—well, a *plan*! So I promptly made one: To make planning itself an object of my mindful awareness. To learn how to live skillfully with a planning mind, without being ruled by it.

That's a good idea, I thought, grabbing for a scrap of paper to scribble it down. *I should plan to write about it sometime.*

As our trip to Guatemala drew nearer, my to-do list drummed relentlessly through my mind, waking me up at two in the morning to bark commands: *Update Forest's hepatitis-A immunization. Buy travel-sized contact lens solution. Get international plan for cell phone.* I loaded *Speak Spanish with Michel Thomas* into my car stereo and began repeating his useful phrases as I drove from errand to errand: *Can I make a reservation for dinner tonight? What do you think of the political and economic situation in Argentina? My friend is a drunk.*

With each mental preview of our future trip, I thought of more items to add to my list. Forest typically got carsick on winding mountain roads: *candied ginger.* Forest should offer a gift to our homestay family's kids: *remote-control helicopter.*

The problem was, I'd squeezed the trip to Guatemala into some white space on my calendar, right between teaching a yoga retreat and rewriting a screenplay. A website that I'd helped develop was due to launch while I was away. Emails were sprouting like kudzu in my in-box. My life felt like a suitcase I'd stuffed too much into. Now I was sitting on top of it, trying to get the lid to close.

Through studying my "planning mind" over the last few years, I already knew some tools for working with it—the first one being, of course, to notice and name it. As my trip grew closer and the planning crescendoed, one of my dharma teachers suggested some other inquiries: How much of my planning was redundant? What benefit did I derive from it? What feelings did it help me avoid? How did it help me bolster the illusion of a solid self?

Again and again, I'd spread out my yoga mat, sit on my cushion, and offer a deep bow to my planning mind: *Thank you so much, but not now.* I'd draw my attention gently back to my body and notice the feelings that lay underneath the plans: the shallow breath, the gripped spine, the emotional cocktail of excitement and anxiety—wildly out of proportion, as if I were Jack Bauer on the TV series *24*, with the clock ticking on my plans to purchase sturdy walking sandals and thereby avert worldwide nuclear annihilation. Apparently, deep in my cells, I believed that if I didn't keep reciting the mantra of my REI shopping list, the entire universe would implode. And as my breath would slow, I'd look straight in the eyes of the demons that muttered and snarled under the veil of my plans: *If I'm not planning, I'm not worth anything. I don't even exist at all.*

The night before we left, Forest was so excited he didn't fall sleep until after midnight. Walking into the airport, our carry-on packs strapped to our backs, he caught my hand and exulted, "We're off on an adventure together! We've been planning it for so long and now it's here!" But as our plane lifted off, he turned pale and droopy. He leaned against the hard plastic of the window and fell asleep, foregoing the usual thrill of watching the San Francisco Bay fall away below us. He turned down apple juice, and honey peanuts, and watching *Megamind* on the seatback video screen. By the time we landed in Dallas for our connecting flight to Guatemala City, his head was throbbing and he could barely lift his backpack.

As I hustled him toward our departure gate, where boarding had already started, I looked at his face—pale and miserable—and knew I couldn't get on another plane. I spoke with the gate attendant, who tore up our boarding passes and issued us new ones for the next day. Fifteen minutes later, we were checking into the airport hotel for what I imagined would be a night of recovery before flying on. Three hours later Forest was vomiting, with a high fever—and I knew we wouldn't be doing a homestay with a family in Guatemala anytime soon.

Forest was not only too sick to go on, he was too sick to fly home. We were stranded at the Dallas airport.

Now, sitting up in his bed overlooking the parking lot, Forest is weeping with disappointment. "I'm supposed to be driving to Lake Atitlán today!" he sobs. "I'm supposed to be giving Selvin his helicopter!"

I ache for him. I know the all-too-human pain of comparing your actual life to the one you had envisioned, and having it come up short. We'd pictured this day so many times—the shimmering water of Lake Atitlán, the bright clothes of the Mayan women washing their clothes at the well, Forest running down the cobbled streets with his new Guatemalan friends. We'd planned it so much that we had thought it was real—a solid future, just waiting for us to come and inhabit it. Instead, it has dissolved like the mirage that it always was. Instead, we are in an airport hotel, hearing the roar of a jet lifting into the air—filled with people, presumably, whose plans had worked out.

Except that's not true, of course, I remind myself. It's safe to assume that every person on that plane has experienced derailments and disappointment in their lifetime far worse than our minor travel setback. What we are experiencing is not one of the big plan-shatterers—the bad blood test results, the phone call at two in the morning, the goodbye note on the kitchen table, the car swerving out of control on the patch of freeway ice. We are comfortable, safe, and well fed, I remind Forest (and myself). For heaven's sake, we have *room service*.

It isn't as exciting as being in Guatemala, of course—but is even *that* true? If Gladis's family could be dropped down in this room with us, would they find it tedious? Or would they enjoy the flat-screen TV with its on-demand movies; the built-in mini fridge stocked with Pringles sour-cream dip, Schlitz beer, and Reese's Peanut Butter Cups? And how do we know what our trip to Lake Atitlán would actually have been like? We are comparing reality with an airbrushed fantasy pinup—and in that context, reality generally comes up looking uncombed and disheveled.

I decide to look at our stay in this hotel room—for however long it would be—as a mini meditation retreat. While Forest naps and recovers, I will meditate and do yoga on the travel mat I'd conveniently stuffed in my backpack. When he is awake, I will embrace being present with him as my practice. I will fully open to the trip that is actually happening and stop comparing it to the imaginary one I had planned. And I'll try to remember that what is most important is not what is happening but how I relate to it.

This has its challenging moments. As Forest's fever climbs every night, he thrashes and moans and calls out in his sleep—"That's my snitch! The snow is two- to three-feet deep!"—apparently deep in a game of nocturnal Quidditch on a ski slope. As I lie awake listening to him breathe like a winded racehorse, the primal fear of a mother facing the unknown for her child surges inside me—entirely disproportionate to the actual danger at hand.

When I was a few years younger than Forest is now, my father was sent to Vietnam on a two-year posting—his third tour of duty there—and my mother took me and my older siblings to the Philippines to wait for him. I didn't learn until years later that while we were there, my father's helicopter was shot down in the jungle behind enemy lines. It was days before my mother heard that he had survived the crash and made his way to safety.

Now, on my improvised meditation retreat at the airport hotel, I feel my mother's fear bubbling up inside me from its lodging deep in my cells. No wonder I like to plan things, I think; no wonder I feel that disaster will strike if I don't. Rattling in the back of my plans is the throb of my father's helicopter flying over the war-ravaged jungles; the terror of my mother, waking up in the middle of the night with her children, far from home.

I lie in bed and try to meditate with my fear—to greet it with metta, loving-kindness; to get to know it, make it my friend. Whenever I can't stand it anymore, I get up and stand close to Forest's bed, bending my face close to his to see how hot he is and if I need to call the emergency room now, or whether I can wait till the morning. The third time, he opens his eyes in exasperation. "*Mom*," he says. "I'm trying to get some *sleep* here."

But for the most part—when I stop comparing things to my imaginary trip—the three days we spend in this one small room are actually quite enjoyable. With Forest dosed up on ibuprofen, we play chess and gin rummy and a Scrabble-like game called Bananagrams. We rent *The Last Airbender*, which we both agree is slightly more entertaining than watching the four-story parking garage out the window. When I want a real thrill, I walk down the hall to the ice machine and look out the window at the runway as I fill a water glass with ice cubes.

When I open my eyes to it, the trip—just as it is—is bursting with miracles. The crunch of hot buttered toast. The glowing red ball of the sun as it drops low on the horizon over the runway I see through the window by the ice machine, and the plane taking off steeply in front of it. The laughter of my boy as he lies on the bed next to me, reading *Syren*, a book in the Septimus Heap series.

And the glorious fact that—other than a couple of calls to the airline to cancel our tickets—I don't make a single plan for seventy-two hours.

After three nights in the hotel, Forest is well enough to board a plane home, though he's still coughing and weak. We pack up our backpacks again and head out. Before I close the door, I turn and bow to the hotel room, as if walking out of a temple.

It hasn't been the trip I had planned. But it has been real—and I have been there for most of it. And that, in itself, is cause for a small celebration.

The Terrain in Spain

. . . . .

THE SUMMER THAT Forest turns eleven, I swap houses for a month with an old friend who lives in Spain, a former yoga buddy I haven't seen or even spoken to in over two decades.

Shawn and I were both in our twenties when we first met. She was a slender, intense yogini from Vermont with a long brown ponytail and Birkenstocks. We were both in a teacher-training program at the Iyengar Yoga Institute in San Francisco. We had drilled side by side on green sticky mats in our eighties-style tights and leotards, parsing the muscular grammar of Downward Dog and Revolved Triangle. We crayoned nerves and organs in our anatomy coloring books and identified—blindfolded—the disassembled vertebrae of a plastic skeleton. After class we'd go out to lunch at a militantly vegetarian restaurant whose hand-lettered menu seemed designed to shame us into veganism. (Eggs, for example, were on the menu as "chicken menstruations.") We visited each other's homes for yoga dates, during which we balanced side by side on our heads while discussing our once and future boyfriends.

But then she fell in love with one of our fellow yogis, a handsome, serious Catalan man on sabbatical from his engineering job in Germany. They married and moved to Barcelona. Shortly after their first baby was born, she wrote me a letter on a flimsy blue aerogram—she sounded lonely, and I meant to write back right away. But I got distracted by a few other things—some long treks through India, a couple of books, a marriage, a child, a divorce.

Now, suddenly more than twenty years have slipped by, and I want to take my son to study Spanish in Spain. Forest's been taking lessons off and on since he was in kindergarten, when I'd enrolled him in an after-school class called Hola Kids, and he's currently studying Spanish in fifth grade. We've made brief trips to Mexico and Costa Rica, but I want him to have the chance to immerse, especially since our planned homestay in Guatemala the previous year never got past the Dallas–Fort Worth airport.

My Google search turns up Shawn teaching prenatal yoga and working as a doula in Sitges, a beach town just south of Barcelona. She answers my email right away: "I still have a photo of you in Downward Dog hanging in my painting studio!" I tour her Facebook page, where she looks exactly the same as I remembered her, until I realize I am viewing a photo of her daughter. I have a warm but disorienting Skype conversation with a European woman with a chic blonde haircut instead of a brown ponytail, who answers to Shawn's name but keeps breaking off to chat in Spanish and Catalan with her two teenagers.

In the decades since we'd last spoken, Shawn and I have each built a thriving life—and along the way, accumulated the usual list of roads-not-taken. I envy her established twenty-year marriage. She envies my fresh new romance with a qigong teacher. I pine for her bicultural, trilingual sophistication. She pines for my local community of dharma yoga friends. She tells me about the first yoga class she ever taught in Spanish—which she hadn't started learning until after her wedding—in which she had instructed a group of pregnant women to "sit on their testicles" (inadvertently confusing the Spanish word for "cushions," *cojines*, with *cojones*). I tell her about the time I led a silent yoga and meditation retreat with my screaming four-month-old son in a frontpack, my milk letting down and soaking my camisole as I guided the retreatants into savasana.

A flurry of emails later, she is sitting at my kitchen table in California—along with her husband, her son, her daughter, and her daughter's best friend—handing me the keys to her house, her gate, her car, and her mailbox; instructing me on how to operate her Persian blinds and put her cat's food bowl in a moat of water so the ants won't infest it.

And then I am doing a seated twist on her yoga mat on her terracotta patio, next to a lemon tree and a garden bed of basil and tomatoes, looking over a valley of rooftops and orange-blossomed trees at the Mediterranean Sea—while in the lawn chairs next to me Forest reads *Pendragon* and Teja plays a flamenco riff on Shawn's husband's guitar.

Travel writer Bill Bryson once said that the great gift of travel is that it puts you in situations where you can't take anything for granted. I've found that, like meditation, it cultivates a kind of beginner's mind in which each experience is fresh.

A house swap, in particular, invites the tantalizing fantasy that you are truly leaving behind not just your own familiar routine but your own familiar and slightly annoying self—swapping it out for a new, improved, more fascinating self, with better outfits and a better shot at enlightenment. Dropped into the middle of another woman's life—sleeping in her bed with her mosquito coil humming, riding her bicycle to the beach while wearing her (only slightly too small) flip-flops, sautéing zucchini from her garden in her kitchen and serving it up in her beautiful Spanish crockery—I feel, at first, as if I've been reincarnated. Yes, I'd learned some great lessons from that Guatemala trip that never happened. But I'm sure I'll have even better insights now that the teachings come with a side of paella.

Our first evening in Sitges, a friend of Shawn's invites me and Forest to a *fiesta de espuma*—foam festival—in a nearby village. It's a giant public bubble bath, in which a cannon mounted on top of a truck fires a stream of soapy foam into a plaza next to a seventeenth-century church, while a salsa band plays with no shirts on. Children in bathing suits and goggles, wrinkled *abuelitas* hand in hand with their grandkids, and papas with toddlers seated on their shoulders all frolic in neck-deep bubbles to a Latin beat. As Forest dances through the crowd with a corona of bubbles, shaking his frothy hips and waving his arms, I think happily, *Toto, I have a feeling we're not in America anymore.*

The next day, Forest, Teja, and I take the train into Barcelona for a bicycle tour through fifteenth-century streets jammed with honking, fuming twenty-first-century traffic. We pedal through the medieval courtyard of the Plaça del Rei, where Ferdinand and Isabella greeted Christopher Columbus on his return from the

New World. We cruise past the sandcastle-like splendor of La Sagrada Familia, the still-unfinished masterwork cathedral of the architect Antoni Gaudí, who spent his final years living as a pauper in its basement. We pause for snack bars and water at a series of memorials commemorating religious and political martyrs who over the centuries had been shot, or burned at the stake, or beheaded; had boiling oil poured upon them, or been rolled through the streets in barrels full of broken glass.

But it isn't just the touristy photo ops that brush the cobwebs of familiarity from my eyes. In a foreign country where I don't speak the language, ordinary life—buying groceries, doing laundry, driving Forest to and from his sailing camp in Shawn's old VW van—is a constant mystery. With the adaptability of youth, Forest learns to sail with the instructions all in Spanish from his slender Argentinian teacher. ("Make sure you understand the words for 'right,' 'left,' and 'watch out!'" I tell him as I drop him off.) But I blunder through my days, bleating the primal phrases of need and want from my introductory Spanish CDs—"*Quiero . . . necessito . . . tienes?*"—and misunderstanding the answers. A freeway sign flashes a warning—*Peligroso!*—which I fortunately know means "danger." But I can't understand the rest of the warning, which in any case has already disappeared behind me.

I also can't understand: Why is the old woman at the roadside fruit stand so irritated that I'd picked up the melon and set it on the weighing scale? Why are the carts in the Supermarque chain-locked together, and how do I get them apart? For that one, I send Forest to inquire in Spanish of the white-coated man at the meat counter—who is standing next to an entire pig, skinned and gutted, dangling by its hind ankles from an overhead hook. (Vegetarianism, we have learned, is a rare phenomenon in Spain. When we request our salads *sin carne*—without meat—they come with ham instead.) In the United States, meat comes tidily packaged in plastic, its animal origins coyly disguised. In Spain, it rolls its eyes and stares right at us: *Hi, I'm Wilbur, and I'll be your tapas for this evening . . .*

Alas, it quickly becomes clear that I have not been reborn into this new reality as an entirely new person—say, for example, a spacious and nonjudgmental person who doesn't get annoyed when her partner plays classical guitar till after midnight and sleeps in till ten, and then drinks strong Spanish coffee from a two-liter measuring cup, even though she has repeatedly told him that the best way to get over jet lag is to get up early and do yoga and meditate with her, and even though she is clearly *so right* about that! Unfortunately, I have packed my mind along with me—as opinionated and prolific as always. Most mornings, Teja and Forest sleep in. I stand on my head on the patio and fume, wondering why no one wants to join me.

A week into our trip, after dropping Forest off at sailing camp, I head home to practice yoga on Shawn's patio. The breeze smells of salt water and orange blossoms. A garbage truck groans up the street, with a sound like a very large animal in labor. The knots in my spine unravel in a gentle twist. And as I drop into the pause at the bottom of a long exhalation, I think, *Now I'm finally here.*

But what do I mean by "here"? Shawn's house is eerily similar to my own: peach-colored walls, a closet full of yoga props, a stack of zafus and zabutons piled in the corner of the living room. And deep in the heart of my practice, I could be anywhere in the world. Folding into a forward bend, I meet with the same familiar body I greet in California—though admittedly more laden with *pan al tomate*. Seated in meditation, I meet with the same familiar mind. Sure, the content of my tumbling thoughts is different: What metro stop will get me to the Joan Miró museum on the peak of Montjuïc? Is it really okay for Forest to eat chocolate croissants for breakfast, and if so, can I have a bite? But my mind's basic structure is the same: the cascade of seeing and hearing and smelling and tasting; the flickering slideshow of planning and judging; the undertow of anxiety laced with longing. Have I really traveled six thousand miles just to do *this*?

It's one of the basic teachings of Buddha dharma, I reflect, as I hoist my pelvis onto a foam yoga block for a supported inversion: the illusion of solid self that I cling to so tenaciously is composed of a limited number of ever-shuffling components. Wherever I go, my experience is created from the same basic elements: seeing, hearing, smelling, tasting, touching, thinking. From the point of view of a yogi, *Spain* and *America* are just abstract concepts. There is no coming and no going; you're always right here, right now. From that perspective, we might as well have stayed home—or gotten stranded in yet another airport hotel for a week.

And yet . . . A pill bug crawls toward my head; when I blow on it, it curls into a ball and tumbles away. A firecracker bangs exuberantly somewhere down the street. My sacrum releases with a pop as I drop my feet to the floor. A high-speed train roars by at the bottom of the hill. My practice invites me into a living intimacy with this specific unfolding moment—a forty-something woman upside down on a patio, with a fat gray cat leaning against her shoulders, wanting his belly rubbed. I'm glad that, this time, our travel plans worked out.

Again and again, I reflect, my practice of yoga and meditation helps me navigate this dance between the universal and the personal, the absolute and the relative. It teaches me to honor my own quirky, specific human body and mind and story while at the same time seeing their ever-changing, impermanent nature, inseparable from the interconnected web of pill bugs and chocolate, garbage trucks and sangria. And it reminds me that I have the opportunity to be reborn in each new moment, wherever I might be on the planet.

My practice reminds me that in travel, as in yoga, the point is not just to get from one peak experience to the next—the poses and destinations are part of an ongoing vinyasa, or flow. As Forest, Teja, and I take the metro through Barcelona to a flamenco guitar concert at the Palau de la Música Catalana, I remind Forest that our day's adventure is not just the hour and a half we will sit in the concert hall, a stained-glass ceiling arcing above us, listening to Pedro Javier González play *Recuerdos de Alhambra*. The adventure is also our sweaty confusion as we puzzle over the metro maps by the train tracks; and it's our rescue by a young architecture student named Maria, who listens patiently to our halting Spanish and leads us through the maze of the station to the right metro line. If we can't be present for Maria and the metro, the chances are that we won't be fully there for the concert either.

My daily meditations help me stay centered as we take a cable car up a jagged mountain to the eighth-century monastery Santa Maria de Montserrat, which now attracts a million tourists a year. "That sounds like a monk's worst nightmare," I say to Teja. But outside the bar by the monastery museum we spot a group of portly, black-robed monks drinking red wine and passing around trays of hors d'oeuvres. Forest takes off his sunhat and sets it on a wall to pose for a photo with a statue of a saint; by the time we have snapped a few shots, the hat has been stolen by one of our fellow pilgrims. I suggest to Forest that perhaps in a few hundred years, Spirit Rock, the Buddhist retreat center where I teach in California, might look like this: a cable car to the hill above the meditation hall, with a café and a bar on top, and a viewing platform where tourists can watch through binoculars as the vipassana students do walking meditation in the courtyard.

And my practice reminds me to stay relaxed as we celebrate Forest's eleventh birthday with a few of his new Spanish friends and a chocolate cream cake with *Felicidades* written in white icing. Forest's dad flies in in time for the party, en route to a business trip in Germany, with his beautiful new girlfriend accompanying him in high heels; I am suddenly conscious that my bare feet badly need a pedicure. The kids play a Barcelona version of Monopoly and argue about the rules in Spanish, while the grown-ups drink sparkling water and make conversation that is not as awkward as I'd feared.

The trip reminds me to be free-spirited in my yoga and meditation practice—to enter it, every time, with the spirit of adventure, open to the surprises that might unfurl in even the most familiar posture, the most ordinary breath. It reminds me to celebrate my body and my life with the unself-conscious exuberance of the women on the crowded Sitges beach, where virtually everyone— grandmother or teenager, slender or billowing flesh—frolics in the waves wearing the kind of tiny bikini that, back in California, you have to be a twenty-something supermodel to flaunt.

At the end of my month in Spain, I fly back home to my own collection of yoga mats and meditation cushions—and Shawn flies home to hers. Forest parks on his desk the little toy airplane that one of his Spanish friends had made for him out of popsicle sticks. "Maybe Leo can come visit us some day," he says wistfully.

"Absolutely he can," I tell him.

And as I practice on my deck overlooking Mount Tamalpais, I often think of my longtime yoga friend, practicing on her patio overlooking the Mediterranean Sea.

It's true that our journeys have taken us in different directions over the past two decades. But in a way, we've both been on the same trip—symbolized by, but not limited to, the pile of yoga props and zafus that sit in the corner of our living rooms.

And sometimes, in the space between one breath and the next, I remember the families dancing together in a plaza full of foam. I remember the guitar player at the Palau de la Música—the way he held his guitar like a lover in his arms, the way his fingers released a torrent of song as they traveled over the strings.

SUTRA 15

The Tempest:
A Meditation Retreat

· · · · ·

ON A RAINY winter day, when my upper back is in knots and my sacrum is askew from hours at the computer writing about yoga postures, I get an email from Spirit Rock Meditation Center, reminding me for the third time that I have not yet sent in the paperwork for my upcoming monthlong meditation retreat.

It's not the only thing that has fallen through the cracks. I recently barely galumphed across the finish line in time to hand in the manuscript for a book about mindful yoga and meditation—and I now know for sure that writing a book about mindfulness is not the same as living a mindful life.

Everywhere I look is chaos: piles of unwashed laundry, a tsunami of unanswered emails, friends' calls not returned for months, dead grass in the yard, pasta growing mold in the back of the fridge. My brain is overloaded with words about wordless presence. Plus, for the past year and a half, Forest—now thirteen—has been homeschooling (or, as we prefer to call it, doing "independent study"). He loved the school he'd attended from third through sixth grade, but his dad and I were curious as to how he would spend his time if left to pursue his own passions during his middle school years. So instead of being able to drop him off at school every morning, I've been coordinating and chauffeuring him to a buffet of local classes ranging from advanced calculus to wilderness fire making without matches.

And into the midst of this chaos, I'm trying to introduce a monthlong silent meditation retreat. Fortunately, Spirit Rock is just a fifteen-minute drive from my house. I've been given permission to sit the retreat as a commuter, returning home for part of each day to keep my family life going. Failing to register on time is just one more symptom of why I need this retreat.

I fire off an apologetic email to Spirit Rock, download the registration forms, and hit Print.

My computer informs me it is looking for my wireless printer, which is sitting on the desk a few feet away, its lights blinking enigmatically. The printer has been quixotic lately—fulfilling certain requests enthusiastically, ignoring others altogether, mysteriously waking up in the middle of the night to crank out documents I'd sent it days earlier. This time, my computer lets me know after a few minutes that the printer is offline.

After restarting both devices and muttering a few off-color mantras, I call in my partner. Teja has computer chops he picked up in his years running a recording studio. After a few minutes, he informs me that my printer driver software is four generations behind.

Well, of course it is. Software Update had rudely interrupted me again and again while I was writing. I always clicked on the button that said *Go Away I'm Busy Writing about Mindfulness.*

Teja begins installing the new drivers. After a few minutes he asks, "Is your modem always this slow?"

Oh, right. I vaguely recall a voicemail from Comcast a few months back, telling me my modem needed replacing. I actually manage to dig up the voicemail and begin following its instructions to order an online upgrade.

But what is my Comcast password? Comcast can't send me a reset message because the email address on file belongs to an account I closed two years ago after it was hacked by someone in Liberia who greatly alarmed my ninety-one-year-old father with their email about my mugging in Madrid.

Comcast offers me a password hint: *What's the name of your favorite pet?* Easy! I triumphantly enter the name of my cat, the only pet I've had in the last forty years.

Comcast disagrees.

I try again, with a capital letter.

No go.

Could it be Teja's cat? The horse I owned when I was eleven? Or the one before her, that my father bought when I was nine because she had the same name as my mother, then sold after the mare bit me and scraped me off under a tree?

No, no, and no.

A text chat box opens up from a Comcast representative: *What can I help you with?*

I want to go on a silent retreat!!! I type.

No response.

Who is my favorite pet? I demand.

Nothing on my screen but what my son calls "the spinning beach ball of doom."

"Well," Teja points out tactfully. "Your modem *is* really, really, slow."

I call the phone number at the bottom of the screen. Due to high call volume, a recorded voice informs me, my wait time for a callback will be fifty-three minutes.

Well, at least that's better than when I called my insurance company recently and was told that my wait would be 917 hours. I think of my psychotherapist friend who came off a silent retreat a few years ago feeling practically enlightened, and while driving home got into a screaming match on her cell phone with the cell service provider.

With forty-three minutes left in my wait time, my dear friend Janice shows up at my door. When our kids were toddlers, our weekly Friday night dinners helped keep me sane. We'd cook huge pots of pasta together while keeping an eye on Forest and Sacha as they paddled in the backyard wading pool. When the kids were a little older, she'd accompanied me to India. Now the kids are both teens, and Janice and I often lead meditation and yoga retreats together. Today we're planning the online course we're going to offer through our website, AwakeningasWomen.com, on the theme of creating space. Our marketing copy offers a tantalizing promise: "How do you create space and ease in the midst of your busy life? We offer helpful tips . . ."

"Those who can't do, teach!" I tell her ruefully.

Janice and I crank through our list: website; delivery platform;

social media—especially challenging for those of us who suffer from what Janice has dubbed MDD, marketing deficit disorder.

The phone rings.

"We can definitely get you a new modem," the Comcast representative assures me with an accent familiar from my spiritual journeys. "But we notice that you don't get cable service—just phone and Internet. Would you like to upgrade?"

"I don't watch television," I tell her.

"Yes, ma'am. But we have a special offer that will save you ten dollars a month over what you are paying now—and will deliver 179 channels of programming."

No! I want to go on silent retreat! I will happily pay you ten dollars a month NOT to deliver me 179 channels of programming! Instead I ask, "Where are you calling from?"

"I am in Kolkata, madame."

Calcutta! That's one of the places Janice and I had traveled together, six years earlier.

Get off the phone! I want to tell the Comcast rep. *Get on a train to Bodh Gaya! I'll meet you there!*

Instead, I tell her I don't want the upgrade, but please send the new modem right away.

A week later, the modem still hasn't arrived. But the cable box for an upgrade has. It's sitting on the floor in the corner of my office, still in its package, the gateway to an almost infinite world of distraction. Why go on retreat when I could watch *Game of Thrones*?

I decide to just make the fifteen-minute drive to Spirit Rock to fill out the overdue registration forms. I tell myself that maybe, when I get back from retreat, I'll have time to send back my cable upgrade.

The truth is, I'm ambivalent about embarking on this retreat.

It feels as if I'd be reenacting on a small scale the renunciation of the Buddha when he slipped out of his palace in the middle of the night to become a wandering seeker, not bothering to make arrangements for family meals and car pools while he was gone. Sure, it sounds idyllic. I imagine myself sitting under the soaring dome of the Spirit Rock meditation hall as the last of the winter rains drum on the roof. Doing walking meditation through hills dotted with spring wildflowers. Taking a shamanic journey into the wilderness of my heart and mind. Leaving behind the clutter on my desk: credit card statements, applications for health insurance, an unread copy of *Social Media Marketing for Dummies*.

Besides, I want to do this retreat to become a better teacher. I'm two years into an intensive four-year dharma teacher-training program—and while I've sat many silent retreats in the week-to-ten-day range, and taught yoga on many more, I've never done the meditation marathons that are a rite of passage in this particular lineage. Most of my childless fellow trainees have sat for months at a stretch in mountain hermitages and Burmese temples, riding the samadhi elevator into deeper and deeper levels of absorption and insight. Meanwhile I've been juggling my formal practice with my life as a divorced working mom, struggling to remember to stay present as I take out the recycling. Sure, I know that spiritual awakening can happen anywhere, anytime—but meditation practice has not erased my drive to excel. In the race to the here and now, I'm worried that I'm falling behind.

But as Forest gets older, I'm finding that my daily presence still feels vital for both of us —just in a different way. Yes, he's more and more independent, spending most of his time engaged in his own activities or with his own friends. He spends hours each day writing sci-fi novels, which he self-publishes through CreateSpace. He roams the slopes of Mount Tam with the "Dire Wolves," his pack of buddies in "Dirt Time," the homeschooler's nature education program.

My own life has expanded too. Three years earlier, Teja had moved in with us, and his college-age daughter, River, had spent the previous summer with us as well—so it's rarely just me and Forest at the dinner table anymore. When Forest's at his dad's house, which is half the time now, I get to revel in "date night." I'm spending my early mornings snuggling with my sweetheart instead of processing angst in my journal, where I've also almost stopped taking notes on my adventures with my son. Especially since the most recent time he got sick, when immediately after throwing up he looked up from the toilet and begged me, "Don't write about this, okay?" (Oops—I guess I just did. But I ran it by him first.)

But our increasing individuation makes it feel all the more vital that I'm around in the background for Forest—available to run his Shakespeare lines with him when he walks into the kitchen for a snack; to read the latest hot-off-the-press chapter of his Underwater Waves trilogy; to hear the stories of his day bushwhacking as I drive him home from Lake Lagunitas.

And now that I have the happy family I always wanted, I want to be home with them as much as I can, laughing around the dinner table. Is this really the time to sneak out like the Buddha in the early hours of the morning, aspiring to enlightenment?

DAY 1

It's the first morning of my retreat, and I'm sitting with a hundred other meditators in a high-domed meditation hall with floor-to-ceiling windows looking out onto rain-greened hills. After the frenetic pace of the last few months, I'm grateful to be somewhere where all that's on the printed daily schedule is "Sit. Walk. Sit. Walk. Sit. Lunch. Sit. Walk. Sit . . ."

Some of the yogis on the retreat have already been in silence for a month, and the stillness in the meditation hall is palpable and contagious. I track each breath—the beginning of the inhale, the ripple of its movement through the interconnected web of the body, the beginning of the exhale, and its ripple on the way out. My mind folds in on itself in the momentary space after each exhalation—diving deep inside like a humming bird dipping its beak into a flower and tasting the nectar.

This retreat at Spirit Rock is normally reserved for meditators who can step away from their busy lives and do a deep dive into practice in the protected bubble of silence.

This seclusion—once available only to monks and nuns who gave up sex and family life in exchange for silence and a shot at liberation—supports the mind to enter into samadhi, or deep concentration, and to see the true nature of self and of life—interconnected, everchanging, and impermanent. When you see how things really are, you're less likely to get caught in delusions and clinging, and you're more likely to make choices that lead to true happiness.

But late that afternoon, I walk out the retreat center gates toward my parked car. Because for *my* monthlong retreat, I'll be experimenting with what my mentor and I call "integrative practice." I won't be in that protected bubble, burrowing deeper and deeper into samadhi. To keep our family life on track, I'll be maintaining my usual schedule of shared custody with Forest's dad. Teja, who would normally be happy to help out, won't be available to do so, because he's teaching qigong on the very retreat that I'm sitting. Roughly half of my time this month will consist of the usual retreat routine—sitting meditation, walking meditation, qigong, dharma talks, silent meals chewing every bite in exquisite slow motion. The other half will consist of shopping for groceries at the Good Earth, cooking and eating meals while talking over his day with Forest, and occasionally checking my urgent-parenting-messages-only temporary email address, anneonretreat@gmail.com. I'm hoping I can slip into the field of deepening calm in the meditation hall, like a snake gliding into a pond, then slide back into the world without leaving a ripple.

As I head to the parking lot, I walk extra slowly, trying to display my uninterrupted continuity of practice. I feel like I'm playing a mindful mother in a film about spiritual practice. I get into my car to drive serenely home. I switch on my phone. And I am greeted by the ding of a text—"Can you drive the carpool to the *Tempest* performance in Sausalito tomorrow morning?"

Because, this month, my daily domestic routine happens to include fourteen productions of *The Tempest*—in which Forest is playing the villain, Antonio—at an array of local schools, theaters, senior centers, and retirement homes.

My calm immediately shatters. Tomorrow's show was supposed to be at a high school in San Rafael, just a fifteen-minute drive from Spirit Rock, which would have meant that I could do my early morning "yogi job" at the retreat (cleaning the bathrooms by the meditation hall), drive home to pick up Forest, drop him off for the performance, and make it back to Spirit Rock for the morning instructional sitting. Then I could spend the morning sitting and walking in silence, picking up Forest at lunchtime after the show was over.

But the director apparently changed the schedule, so the first performance is now at a middle school in Sausalito, a half-hour drive farther south. I stick the phone out the window, trying to catch the flickering signal, and send off a snippy text: "You really should be more clear in your communication with the parents!"

Suddenly my meditation retreat feels not like a respite, but just another obligation to add to my busy schedule.

As irritation swells inside me, I belatedly remember to pause and name it, just as I would in the meditation hall: *Irritation feels like* this. *Judgment feels like* this. This *is a contracted mind.* I remind myself that my retreat practice is supposed to be about cultivating my ability to maintain a continuity of mindful embodied presence, whether I'm sitting in the meditation hall focusing on the in and out of my breath or driving a carpool of teenagers at sixty miles an hour down a freeway to a play performance.

Will it work? A half day in, I'm having my doubts.

DAY 5

"Why are the ceilings in this place so low?" asks the fourteen-year-old girl I'm trailing into the retirement home where the Teen Touring Company is about to perform. She is wearing shorts and a bright pink crop top. She has miles of silky tan legs, yards of shimmering brown hair. She's not addressing me—I'm invisible to her, just the mom who drove the car pool here this morning. She's talking to the teenage boy who's walking next to her, their arms laden with stage props: a black velvet curtain and ropes to hang it from the ceiling; a billowing piece of blue silk to represent the stormy sea upon which their ship will be wrecked.

His answer is confident: "Because when you get old, you *shrink*."

Standing a little taller, I follow them into the reception area, pausing for a spritz from a hand sanitizer dispenser the size of a beer keg. As we pass the front desk, I hear the receptionist on the phone, speaking calmly but urgently: "Can you tell if she is still breathing?"

In the cafeteria, instead of chatting with the handful of theater parents milling around a table of coffee and pastries, I sit down in one of the empty folding chairs set up for the audience who will arrive in an hour. As the kids begin to string up the curtain, put on pantaloons and flounced skirts, and slide stage daggers into scabbards, I close my eyes and remind myself of the mindfulness acronym one of my retreat teachers had offered in the dharma talk the previous night: SLOW. *Stay. Lovingly. Open. Wonder.*

I'm five days into my commuter retreat, and here's the question I keep exploring: *When am I "on retreat," and when am I not?*

Clearly, I'd been on retreat that morning as I'd done walking meditation under the trees. I'd slipped off my shoes and walked barefoot on the grass by the creek, mindfully avoiding blobs of wild turkey poop. I'd stepped over the leg bones of a deer on the hill, scattered and sucked clean by teeth, rain, sun, and time. With each step I'd recited a word of a walking meditation mantra I'd learned years ago from Thich Nhat Hanh: *Yes. Yes. Yes. Thank you. Thank you. Thank you.*

And I'd definitely been on retreat the previous evening, when one of my teachers—a former midwife with a solid, grounded presence—had given a talk titled "The Freedom Map of Transcendent Spiral Conditionality." She had expounded on the twelve steps of transcendental dependent origination—the Buddhist train ride from suffering to liberation, with stops on the way at stations such as faith, rapture, disenchantment, and deliverance.

But how about now, as I sit in the cafeteria of this senior home, watching the audience roll in in wheelchairs, shuffle past with walkers? A woman with coiffed silver hair, faded blue eyes, and red lipstick lowers herself carefully into the folding chair next to me. She is wearing a gorgeous turquoise silk blouse patterned in Chinese characters, a soft purple knit cardigan over it. I suddenly feel scruffy in my yoga pants and hoodie—maybe by the time I'm eighty I'll learn to adorn myself too? She smiles at me as she leans her cane against the edge of the chair. Her cane has a silver parrot's head on the top. With the heightened attention of my "integrative practice," I catch myself: *Am I really experiencing cane envy?*

The music starts to play, the recorded storm noises begin, the cloth sea billows, and in front of us the fateful shipwreck unfolds. As the castaways come ashore, the beautiful young Miranda, who has been stranded on this island with her father since babyhood, marvels upon seeing other humans for the first time:

How beauteous mankind is!
O brave new world,
That has such people in 't!

Around me, the residents of the senior center watch, riveted. (Well, okay—a few of them fall asleep.) During pauses in the dialogue, I can sometimes hear the actors whispering and giggling behind the curtain. I've already seen this production a couple of times. But I still perk up with pride when Forest as Antonio plots murder:

Here lies your brother,
No better than the earth he lies upon,
If he were that which now he's like, that's dead;
Whom I, with this obedient steel, three inches of it,
Can lay to bed for ever; who
Should not upbraid our course?

After five days of focusing on being present, the story feels more vivid and poignant to me—an enactment on stage of the human dramas of power, betrayal, forgiveness, and repentance that play in one form or another through every human heart. The scenes come and go, like stories in my meditating mind. As I watch the teens performing for their elders, I wonder: Would I have learned any more about impermanence if I had stayed in the meditation hall, watching my breath?

After the show is over, the woman sitting next to me raises her hand and tells the kids that she played Miranda in her school play when she was in high school, back in the 1930s.

Stay. Lovingly. Open. Wonder.

DAY 7

This weekend, Forest is at his dad's house, and I finally have a few uninterrupted days for formal meditation practice at Spirit Rock. In the morning I have a couple of blissful sittings—fully absorbed in the subtle movement of breath deep in the pelvic floor. As I sit in a wash of gratitude, my head begins to slowly rotate on its own to the left, as if turned by the hands of an invisible ghost chiropractor—releasing waves of tingling down my spine. The bell rings, and we all file mindfully to lunch.

Back in the hall after lunch, as if it has been waiting in the wings— misery. My upper back gradually hardens into a column of iron. The trapped bird of my breath flaps its wings, helpless, against the steel cage of my ribs. A carapace of armor encases my whole upper thoracic. The classic hindrances of meditation descend like a flock of vultures—grasping, restlessness, sleepiness, aversion and, above all, doubt. *What am I doing here? Is this the right path for me? There's way too much sitting for my tastes, not nearly enough dancing. It seems like the day will never end.* My only refuge: at the end of the evening, unlike the other prisoners here, I get to drive home and sleep in my own bed.

Later that afternoon, during walking meditation, I pace irritably back and forth on the beautiful path, under spreading oaks and a blue sky, next to a babbling brook. All that beauty feels as if it's on the other side of a glass wall. As the bell rings for the next sitting, I realize I am walking toward the hall with dread, as if approaching an execution. I pause: *What am I afraid of? All I will be doing is sitting still in a beautiful quiet room full of kind people, doing nothing. Is the pain in my back really that bad?*

Then it hits me—I am dreading *me*. I am dreading the way I will bully myself, try to control myself, punish myself, criticize myself.

I see it now: In my mind I've been comparing myself unfavorably to another mother and meditator, a dharma teacher who sat the monthlong as a commuter last year, just as I'm doing now. In my training, I've heard teachers speak glowingly of her meditation practice and her insights on that retreat: how she'd dropped deep through the levels of *jhana*, meditative absorption; how she'd followed the classical arc of the "progress of insight," the stages a meditator is said to pass through on the path to full awakening, as outlined in the fifth-century Pali text the *Visuddhimagga*.

I've been feeling that I have something to prove, not just to my mentors in my teacher training but also to myself: *I'm a good medita- tor, even though I'm a mom.*

But *my* progress of insight includes Shakespeare and cane envy.

I enter the hall and drop to my cushion. I don't try to control my mind. I don't look for evidence of progress. I just sit there and watch the stories that spin through my mind—as if I'm watching teenage actors on a makeshift stage.

My mind wanders, just as it does when I am trying desperately to control it. But everything feels more spacious, and my back doesn't hurt nearly as much. And I have learned something—at least temporarily—about relaxing into awareness, as a meditator and as a mom.

DAY 12

It's almost two weeks into my monthlong retreat, and I'm spending my morning at home doing "laundry practice" while Forest sits at his computer, discussing Dickens with kids in Texas and Hong Kong as part of the English class he's taking through Stanford Online High School. I am sitting in the middle of my bedroom floor, folding and putting away clothes.

Flowing back and forth from home to retreat has been shining a bright light on where my habitual patterns do and don't support mindfulness. Just as I often don't realize, until I sit down on my cushion, just how fragmented and chaotic my mind has become, I haven't realized until I train the lens of heightened awareness on my home what a palpable trail of chaos my lapses of mindfulness have been leaving.

Who is this person who has been galloping through my life, neglecting the mundane tasks of the present moment as she charges toward her goals? Whoever she is, she has left snack bar wrappers stuffed into the cracks in her car seat cushions, half-nibbled bags of almonds at the bottom of her purse. The bottom of her laundry basket is stuffed with items she put there months ago and never got to: a Christmas tablecloth stained with red wine and candle wax, a sleeping bag mildewed from a rainy camping trip. Her life, like her sock drawer, is stuffed to overflowing.

At Spirit Rock, everything is tranquil and orderly, from the neatly labeled cleaning supplies for my bathroom-cleaning job to the yogis themselves (although I've been practicing long enough to know that behind the downcast eyes and expressionless faces might rage dramas to rival any Shakespeare play).

Outside the hall I'm learning to generate my own force field of calm. Setting my intention to do a half hour of dishwashing meditation with the same care and attention I'd give to a meditation period in the hall. Driving to Spirit Rock through the brightening dawn with the same precise awareness I'd bring to walking meditation. Buying broccoli at the supermarket with the mindfulness I bring to my breath.

I tell myself that the daily reminder that "I'm on retreat" lends extra gravitas to these acts of mindfulness and turns them into constant learning opportunities. Vowing to use driving as a meditation practice, for example, I am startled to see how habitually I'd been using it as a time to daydream about plans to write another novel or take Forest on a trip to Argentina. Instead, I focus fully on the road: the jewellike stoplights changing from red to green, the vibration and hum of the moving car, the green pastures I'm driving past, the expressions on the faces of the other drivers.

But part of me still feels as if I'm cheating, pulling a hoax on myself and my meditation teachers. This isn't a *retreat*. This is just— *life!*

Or maybe that's the point?

I put in another load of laundry. I'm making my way all the way down to the bottom of the laundry hamper. I keep thinking of something Gil Fronsdal, one of the teachers on the retreat, had said in his dharma talk the night before. As a Zen student, he had been taught that "everything is to be respected." You bow to your cushion. You bow to your teacup. You bow to your teacher. Nothing is left out. Not your rage and disappointment. Not your dirty underwear. Not your wandering mind. Not the cat sleeping on the bed.

This morning I am bowing to everything: the wax stain on the carpet from where I knocked over a candle after meditation five years ago; the laughter from the next room; the sock I can't find a match to; the squirrel who runs along the wooden railing outside my bedroom, holding a bay nut in his mouth.

What is a meditation retreat? I decide that it is any moment I set on my altar.

DAY 17

While Forest sleeps in, I drive over to Spirit Rock to do my early morning yogi job—cleaning the women's bathroom outside the meditation hall. I scrub the mouth of the already gleaming toilet with the brush, swoosh the bristles in and out, and spray vinegar on its seat. I try to imagine that I am tending an altar. I try not to imagine the naked buddha bottoms that will sit on it. I wonder if the people who use this bathroom will ever think: *My, this is a clean toilet! Whoever cleaned it must be enlightened. Look at how they wiped down the top of the tank before arraying the three rolls of toilet paper on it so neatly!* I already resent them, a little, for messing up my work. How carelessly they will come in here and sit, without thinking of me at all, their own stories spinning in their own heads.

Also, I kind of wish I were at home, cleaning my own bathroom—which, I noticed as I dashed out the door that morning, really needs it. Am I so busy with my meditation retreat that I am going to need to hire someone to scrub my toilet?

After my yogi job I head home in the now full light of morning. While Forest does his Spanish homework, I go outside to meditate on the deck in the shade of an oak tree, removing myself a little farther from the sound of the Rosetta Stone language app. I try not to reject the movements of my mind, endlessly reciting its plans for the rest of the day: meditate, drive Forest to Spanish class, buy dental floss. Instead, I soften and widen to include the whole moment, just as it is: the squirrel in the tree scolding the cat; the voice in my head scolding me.

At the retreat center I cleaned a toilet. At home I meditate.

Wherever I go, everything I think of as solid—my house, the meditation hall, a tree, my opinions, my son—is actually ever-shifting. It's all as temporary as a *Tempest* set—assembled to create an illusionary world where a drama can play out for a little while, before the actors take off their costumes and go home. I feel the futility of clinging to cobwebs, hoping they will support my weight.

Strangely, that's an image that makes me happy.

Forest steps onto the deck. "Mom? Is there anything for lunch?"

DAY 21

It's three weeks into the retreat, and my senses are heightened. In my journal, I find myself writing a prose poem to the retreat cooks, which I know I will never send them: *Your food is so sensuously delicious it is almost indecent—it is amazing that we are allowed to eat it in public. You must have laughed out loud as you made that raisin orange chutney—knowing how its flavors would unfurl in layers in the mouth like a time-release capsule of ecstasy, first the languid sweet of the raisin, then the bright notes of the orange, then the fireworks of ginger. I want to devour in two bites that chewy tofu with sesame sauce. At the same time, I want to go on eating it for all eternity. Is that too much to ask?*

Both at Spirit Rock and at home, I'm tuned in to the beauty of life—the clover blooming bright pink on the hills, the deer nursing her fawn, the joy of sitting at home laughing over a bowl of parsley-flecked pasta with Teja and Forest.

Later, I sit on a bench at Spirit Rock, watching the flamboyant male turkeys spreading and fluttering their great fans of tails, trying so hard to get the attention of the drab females who play at ignoring them. It's a rampant display of sensuality and passion amid the renunciation of the yogis. I remember the gatha, the meditation verse, that I learned from Thich Nhat Hanh: *Present moment, wonderful moment.* And I realize that what is satisfying is presence itself, more than *what* I am present for. Present Moment Wonderful Moment doesn't mean that this moment is always wonderful—often it isn't. But in a moment for which I am present, presence itself is wonderful, even if the content isn't.

As my mind gets quieter, I'm also intensely aware of the way it skitters away from staying present with joy, just as surely as it skitters away from pain—perhaps to avoid the sorrow and frustration of discovering that joy, too, is impermanent, ungraspable. My mind would rather fantasize about some future satisfaction that it imagines would actually have the power to satisfy in a way that the actual thing happening does not, even when the thing happening is what I have always dreamed of: a family dinner with a partner and a child, for instance.

When I look closely at some of my most intense pleasures, I'm aware of the anxiety that pulses just below the surface of my enjoyment. This examination is like looking into one of those makeup mirrors that dispels the soft ambient light of delusion and reveals every pore, magnified. Even while pleasure is happening, I want *more* of it. I'm aware that I'll miss it in the future. As the poet Bashō writes, "Even in Kyoto, I long for Kyoto."

That night I come home and crawl into bed with Teja. When the retreat began and the usual precepts were recited, I'd been careful not to vow myself to celibacy. I'm not a nun. I kiss him and say, "This is even better than the parsnip soup at lunch."

He says, "That's the sweetest thing anyone has ever said to me."

I wrap my arms around him and say, "We are both alive, and we are together." We kiss again, and then I add: "It won't always be that way."

DAY 26

I'm in the last week of my retreat, and attending yet another performance of *The Tempest*, this one at an elementary school in a primarily Latino neighborhood. Most of the students have never seen a play before, and they are wild with excitement. When the demon dogs roar in in act 2 and drive the other actors off the stage, the kids leap to their feet, cheer and squeal for almost five minutes, shout for an encore.

Watching, I'm aware of a sense of well-being and ease—a steadiness in my nervous system, a quiet warmth in my heart. This is different from the way I felt when I began this monthlong journey into "integrative practice."

There was no breakthrough moment on this retreat. The notes in my journal don't build in a crescendo to a grand realization. Instead, the retreat has been a collage of moments, arising and passing away. There were mini awakenings, moments of profound gratitude, moments when the gates of my heart swung wide open. There were also moments of distraction, annoyance, judgment, just like any retreat. It was joyful and messy and chaotic. It was ever-changing. It was my mind, my life. And at this moment, I wouldn't want it any other way.

On stage, the play churns on to its happy ending. After the curtain call, the kids in the audience swarm onstage, surrounding the actors, clamoring to touch Forest's sword. "Is it real?" they ask him.

What is real and what is illusion? I wonder.

As I hang back and watch the kids, Prospero's closing words echo in my heart. I've watched them recited over and over by a teenaged boy—to fifth-graders, to high schoolers, to a gray-haired audience with a bevy of walkers and wheelchairs parked to the side of the improvised stage. They are the words of an aging magician, written by a playwright for his final play—words that sum up the truth of impermanence, the ever-changing nature of life:

Our revels now are ended. These our actors,
As I foretold you, were all spirits and
Are melted into air, into thin air.
And, like the baseless fabric of this vision,
The cloud-capp'd towers, the gorgeous palaces,
The solemn temples, the great globe itself,
Yea, all which it inherit, shall dissolve
And, like this insubstantial pageant faded,
Leave not a rack behind. We are such stuff
As dreams are made on, and our little life
Is rounded with a sleep.

Singing My Mother to Sleep

· · · · ·

WHEN MY MOTHER was ninety-one years old, she stumbled in her pew at weekly Mass and gashed her leg on the edge of a kneeler.

By that time, she and my father had been living in a military retirement home in Washington, DC, for the past decade, and they had been, as my mother put it, "in *appropriate* health." But the next day the cut was infected. Her doctor prescribed oral antibiotics. But she had been having trouble swallowing—a symptom, I'd been told, of the dementia that had begun to erode her short-term memory. My conversations with her about daily life and recent events had increasingly cycled through repetitive loops, which embarrassed her—"I don't like feeling so confused," she told me. Yet she was able to vividly recount details of her Army childhood in the 1920s—the mule-drawn wagon she'd ridden to school in Hawaii, a trip to Yellowstone with her parents and brother in a Model T.

When she tried to take the antibiotics, one of the pills lodged in her throat and partially dissolved, burning the lining of her esophagus. She refused to take more. Her fever soared along with her white blood count, and over her protests—she had already said that she didn't want her body to be forced to outlive her mind—she was taken to Walter Reed Hospital and put on intravenous antibiotics.

I didn't know any of this while it was happening. Teja and I were leading a meditation retreat for corporate executives in a rustic Northern California conference center with spotty Internet access, so I hadn't checked my email for three days. When I logged in over lunch for a quick peek at my messages, I found a stream of emails from my six siblings.

I scanned down the thread, trying to grasp the situation, assuming that this was just one more of a series of minor health incidents. In recent years my mother had fallen a couple of times, leaving the bones in her arms with hairline fractures. She had been admitted to the ER with a fever from a urinary tract infection. But she was always still there the next time I visited—marveling at how much I had grown as I walked in the door and slipping dollar bills and napkin-wrapped dinner rolls into my coat pockets as I left.

And as usual, the emails conveyed, my six ultracompetent older siblings were already taking charge. Connie—a lawyer and former nurse, sixteen years older than me—had already taken the train down from New York to be with my parents. My other brothers and sisters—scattered over the East Coast from Long Island to Maine—were outlining their availability.

I looked at my calendar—when the retreat ended the next day, I was supposed to drive home for the opening night of Forest's high school fall play, *Urinetown*, which he'd been rehearsing for weeks. I checked out my frequent-flyer miles, balancing the logistics of love in my head: being present for my teenaged son, being present for my aged parents, being present for the partner I was co-leading the retreat with. I booked a flight for a week later, assuming that was soon enough to be helpful.

Then I went back into the meditation hall to lead the afternoon session.

Between meditation periods, I checked my email. My mother's white blood cell count had dropped and the pneumonia seemed to have been beaten back. But her breathing was labored, and she could only speak in a whisper. Removed from her familiar apartment, she was disoriented and frightened. The doctors wanted to give her a barium test to determine why she couldn't swallow. She didn't want the test. She wanted, adamantly, to go home to my father. They would keep me informed, the emails assured me.

There didn't seem to be anything that I could do right now to help from California. So I carried on with the retreat schedule. That evening, Teja and I led a closing ritual, in which the participants lit candles and proclaimed their intentions to return to their lives more mindful, more present, more connected to their families.

The next morning, just before going into the final session, I checked the message thread again, and finally grasped that this was not just another nick that needed to be patched up. My sister Connie had talked with my mother about her end-of-life wishes. Then they had both conferred with my father and with the doctors. Together, they made the decision to move her to palliative care. They would not continue any medication designed to make her "get better"—discontinuing not only the antibiotics but also all her blood pressure medications and anticoagulants. She was going to leave the hospital and go back home to her apartment, with twenty-four-hour care in place.

My sister Mary wrote, "Mom knows that all of us are planning to come visit one or two at a time in the next few weeks. She said to be sure to say that she would be equally happy to hear from her family by phone. She feels she always says goodbye to us each visit knowing that it might be final, blessed that she has had ninety-one years in this world, and hasn't wanted to linger forever in poor health. She has often said to me that if I hear that she didn't wake up one morning, I should know that she was happy to go home to heaven."

I reached for my cell phone to call my sister Kathleen, who was in California helping her daughter with a newborn baby. Just as I picked it up, it rang.

"I'm on the BART on the way to the airport," Kathleen told me.

"I have a ticket for next Friday. Is that soon enough?" I paced around my cabin, a little cottage in the redwoods, with a triangular window over the foot of the bed framing a vista of red trunks and dark green branches. *I'm so far away from Washington.*

There was a pause. "Anne," she said. "I don't think either of us are ever going to see her alive again."

When I was a child, my mother always carried an enormous purse she referred to as "the Blue Monstrosity." "Never travel without food and water," she used to say. She could reach into this purse at any time and produce a foil-wrapped stack of stale saltines, a baby bottle full of tap water, a carton of raisins, a soft and browning banana. Like Mary Poppins' magic bag, her purse always contained whatever a child might need: a bandage, a book for a boring car ride, crayons and construction paper, a ball of yarn and a crochet hook.

Decades after all of us were grown up, I was on a train with her, and a mother in the next seat was trying to calm a fussy toddler. Mom reached into her purse and pulled out a small toy—a little black-and-white plastic cow with jointed legs mounted on a pedestal that could be pushed up and released down to make the cow dance. That was a toy from my own childhood! Mom's purse was a time portal to 1965. And just as I once had, the cranky child in the next seat stopped crying and started to laugh.

My mom had a magic touch with small children. I was her seventh baby, and she always said that she would have had seven more, if her doctor hadn't insisted on a hysterectomy when she turned forty. She breastfed us in an era when doctors recommended formula. She sang us to sleep and read us aloud the rhymes and stories of A. A. Milne and E. B. White. On my third birthday, she put a paper crown on my head and told me I was Queen for the Day.

Whenever I was sick in bed and had to miss school, she brought me ginger ale and saltines and produced from some hidden stash wonderful books to distract me—*The Phoenix and the Carpet*; *Half Magic*. On frigid Christmas mornings in Kansas, she drove me to the stables at dawn to bring my horse, Kentucky Lady, a hot bran mash with apples and brown sugar.

And it wasn't just her own children she was devoted to. When I was a teenager and we were stationed in Korea with my father, my mother was horrified to learn that Ani, the Korean woman the Army employed as our family's housekeeper, was leaving her five-year-old son at home when she came to work for us. Insisting that Ani bring her child with her, my mother watched the little boy all day herself.

But she basically stopped understanding her children when we hit puberty. Born in 1924, she'd led a sheltered childhood even for that era. When my father met her, she was a nineteen-year-old at Connecticut College, and he was astonished to learn that she'd never had an ice cream soda. Her fashion advice to me and my four older sisters was always to look "sweet, simple, and girlish." Based on the media recommendations of the Catholic Church, she deemed *The Sound of Music* too risqué for us to watch. In 1976, when my father was commander of Fort Leavenworth, Kansas, she forbade me to wear jeans or shorts to Patton Junior High School—I was the only girl at my eighth-grade dance trying to do "the Bump" in a polyester pantsuit. After a lifetime as a military daughter and wife, she saw potential disasters everywhere: when my friends came over to spend the night, my mother would greet them with instructions on how to escape out the bedroom window in case a fire were to occur in the night.

The summer before my freshman year in college, when STDs made the cover of *Time* magazine, my mother told me, "Dear, you may have read that herpes is epidemic now. So always wash your hands after handling money." This was the first conversation we'd had about sex since I was five years old, when she told me about the little hole that babies come out of—a conversation that had left me with the impression that the little hole was somewhere in the region of my belly button.

As I grew up, I didn't want to hurt her by revealing who I was becoming. After I went off to college, I hid all traces of my actual life—the one in which I was having sex, and experimenting with hallucinogens, and trading in weekly Mass for yoga satsangs and Zen sesshins. I called every month or so, made brief visits at holidays, and rarely wrote letters. I moved to Santa Fe, then to California. I left the regular family visits to my older brothers and sisters—all married, with several children apiece, and living on the East Coast within a few hours' drive or train ride of my parents. I created an edited version of myself I could trot out at family gatherings a few times a year. I loved my mother. But I assumed that she couldn't handle knowing who I really was. Whenever I visited, the unspoken rule seemed to be "don't ask, don't tell."

But as I dived into my practice of meditation and yoga, I also came to understand that I hadn't left her behind. Thich Nhat Hanh writes, "If you look deeply into the palm of your hand, you will see your parents and all generations of your ancestors. All of them are alive in this moment. Each is present in your body." My mother was always with me—in my awkwardness at parties and the warmth of my smile; in my poetic word choices and my starkly sensible shoes;

in the precise way I sighed in exasperation as I rummaged in my battered, voluminous purse for my keys. Her voice echoed in my throat; her anxiety woke me up in the middle of the night; her sensitivity made me bolt from noisy restaurants, violent movies, and people who mispronounced the word *nuclear*. (Her only commentary on President George W. Bush: "I think the leader of the free world should be able to correctly pronounce the name of the bomb.") In my mind, her cheery sayings narrated my life. After a setback: "Onward and upward!" In a messy house: "If everyone picks up ten things . . ." When it's necessary to go to a party or a parade you don't want to attend: "It's a command performance."

When Forest was a toddler, I read aloud to him in her exact inflection: "Oh, *poor* little kittens! You've *lost* your mittens!" And when he was a teenager, telling me about his adventures, he'd look at my face—which I thought I was keeping carefully neutral—and say, "*Mom*. You look really *worried*. There's no need for your *death face*."

I guarded myself, constantly, against judgments from her, but they rarely materialized aloud. When I announced that I was pregnant at age thirty-five—several months before my wedding—my mother expressed nothing but delight: "I was afraid it would be too late," she said, as she beamed at me over her crocheting. (She was always crocheting—mainly baby blankets and soft yarn balls for her ever-expanding brood of grandchildren and great-grandchildren.) For my wedding at Green Gulch Zen Center, she gamely slipped off her shoes before entering the zendo—the very same shoes, my older sister Celia pointed out, that she had worn to Celia's wedding thirty years earlier.

When my baby daughter Sierra died at birth, my mother was the only one who understood both the immensity of my pain and the way that my love for Sierra would endure past the heartbreak. "Sierra will nestle down into permanent remembrance," she wrote me. When Forest wouldn't sleep through the night as a baby, or didn't know how to make friends in preschool, she didn't sound the alarm bells. She took the long view, instinctively echoing the wisdom that a traditional Persian story gives as the magic incantation that will make you sad when you're happy, and happy when you're sad: "This too will pass."

And when I'd last visited home, as I prepared to walk out the door, my mother had grabbed me by my hands. She had looked urgently in my eyes. She had said: "I want you to know this: *I have no criticism of you.*"

I finished that final morning of the meditation retreat in a daze, giving the instructions I myself needed to hear: *Everything is changing, moment to moment—your breath, your emotions, your thoughts, your world. All slipping through your fingers like water. So be gentle with yourself.*

Teja and I packed up the car with our zafus, yoga mats, Tibetan singing bowls, suitcases. While Teja stopped in at Peet's Coffee Shop for some caffeine, I sat in the car and called my sister Connie.

"Mom is adamant that you should not come out here," she told me. "She feels that she said goodbye to you on your last visit, and she wants you to stay home and take care of Forest."

"Can I talk to her on the phone?"

"She's asleep. I'll call you when she wakes up."

The call came as Teja was driving us through the heavy Friday traffic clogging 19th Avenue in San Francisco. We were stopped at a stoplight with cars and trucks rushing by on the cross street.

"I love you, Mom . . ." I began, as my sister held the phone to my mom's ear, three thousand miles away. But she was already pouring out a torrent of words, her voice a hoarse, windy whisper as she gasped and wheezed for breath.

"You are my precious baby girl. I love you. I have always loved you. Trust yourself. You know what is right for you. You are so far away. Why did you move so far away?"

I could barely hear her over the engine and traffic noise. Teja put his hand on my knee as the car moved forward. Was I really saying goodbye to my mother like this, with a cell phone pressed to my ear as we drove past a Juice Box Vapes store? I thought of climbers trapped on Everest in a blizzard, knowing there is no hope of rescue, who call home to say goodbye.

"I love you, Mom," I said again. "I'm right there with you. Every time I look at Forest's face, I see your smile."

She was saying something about California, about how far away it was, about how she didn't know why—something. Something. Something. "Can you hear me? Do you understand?" she whispered.

"I hear every word you are saying. I understand everything," I lied.

Her voice flickered out, then came in strong and urgent, a breath at a time. "I have not—[gasp]—always—[gasp]—understood you. But I have always—[gasp]—loved you."

This is a central teaching of dharma: *This is like this, because that is like that.* The older I get, the more I understand how my mother's story has shaped my own.

Like my father, my mother, Nancy, was born into an Army family. Black-and-white home movies from the 1920s show a radiant, short-haired, athletic little girl who looks just like my childhood photos—hula dancing in a grass skirt in Hawaii, riding a horse through the hills, playing jacks with her little brother. But the movies don't show the sadness that was already laced through that family's joy. When my mother was three years old, her five-year-old sister Anita Jane died of spina bifida. Her picture still laughs from the pages of the family album—a bright-eyed little girl in a wool sweater and a white beret. For years, a torn piece of sheet music sat on my grandfather's piano, never to be thrown away: "Anita Jane ripped that," he'd say.

Determined to protect his other beloved daughter, my grandfather refused to consent to her marriage when my father first proposed. World War II was still underway, and he'd seen too many friends' daughters become pregnant widows. So for two years my father wrote daily letters home to my mother from the Philippines, where he was building an airstrip with the Army Corps of Engineers. My mother lived with her parents and worked as a nurse's aide, then as a typist in a signal corps office in San Antonio. Years later, she said to me, "I did what my parents wanted. But I thought that if he were killed before I could have his baby, life would not be worth living."

When the war ended, my father came home on leave with two weeks' notice, and my parents got married. My mother began her life as an Army wife. She had baby after baby while traveling the world with my father from post to post—Japan, New Mexico, Germany, Kansas.

When I was six weeks old, my father left for the first of three tours in Vietnam. Home alone with seven children, my mother comforted friends whose husbands came home in body bags. One day when I was six months old, my mother got a call, crackling and hissing over long-distance wires. The operator told her it was a call from my father's battalion commander. Then the line went dead. My mother could never remember exactly what happened over the next few minutes, as she waited for the call to come again—a call she was sure would tell her that her husband had been killed. When the call came through again, the battalion commander gave her the news that her husband had been promoted to full colonel. She hung up the phone and looked around the room to find that she had pushed all the furniture away from her to the walls, like an animal, clearing a place where she could fall down to die.

On my brother's tenth birthday, when I was five years old and my father was on his second tour in Vietnam, my mother took us ice-skating before the planned birthday party. My mother fell and shattered her hip. That week, I would learn years later, my father was fighting in one of the deadliest campaigns of the war. The rivers in the Delta were running red with blood. When my grandmother tried to get through to my father in Vietnam to tell him my mother was in the hospital, she was told that he was flying a helicopter in battle and that they could only contact him if my mother died. So my oldest sisters came home from college to take care of the kids who were still at home.

My father finally got permission to cut his tour short and come home to take care of his family while also escorting back the coffin of a young soldier in his battalion. My father arrived in our front hall at night in a swirl of cold air, with shrapnel in his leg and a Raggedy Ann doll for me in his camouflage trunk. My mother's hip was badly mended, wasn't healing properly, and the hip joint began to rot away. The doctors gave her barbiturates and told her that in a few years technology would be available to replace her hip with an artificial one.

My mother was still on crutches when my father went back to Vietnam for a final, two-year tour, and we moved to the Philippines to be closer to him. She took painkillers for her hips, tranquilizers for her nerves, sleeping pills to get her through the night. Every month or two my father came home from the war for a weekend visit. Then my father's helicopter was shot down behind enemy lines, and for three days—before he was rescued—no one knew if he would come back. My mother's hands began to tremble. The military doctors theorized that it might be Parkinson's and prescribed dopamine pills, which made her wake up screaming in the middle of the night. Pouring my orange juice one morning, she spilled it across the counter and burst into ragged sobs that wouldn't stop.

Eventually, my mother stopped talking to me. She stopped talking to anyone. Then she was in the hospital and our Filipina maid, Remy, was taking care of me and my two older brothers, the only children still living at home. My father came home from the war to fly us all back to the United States. Our departure flight rolled down the runway, past the caribou grazing in the rice fields, and lifted into the air; the islands green below us, and then veiled in clouds.

Years later, one of my sisters would refer to those periodic collapses into grief, pain, and hospitalization: "We sometimes call them Mom's 'nervous breakdowns,' as if they were abnormal responses to a normal situation. But they were really normal responses to an abnormal situation."

When I was in my twenties, I went to a retreat for Vietnam veterans and their families, led by Thich Nhat Hanh, who is Vietnamese. "You are the flame at the tip of the candle," he told them. "You hold the fire and pain for the whole country." At one point in the retreat, someone raised his hand and asked, "Was the Vietnam War just part of the karma of the Vietnamese people?" Thich Nhat Hanh took a deep breath and answered, "The Vietnam War did not just happen to the Vietnamese people. It happened to everyone who was involved. And America is still feeling the pain of its participation."

Through decades of yoga, meditation, and therapy, I've found my mother's terror during that war stored in my bones, my breath, my heart. But we never talked about it. In my late twenties I read a book called *Military Brats*—part autobiography, part sociological study—written by the daughter of an officer who had served with my father in Germany. It outlined the three characteristics of a military family's constellation: stoicism, secrecy, and denial. I recommended the book to my mother. But she responded, "I loved being an Army wife. It's the best life in the world."

Back at home, I unpacked my suitcase and threw my yoga clothes in the laundry. Forest was still at school. I took a shower and washed my hair, getting ready for the opening night of Forest's play, the dark satirical musical *Urinetown*. I had to be there. My mother had always put her children first and wanted me to do the same, I told myself. I'd been gone for a week already, and I knew that with teenagers, proximity is everything. Quality family time can't be planned—it happens in the random late-night moments when your teen wanders out to the kitchen where you are eating yogurt because you can't sleep, and sits down to tell you about the blind date he went on a few weeks ago, the one you never even heard about, and how afterward he was "friend-zoned." What he will remember, years later, about his teenage years is just this: *You were there. Or you were not there.*

But I lived that night with double vision, torn between *being* a mother and *having* a mother. One Anne was in the audience at the school theater, holding hands with her partner, Teja, and her stepdaughter, River, and beaming with pride as Forest sang and danced around on the stage in a business jacket and board shorts as sidekick to the evil boss of the Urine Good Company. The other Anne was in my imagination, sitting by her mother's bedside as she struggled for one breath after another.

When I got home, I changed my flight. The next morning, I was on the plane to Washington.

When I arrived at my parents' apartment, my mother had been sleeping all day, heavily dosed on morphine and Ativan, following what my sister Kathleen told me had been an anxious night. When she was still conscious, my mother had been adamant that she did not want to be forced to eat or drink. That meant she was going to die from dehydration, which my sister explained could be a peaceful way to go. Her kidneys would shut down and she would go unconscious, fall asleep, and never wake up.

I sat down on a chair next to the bed, Kathleen sitting on the other side. My mother was breathing with her mouth open, her white hair loose and her face slack—without her familiar expression of love and worry, she didn't look like herself. She was covered with one of the blankets she loved to crochet, in squares of yellow and green. A little plastic device at her nose was delivering oxygen, the tube running out the bedroom door and around the corner to a machine that made the living room sound like an airport runway. Over the years she'd paneled the wall by her bed with family photos: my father getting out of a jeep in Japan, just after World War II; me in my college graduation cap and gown; multiple grandchildren holding multiple great-grandchildren in their arms.

I got out of my chair and lay down on the bed next to her and wrapped my arms around her. Her head turned toward me as I told her I loved her, but her eyes stayed closed.

After about fifteen minutes, my sister began to sing lullabies: "Down in the Valley," "Hush Little Baby," "Lullaby and Goodnight." The room was dark, and my sister's voice touched some long-ago memory buried deep inside the oldest part of my brain. She must have sung these songs to me when I was a baby, I thought. Then I realized that, of course, it was my mother who had sung them. I was remembering my mother's voice—so much like mine and all of my sisters'—as she rocked me in her arms and sang, "And if that pony cart turns over, mama's gonna buy you a dog named Rover . . ."

The tears ran down my face into the rough wool of the crocheted blanket. As the youngest child, unlike Kathleen, I hadn't sung these familiar songs to a little brother and sister. But they were the same songs that I had chosen to sing to Forest, thinking that I was randomly selecting them, looking up the words online after the tunes bubbled up in my mind as I held him. For the first time, I realized that I had been singing the songs my mother had sung to me.

"Rock my soul in the bosom of Abraham . . ." sang Kathleen. I had sung that one too—wondering why on earth, as a Buddhist who hadn't gone to church in a quarter century, I had chosen it.

When I left the bedroom, my sister Mary was waiting in the living room. She told me that the day before, my mother had told her, "There must be a nursery in heaven. And my job will be to help take care of all the baby angels."

By the next day, all of my six brothers and sisters had arrived. We took turns going into my mother's room to sit by her bedside with her, put Vaseline on her dry lips, hold a damp cloth to her forehead. In between shifts we sat in the living room catching up with each other over the roar of the oxygen machine, eating the oatmeal raisin cookies my sister Celia had baked from my mother's recipe.

My mother still hadn't returned to full consciousness, and I began to understand that she probably would never speak again. But she still gestured to my sisters when she needed to use the commode that sat next to her bed. And she turned her head toward me when she heard my voice.

In order to watch a high school play, I had missed my chance to speak with her in person one more time, and I tried not to second-guess my choice. For my mom, I reminded myself, staying with your child was *always* the right choice to make.

I was sitting with her that afternoon when she became anxious and agitated, trying to sit up, clawing at the air, gazing with blank eyes at things I couldn't see. I took her hands in mine and told her, "You have generated so much love in your life. You have created all of these beautiful children. And now all that love is coming back to hold you. Love is holding you in its arms. You are floating in an ocean of love and you can just relax into it. You can breathe in love and breathe out love. You can breathe in peace and breathe out peace. You are dissolving into love."

She relaxed back onto the bed and became quiet again.

"Her body was very strong," the hospice worker said when she came for her daily visit. "So it is giving up slowly." Part of me cried out, *Why are we doing this? Give her an IV! Hydrate her! Bring this little sponge of my mother back to life, like one of the tiny, dried-sponge animals we used to toss into the bathtub when we were children to watch them swell up!*

. . .

By the next day, she was worse, her breathing restless and agitated. The hospice nurse told my sister he thought she was nearing her final moments. My father and all seven of her children gathered around her bed.

"Goodbye, Nancy," said my father, his voice shaking. "We've had so many good years." We each called out our names to her and sang "Lullaby and Goodnight" through our tears.

But my mother kept on breathing.

We began calling out the names of all her grandchildren. By the time we got to the great-grandchildren, we started getting the names wrong. "Child, what *is* your name?" joked one of my sisters—the line my mother used to use when she slipped up and called one daughter or great-granddaughter by another's name. Then, improbably, we were laughing.

There was another breath, and another, and another. "I hope she doesn't feel like this is a 'command performance,'" said another sister. And we all laughed again—my mother's quick-witted children, awkward and embarrassed by excessive emotion. It appeared that she was not dying at that moment, anyway.

The sweet male hospice nurse explained to us that the presence of all of us in the room might be keeping her from letting go. What mother wants to leave with all of her children—and their father— standing there singing to her?

So we all went back to the living room again and had more cookies.

I wanted to hold my mother's death as a sacred ritual, as a sacrament, as a kind of yoga—with calm, dignity, depth, and presence.

But as with everything else, the sacred and the mundane seem to be inseparable. Death is a holy transition from one world to another. It is also a grimy passage that demands rubber sheets, disinfectant wipes, latex gloves, and Vaseline. It insists upon plane reservations and babysitters. It is inseparable from the human messy details that make it . . . well, life.

My mother's death room became my meditation hall now. I would sit by her bed for an hour at a stretch with her in silence, following first my breath, then hers. Her breath was openmouthed, loud, the air wheezing across her vocal cords. Slanted light came through the blinds of a window that opened onto the courtyard where she used to love watching the squirrels and the birds flitting and scampering in a massive oak tree. Connie would give her morphine, wipe her lips, put small chips of ice in her mouth. She'd turn her every few hours so she didn't get pressure sores. One of these times, I walked into the room and there was my mother, her legs exposed, in her underwear. I realized I had never seen this much of her body. She always wore such modest bathing suits—had I ever seen her belly before? I recognized its shape, its curves, the shape of the legs and pelvis. It looked just like *my* body.

Outside in the living room, it was a family reunion. We talked about the big climate change story that my brother had just broken in his job at an online news organization. We exchanged stories about our children and grandchildren.

My father, meanwhile, was coping by planning my mother's funeral. He disappeared into his office and came back with a printout of a beautiful program that he and mom had designed together ten years before, with a picture of her as a young bride on the cover, and her choices for scripture readings and hymns inside.

He passed it around the room and told us that he had planned a service here at their retirement home, followed by a full Catholic funeral at West Point.

He said, gruffly: "Of course, she's got to die first."

When I was a teenager and my mom was in her fifties, she promised to write a letter every week for a year to an elderly friend, the aunt of a parish priest, whom she had adopted years ago as her own Aunt Anne. The letters were intended to brighten Aunt Anne's life, and to be the "memoir" that Aunt Anne had always begged her to write.

So every week she banged out a double-spaced, three-to-four-page chapter on the old Smith-Corona manual typewriter that her father had given her when she went to college in 1939. She wrote about the time she helped a teary-eyed sergeant find a place on Fort Leavenworth to bury his children's dead collie—"under a tree adjacent to the Prisoners' Cemetery (Kyrie Eleison!) where the unclaimed prisoners were laid to rest." The time she refused an invitation, as the wife of the commander of Fort Campbell, Kentucky, to be the judge for a local beauty contest for girls ages three and four: "In my heart, all little girls that age are winners." The time her granddaughter wept for a lost doll: "We understand this, Aunt Anne and I. We too have had the loss of possessions—the precious music box purloined, the favorite garment ruined, the beloved claimed by death. We too have wrapped ourselves in forgetfulness." After Aunt Anne died, my mother's letters were returned to her—all of them lovingly tied up with yarn and saved in a shoebox.

It's only now—with my own son approaching college age and nearly ready to leave home—that I understand what a gift this project was to my mother as well. She had raised seven children while traveling the world as a military wife; she was living in a strange town with an empty nest, and my father, recently retired from the Army, was gone most of the time, attending law school at night while trying to build a new career as a traveling consultant to the defense industry. I, the youngest, was away at boarding school. My mother was in her late fifties—just a little older than I am now—living mainly on her own. This project gave her something meaningful to do with her time—and a way to reflect on her life.

I can also see the stories that aren't in this memoir for Aunt Anne. The exhaustion of traveling the world as a military wife, moving every couple of years with three children in tow, then five, then seven. The loss, loneliness, and sheer terror of being married to a soldier at war for years at a stretch. The strain of being a shy, spiritual introvert required to socialize endlessly as the wife of the commanding general—at glamorous parties where she drank cocktails to overcome her social anxiety. The anxiety and physical pain she numbed out with prescription painkillers—and by drinking too much white wine in order to get to sleep. And the way all these things kept her from being present with her children—with me—the way she most wanted to be.

Sitting at my mother's bedside, I thought of the things I wished I had said to her, once I was an adult: *Mother, you must have been so sad and frightened and unhappy. Mother, you must have felt so alone. Mother, I was scared too. Mother, I too felt so alone. I'm sorry, Mom. I forgive you, Mom. Please forgive me too.*

But I hadn't said them. The code in our family was that we didn't speak such things aloud.

Thich Nhat Hanh's words came back to me: "You are the continuation of your parents." He wrote, "There are people who are angry with their mother, and . . . they want to forget her. They don't want to have anything to do with her. Is that possible? No. They are the continuation of their mothers. They are their mothers. They cannot escape. That is why the practice is to go back and to reconcile with the mother within."

On the third day of my visit, in between shifts at my mother's bedside, I went into my father's office with him and watched a DVD that he had edited together of movie clips from my mother's life.

There she is, in black and white, filmed on a hand-cranked 16-millimeter movie camera, turning cartwheels on a beach in Hawaii in 1929. There she is riding horseback and then watching my grandmother, in jodhpurs and tall riding boots, shoot a tin can with a pistol. There she is in her wedding dress, standing next to my uniformed father, two weeks back from World War II, as he cuts a wedding cake with a silver sword. There she is rushing into the surf with my father on their honeymoon in 1944, dancing with him in the front yard of their borrowed cottage, rubbing sunscreen on his back. There she is with her children on a beach at Sullivan's Island, South Carolina, on family visit after visit—first with one baby, then two, then three, then a whole litter, with the youngest—me—in a swim cap and bathing suit, looking just like my mother in 1929.

Then I went back into her room again and sat in silence with my sister Kathleen by her bed. Light spilled through the blinds tilted toward the ceiling. Her breath rattled in, then out. In, then out. It got faster, more shallow—then slower, with spaces opening between it.

Death is like labor, I thought, *only we can't see the baby.* On the other side, were a midwife's arms waiting to joyfully receive my mother's spirit? I didn't know. All I knew was that sitting with her, I was so grateful for the training I'd had on countless meditation retreats—to be still and present, hour after hour, in silence. To follow a breath coming in, and going out, and coming in again.

But in this situation, it was clear that the breath was not an anchor for settling the mind and heart in life. What I needed to do now was drop into the vast stillness and spaciousness that holds that coming and going. To rest my heart there. To be still. To just listen.

I had been rereading those letters my mother wrote to Aunt Anne. In one of them, she named a list of the blessings she dreamed of for her eighth grandchild, about to be born. I would read it again later, many times: "May this child, while still a nursling, hear the serenade of a mockingbird through an open window in the still of a moonlit night. . . . May this child, still discovering, gaze into a nest of robins while the baby birds emerge from their shells in the branches below the veranda rail. . . . May there be marching bands and a father who whistles, and some old dear man who whittles and a lady who invites flower-picking in her gardens, and a secret hideaway, and hours of jackstones with a little rubber ball, and the discovery of the endless skein of rubber inside an old golf ball. . . . Most of all, may the child grow to maturity surrounded by family and friends, conscious of God everywhere and in everything, and welcoming the magic that gleams beyond reality in fleeting moments."

I watched the light and shadows shifting as the sun moved into the afternoon. I felt the river of my mother's life—how much she had seen, and felt, and loved, and lost. I felt how much of her life had been invisible to me, lived behind the screen of my projections onto my ideas of *Mom*. I felt—still alive inside her—the little girl who had turned cartwheels on a beach; the radiant young woman who had fallen in love with my father; the mother of seven with a shattered hip and a husband in Vietnam; the mystic grandmother who had sat crocheting in her rocking chair, watching the squirrels in the oak tree out the window, seeing God in everything.

As the light slowly changed, my sister and I sat beside her and listened to her breathe. I felt her spirit. I felt my deep kinship with her—how I came out of her body. How I shared so much with her: bowed legs and big green eyes, warm smiles and dark worries at midnight, an inability to have a conversation with a television on in the background. She had loved me, hurt me, taken care of me, let me down—all the things that I knew I had done and would do to my loved ones as well.

And I made her a promise in silence: *Mom. I promise that the very best of who you are will live on through me. I will carry it out into the world as your ripple, as best as I can. And I will let go of the rest.*

She breathed out. She breathed in, with a gasp—and then didn't breathe out again.

The pause went on and on. I opened my eyes and looked at my sister. The home care attendant, sitting quietly in the corner, got up and closed my mother's mouth. She said, "Get your father."

I didn't know, in that moment, the details of what was about to come. How my father would come to her bedside to say goodbye, and my sister Connie would remove the oxygen tubes from my mother's nose and place my mother's left hand on top of the coverlet and slide off her wedding band and engagement ring, and hand them to my father: *Till death do us part.*

How we would sit there together around my mother's body as my father would tell us all again the story we had heard so many times before: How he bought that West Point miniature class ring, had it engraved with their names, and presented it to her without having first asked her to marry him. How she was outraged and gave it back to him until he made a proper proposal. How as a newlywed, pregnant and thin with morning sickness, the ring had slid off her finger while she was doing holiday cooking and got baked into a fruitcake—and how she had to cut all the fruitcakes apart to find it.

Connie would cover my mother's body with the black and green crocheted afghan that her grandmother had made for her when my mother was a baby—the one my mother had asked to be buried in. The medical examiner would be called. My mother's body would be wrapped up in a blue microfiber blanket, with her face covered, and strapped to a gurney. My brothers would push it down the hall, me and all my sisters walking along with it, my father in a wheelchair. We would try to sing "When the Saints Go Marching In," but none of us would know all the words. We would ride with the body in a freight elevator down to a loading dock, where it would be put in the back of a van.

As the van would drive away with my mother's body in it, we would all stand and watch it go, waving goodbye until the vehicle pulled out of sight—just as my mother always waved goodbye when one of us left after a visit, so her wave would be the last thing we'd see when we looked back. One of us would say, through the tears, "Onward and upward!"

There would be a funeral at West Point, where my mother used to visit from Connecticut College for dances and dates when my father was a cadet. This time the West Point gym would be hung with banners for the Army-Navy football game that coming weekend. My sister Mary would pass around my mother's datebook from 1943—a gift from my father, with the West Point chapel on the cover and my mother's appointments recorded in it in her loopy nineteen-year-old handwriting: Logic exam. English exam. Meetings for the college newspaper staff. And increasingly, every weekend, my father's name—*Jack. Jack. Jack.*

We would look to see what she was doing that week in 1943, seventy-three years ago. We would discover that she had been going to the Army-Navy game at West Point with my father, the young cadet with whom she had just fallen in love.

After the funeral, we would drive to the cemetery and that beloved cadet—now a retired general, unsteady on his feet—would watch her body be lowered into the ground, a mile from the path along the Hudson River where they had taken their first walk together, a few weeks after they met in Georgia.

At the time of that walk, she had just returned to Connecticut College, so he had invited her for a West Point visit—surprised but undeterred when she brought her mother along as chaperone. He had taken my mother for a stroll past Flirtation Rock—named for the legend that if a cadet didn't get a kiss from his date when he passed it, the rock would fall down.

"Did you kiss on that first date?" I once asked my father.

"Well," he said, "the rock is still standing."

Finding My Daughter

· · · · ·

WHEN A CHILD enters your life through conception and birth, or as a baby, there's a clear beginning to the story: a moment when you feel a kick in your belly, or hold a squalling infant in your arms, and know that a new relationship has begun.

When a child enters your life through a different door—as an adolescent, a teenager, or a young adult—it's harder to know when your story together begins. Sometimes it only becomes apparent in retrospect, when you notice that your family—and your heart—has gotten bigger through the long accrual of ordinary moments that build into something precious, like stones added one on top of another to make a temple.

I'd always wanted to have a daughter as well as a son. When I first envisioned having a child, it was always a little girl I could mother in some of the ways I had been mothered—and some of the ways I only wished I had been. I would read aloud to her all my favorite horse and dog stories, which Forest was never interested in: *Misty of Chincoteague*, *Black Beauty*, *Lad, A Dog*. She would be quirky and sensitive and brilliant and a little eccentric, but because of my wise and skillful mothering she would be the trendsetting adventurer of her middle school, not the weird kid who no one wanted to sit with at lunch.

But instead, for most of my years as Forest's mother, what I had was the memory of a daughter's loss: a beautiful baby girl who never breathed, lying in my arms with rosebud lips and a swirl of dark hair on her forehead.

My urgency about having another baby girl had fueled my dating in the years after my marriage fell apart. I studied the face of each man I grew temporarily close to—what might those blue eyes look like gazing up at me from a daughter's face? I researched still-experimental sperm-sorting methods that maximized the chances for those double-X chromosomes. But I learned that since I was already in my late thirties, I was too old to qualify for the experiments. I investigated adopting a baby girl from China but decided that as a single mom with a financially shaky career as a freelance writer and meditation teacher, I couldn't take the leap.

By the time I got together with Teja, I was forty-six and my baby-bearing years were basically behind me. I stopped using birth control, telling myself that if I became a fertility miracle, whose picture turned up on the cover of the *National Enquirer*, that would be fine with me. But the urgency had waned along with my estrogen levels. I adored Forest and was grateful for him every day, and I told myself that was enough.

But I still felt a pang when my friend Janice took a road trip down the coast with her preteen girl, windows open and their long hair tangling together in the breeze as they sang along with Taylor Swift's CD; or when Rachael showed up at a potluck wearing a pair of skinny jeans and boots she'd borrowed from her daughter.

I'd grown up as one of seven children. In one of my earliest memories, the Thanksgiving table actually collapsed from the weight of the food. It had never felt quite right, sitting at the dinner table with just one child and an irritable cat. I loved it when Forest's friends came over for sleepovers and I could cook blueberry pancakes in the morning for more than just one hungry boy. But in my imagination, sometimes I set the table for Forest's big sister, Sierra, too.

Starting with our very first date, Teja had told me stories about his daughter, who was sixteen when I met him.

When she was a baby, he used to do qigong with her in his arms—sweeping her high over his head and then low to the earth as he spiraled through the movements. When her mom went back to work at an office job when River was six weeks old, Teja took care of her all day—then stayed up late in his recording studio, producing albums for other musicians while keeping one ear tuned to the baby monitor. He parked her in her playpen at his dojo while he taught aikido, and she giggled and shrieked as she watched him roll and throw and high-fall on the mat. For her ninth birthday party, he and his sister threw a party and invited River and all her friends to paint his old truck with house paints—the girls painted it bright blue and decorated it with flowers, kittens, and stars. Whenever he used it to haul debris to the dump, people waved and honked. When River won a telescope in a science essay-writing contest, he took her out at night to view Saturn's rings and identify the craters on the moon.

But in the aftermath of his divorce, when River was twelve, she had gone to live with her mother. When Teja moved in with me and Forest during River's last year of high school, River didn't come with him at first. Instead, on the bookshelf over his computer, he set a letter from River written when she was eleven—"You are the best dad in the world! I will love you forever." As the holidays came without a visit, we put a picture of three-year-old River on the piano in our living room, laughing with a tangle of Christmas lights in her hair.

River first came to stay with us the summer after her sophomore year in college. I was thrilled for Teja that she was coming, but also a little nervous about what this might mean for me. I didn't dare dream that I might be getting a daughter—I just hoped she didn't hate me.

But when River met me that first night, she greeted me with a hug and a smile that reminded me of her dad's. Later that week she suggested that we get a pedicure together, and she helped me pick out wine-red polish for my normally scruffy toenails. As we sat with our feet in the warm, soapy water at the nail salon, she asked me candidly what I thought our connection was supposed to be.

"Let's not decide that right away," I answered, touched by her directness. "We don't have to force anything. You already have a mother, and I'm not trying to replace her. Let's let our connection grow, and just see what it becomes."

It was different, living with a girl. In the mornings that first summer, I delighted in the smells of floral shampoo and body lotion that flowed up the stairs from her bathroom, perfuming the house.

I was still having to remind Forest, just turning thirteen, to bathe at all. Before special occasions, there was the sound of a blow-dryer and the click of high heels on the tiled hallway. And there were more special occasions for all of us than there used to be; with River around, a simple family dinner out became a celebration. She had a natural gift for noticing daily delights the moment they appeared—a hummingbird at the window, the smell of bread baking in her dad's bread machine.

Several nights a week, she and her dad stayed up late—a huge bowl of homemade popcorn between them—watching the animated feature films they had loved when she was a child (*Kiki's Delivery Service*, *Pocahontas*) and the action flicks they both loved now (*Captain America* and *Star Trek*). She introduced him to the syncopated electronic bass lines of dubstep, and he played her the classical guitar pieces and folk songs with which he used to sing her to sleep. One night she flat-ironed my hair and did my makeup for me, and she, Forest, and I went to hear her dad's band play at a pub in our town.

The four of us settled into the ordinary rhythms of family life: daily walks around the wooded banks of the local reservoir, spotting coyotes, egrets, and owls; trips to Costco to buy bulk perishables—broccolini, spinach, salad greens—in quantities that had never made sense for a family of two; blueberry waffles on our deck on weekend mornings; home-cooked family dinners, where we swapped stories about our day as we sautéed veggies and scrubbed pots.

I taught her how to chop an onion and how to make a grilled cheese sandwich. With exquisite tact, she let me know which of my handful of party dresses were hopelessly out of date—*before* I wore them to parties—and then offered me hers to borrow. We discovered we shared a passion for reading and made trips to the library together to pick out piles of novels.

To my delight, she and Forest slipped into an effortless rapport. Eight years apart in age—and different genders—they felt no need to compete with each other for love from me and Teja. He showed her the best hiking trails near our house. She gave him advice about girls and began referring to him as her "little brother."

I marveled at her warmth, sweetness, and sensitivity. She was as emotional, intuitive, empathic, and heart-based as Forest and I were geeky and cerebral. She loved to hold hands or link her arm through mine or her dad's as we walked, and to lean into us for long, melting hugs. She sensed the emotional undercurrents when people were talking, sometimes even before the speaker did—when someone else in the room was sad, tears came to her eyes.

She was an artist and tuned in to visual details I was oblivious to—laying out brightly colored placemats and napkins on our dining room table, picking a bouquet of flowers that I hadn't noticed had bloomed in our garden, and putting them in a cobalt blue vase that had been gathering dust on a top shelf. She had bright, lacy underwear and pretty bras arranged by color with their cups neatly nested inside one another; *my* underwear was drab and utilitarian, with frayed elastic, tossed in a jumble in a drawer. She had high-heeled boots and a bathroom drawer full of eyeshadow and mascara and foundations; I had sneakers with orthotic inserts, and a single tube of lipstick I'd used since Forest was in kindergarten.

And yet I recognized myself in her. My childhood had been fractured by war and boarding school. Hers had been fractured by divorce. Now we were creating a new family together. This was a fresh start not just for her but also for the young woman who still lived inside me. In embracing my partner's daughter, I was also taking myself in my own arms.

At the end of that first summer with us, River headed back to her Southern California college for a semester, then flew to Marseille for a yearlong exchange program in international business. Midway through the program, knowing she was hungry to balance her business studies with creative expression, I helped her apply for a summer work-exchange residency where a friend of mine had taught, in an artist's colony in the countryside of the south of France. The excitement I felt when she called me to say that she had gotten the position was a clue to me about how deeply I had taken her into my heart. For hours after our conversation I kept finding myself smiling with joy at odd moments—as if *I* were the one who was about to spend my summer doing watercolor paintings and helping change the sheets in a stone farmhouse in Carcassonne.

After her year in France, River came home for our first family

Christmas together. Our family relationship had leaped ahead in the time apart, as if we had all come to know that it was something we could count on.

She and I laid out the makings for sugar cookies. Teja put on a CD of guitar music—a holiday collection he had released before River was born. "I grew up listening to this," she told me and Forest, as we rolled out two big balls of dough into flat sheets.

As the music played, we used cookie cutters to make Christmas trees, stars, Santas, and a menagerie of tigers, deer, and bears. We slipped them in the oven to bake. Then we took the leftover scraps from the two batches and kneaded them together into one big ball for the final batch.

"Keep kneading until all the seams disappear, so when you roll it out you don't have cracks in the cookies," I told River and Forest as they took turns kneading the dough.

I was so happy, I almost couldn't bear it. I wanted to inhale the whole moment deeply—the smell of baking butter and sugar, the laughter of my two children, my partner's arm around me.

I could feel the way that the four of us were being kneaded together into one batch of cookies—the seams between our separate, fractured families disappearing.

An international internship was a graduation requirement for River's program, so over that holiday, Teja and I helped her apply for one at a multinational company where we'd been leading executive meditation retreats. As a writer, I generally guard my time tightly, but I was thrilled to help her write and rewrite her application and slog through interminable work permit application forms in French and Dutch (with the help of Google Translate). I realized that I was feeling the same way about helping her that I did about helping Forest—that her well-being and success made me happier than my own.

Early one morning, both of us still in our pajamas, we checked her email together at dawn and found out that her work permit had come through and that she would be flying to Amsterdam in two weeks. We jumped up and down together and squealed as we hugged each other.

While River worked in Amsterdam, Teja and I Skyped with her every week—helping her find an apartment overlooking Rembrandtpark; meeting her new roommate; meeting her new Dutch boyfriend. When she finished her internship, she came home to live with us again while she wrote her thesis. She painted the walls of her bedroom in marbled layers of peach, she and her dad working side by side as they dabbed at the walls with sponges to create the faux effect. Then she settled down to write her case study, an analysis of the mindfulness-training retreats that her dad and I led for the company where she'd worked.

One day River suggested we clean out the kitchen spice rack together. The inspiration for this came when she opened a jar of cayenne for her refried beans and found bugs wriggling in it. I do *know* that it's a good idea to purge one's spice shelves periodically. It's just that it hadn't been on my priority list for . . . oh, maybe a quarter century or so?

So digging through the spices was an archaeological expedition through my culinary past. There were jars of cardamom pods and sulfurous asafoetida from the time I reviewed an ayurvedic cookbook for *Yoga Journal* and got inspired to make mung-bean kedgeree to calm my fly-away *vata* energy. There was faded saffron I picked up in Mysore while studying ashtanga yoga and which I had daily simmered in fresh milk from the cow stabled below my bedroom. There was yeast from a brief foray into bread baking when my now six-foot son was in kindergarten, and red curry paste from an adventure with Thai cuisine.

There were two unopened jars of faded tarragon, an herb that I can't recall ever using—my best guess is that one arrived when my ex-husband moved in with me, and the other when Teja did. There was fenugreek seed that I had bought without having any idea what to cook it with, because—back in my own premotherhood, twenty-something life when I wrote down my dreams every morning—a dream owl had informed me that I needed to eat more fenugreek. Especially with items like these, with expiration dates before she could talk, River helped me be ruthless.

And as we made our way through the spices, we told each other stories. Running hot water into a jar of clumpy powdered garlic, I told her about how I tried to make cold cucumber-yogurt soup from my very first cookbook, *The Enchanted Broccoli Forest*, when I'd just graduated from college. "It would have come out great, except that the recipe called for three cloves of garlic, and I didn't know what a clove was. So I put in three entire heads. I served it to my boyfriend and we tried to eat it because we didn't want to waste the money we had spent on yogurt and cucumbers."

She told me about learning to cook in her roommate's kitchen while she was doing her internship in Amsterdam—how her Dutch boyfriend had taught her how to make lasagna, and then the proper Dutch way to do the dishes afterward. "In kitchens in Holland, there are two kinds of towels—tea towels for drying dishes and hand towels for drying your hands. And people get really shocked and irritated if you use the wrong ones."

Cleaning the spice rack was just one of a series of projects we embarked on together, each one bringing us closer. And over time, as we swapped stories, I had the sense—one that I often have with her—that we were fleshing out our histories for each other, as if we were handing each other coloring books filled with outlines of our past selves and then coloring them in together.

Meanwhile, she and Forest bonded over music—they huddled in front of their computers, playing each other their favorite songs. He inundated her with songs by his favorite band, Muse. She introduced him to Twenty One Pilots and they sang along to "Stressed Out" as they washed the dishes together.

Together, River and I watched the HBO series *Girls*, agreeing that we were comfortable enough with each other to sit through the graphic sex scenes. One day, when it was just the two of us for dinner, we went to the farmer's market together and bought peaches, which I sautéed with butter and brown sugar. We poured them on top of ice cream and sat down to shovel our dessert into our mouths before the ice cream melted. When we both involuntarily began to moan with delight, we burst out laughing so hard we spattered ice cream and peach juice all over the table. It was the kind of mother-daughter moment I'd always imagined.

One evening when I was nervous about going to an event where I expected to see my ex-husband's new wife, River helped me pick out an outfit that looked both sexy and maternal, and did my eye makeup. Then, before I left, she slipped a small, polished, heart-shaped stone into my hand.

"Carry this in your purse," she said. "It's to remind you that I am your rock. I'm with you always."

For our first Mother's Day together, she decorated the table with flowers, then she and Forest presented me with a handmade card and several handmade gifts. I have never doubted Forest's love for me, but I am confident it was not *his* idea to shape little jewelry dishes out of modeling clay, paint them with gold hearts, flowers, and "We Love You," and stay up late firing them in our kitchen oven.

That same night, River also made me a picture frame decorated with purple and turquoise tissue paper—my favorite colors—with a picture in it of the two of us, laughing, our arms around each other.

I had wanted a nuclear family—me, a husband, and a couple of children, all sitting around a table together. That's what I finally had. It just hadn't arrived the way I had planned.

It was as if I'd been sitting and waiting impatiently for the front doorbell to ring, looking at my watch, pacing from window to window watching the street, and, in the meantime, the family I was waiting for had already come in the back door, sliced apples, rolled out dough, and put a pie in the oven to bake. The sweet smell of cinnamon and apples was already permeating the house, just waiting for me to sit down at the table.

What I learned from finding family with Teja, River, and Forest is that what makes a family is something deeper than genetics. And what makes someone your child is not just that they grew inside you or got birthed through your body—or that you changed their diapers, and took them to their first day of kindergarten, or took their first lost tooth from under their pillow and replaced it with a quarter and a note from the tooth fairy. Yes, there is something unique in the slow accrual of family intimacy over years and decades of shared moments. But love can flow backward in time, so you can know someone in the present and come to love all the different people they were before you met them.

I loved a little girl before she was born, who died before I could hold her. And I love a little girl laughing with Christmas lights in her hair who grew up before I met her. I love a man who beams at me from a photo with that little girl in his arms—a man with brown, curly hair flowing past his shoulders that had turned short and gray by the time we met.

It wasn't that River had replaced Sierra or that Teja had replaced my ex-husband. It was that together we had built a family out of the broken pieces of our past. And I knew that it was a beautiful, complete, and radiant thing, not a cobbled-together substitute.

Seventeen years after Sierra's father and I scattered our baby's ashes in a remote mountain lake, I am back there once again, this time with my new family.

Lake Ralston sits in a rocky cairn high above Echo Lake, where my ex-husband's family still maintains their summer cabin. Forest and I still spend a couple of weeks there every summer, often inviting friends to come with us.

Every year, I've made the pilgrimage to Lake Ralston. I sit on a rocky ledge and gaze across at the ribbon of water splashing down the granite ledges and rockslides, then scrabble my way around the lake and sit at the base of the waterfall where we released Sierra's ashes into the stream. I jump into the clear water, gasping at the cold, and then haul myself out and bake on a slab of sun-warmed granite. As the years have gone by, it has slowly become a place of bittersweet joy for me again, rather than a place of ragged mourning.

This year, my hike to Ralston is not alone. I'm going there with Forest, now age sixteen; with River, age twenty-four; and with Forest's best friend, Vaughan, who has been coming up to Echo with us almost every year since the boys were eight and six.

We climb up the familiar white-granite trail with daypacks full of sandwiches. It's River's first time at Echo Lake, and we are all excited about introducing her to the land we love so much. We point out the junipers, the white pines, the red firs; the ground squirrels and marmots who poke their noses out between the boulders. We point out the Indian paints and asters.

Harder to point out are my memories, embedded at every turn of the trail: rowing across Echo in a canoe at age nineteen with the boy who would become Forest's father, inhaling for the first time the distinctive mountain scent of pine and snowmelt; leaping naked off the rocks into the water in my twenties holding hands with that young man, both of us stoned and laughing; the two of us with one-year-old Forest between us, holding our hands as he waded into the shallows in his diaper.

And, of course, the two of us walking up this trail seventeen years earlier, carrying Sierra's ashes in a little ceramic urn painted with flowers that had been a wedding gift meant to hold sugar.

We pause at a familiar bend in the trail, the twin ovals of upper and lower Echo Lake below shining like blue jewels in the valley. I snap a picture of River and Forest on the edge of a granite ledge, their arms around each other.

When we get to Lake Ralston, we sprawl on the slabs of sun-warmed granite at the edge of the water and eat our sandwiches. Forest and Vaughan play hacky sack. I slip away and sit down by a twisted old pine for a moment of meditation. River follows and sits down next to me. In silence, we look across the jewel-blue water.

"You see that waterfall over there?" I point across the lake to where a band of silver winds down the craggy granite. "That's where we scattered Sierra's ashes."

She nods. "I know. Forest told me." She dissolves into tears. "I'm so sorry."

She leans against me, and as I wrap my arms around her I marvel, as I often do, at her emotional attunement. It feels as if she is crying out the tears that are too painful for me to allow right now.

She says, "I will always hold Sierra in my heart as my sister. It's like I can feel her presence here—that if we were just still enough, we might see her peeking around the side of a tree, a teenage girl. I'm so sad that she didn't get to grow up with you as her mom."

"Even with a loss this big . . . time passes, and the pain becomes less sharp," I tell her. "Eventually, I think, all that remains is the love."

As I say it, I know this is becoming true for me. The love I feel in that moment is big enough to fill the whole lake, the whole basin of granite rockslide and clear, blue-green water, reflecting the vast mountain sky. My children have carved a space in my heart the way the ancient glaciers carved cairns into the valley.

I wrap my arms around my daughter and say, "The pain recedes. The love goes on forever."

Epilogue

AFTER TWO YEARS living at home with us, River moved to Portland to find a job and study art. Then Forest was a senior, filling out college applications. Blink: River was back with us again, working for a catering company and studying to be a web designer. Blink: Forest got accepted to a university on the East Coast.

Family life rubs your nose in the truth of *anicca*, impermanence. Because even if everything goes perfectly, you eventually lose everything. You lose the early mornings rocking your breastfeeding baby as the dawn brightens the sky. You lose snuggling together on a sofa reading aloud: "One berry, two berry, pick me a blueberry!" You lose riding a bike with an extra seat and an extra wheel screwed onto the back and a four-year-old pedaling furiously behind you to "give us some extra gas!" as you go up a hill. You lose a six-year-old singing "Oh, What a Beautiful Morning" on the toilet, then you lose a seventeen-year-old belting out "Brain Damage" by Pink Floyd, also on the toilet. You lose a girl's watercolor paintings strewn across the kitchen table, and the guitar riffs blasting from a teenage boy's room at 1:00 a.m.

But along the way, you gain the whole world. Family life powers its way through your heart in a torrent of lost sweatshirts and runny noses, school concerts and school suspensions—and leaves it bigger, more tender, more vulnerable and alive and connected.

The end of the summer before Forest's senior year, the four of us—me, Teja, Forest, and River—went on a camping trip around the Olympic Peninsula in Washington. We rented a van with a pack of wolves painted on the side. We paddled kayaks around a mountain lake and roasted marshmallows for s'mores over a campfire. We pitched a tent on a windy bluff overlooking the Strait of Juan de Fuca, and on the banks of a river in the Hoh Rain Forest.

Near the end of our trip, we took a hike through the rain forest on a trail that wove through a lush tangle of massive roots under a dense green canopy of Sitka spruces, hemlocks, cedars, and

Douglas firs dripping with moss. Signs along the way explained the ecosystem of this temperate rain forest: how massive trees capture the sunlight, while shade-loving mosses, mushrooms, and ferns carpet the forest floor.

We paused to read a sign by a fallen tree called a "nurse log." Nurse logs, we read, are fallen trees—often massive evergreens that had lived up to five hundred years by the time they uprooted and tumbled. But you can't really call them dead. In falling, they tear a hole in the canopy, letting in light that enables new seedlings to take root. As they decay—which may take another five hundred years—they teem with far more life inside them than they had when they were rooted. With the help of insects, microbes, and fungi, the log becomes an elevated bed of nutrient-rich, spongy soil that cradles the growth of new trees.

There's a metaphor here about family, and love.

When Forest was six, he woke up sobbing from a nightmare in the middle of the night. I lay with him and sang him songs until he started to drift off to sleep again. As I stood up to slip away, he opened his eyes and said, "Love is the most powerful thing there is."

"That's right," I told him.

"Do you want to know why it's so powerful?"

"Yes, tell me why."

"Because it goes on forever in all directions," he told me. "No one ever started it. And no one can take it away from you."

Acknowledgments

A book, like a child, is born from the vast, creative, mysterious generosity of life itself, so it's hard to know where to begin saying "thank you." Without my close family, there would have been no story—I'm deeply grateful for their love, support, patience, and willingness to let me write about them. Special thanks to my son for lighting up the past eighteen years with laughter and song—and for being the main character in so many of my tales. To his dad, for being the best father to him I could have imagined, even after we stopped living together. To my life partner, Teja, for healing my heart, awakening my body, and creating a home with me. To Teja's daughter, who helped give this story a happy ending by becoming my daughter too.

My sister Kathleen is my lifelong confidant and writing mentor—many of these stories began as letters to her, and she held my hand through multiple drafts over many years. My writing coach Shoshana Alexander's faith and wise edits kept me from collapsing before I reached the finish line. My dear friend Katy Butler is an exquisitely precise writer and editor—our semiregular manuscript exchanges and tea meetings made this into a far better book.

Never-ending hugs to my fellow moms and beloved friends—Rachael, Janice, Amy, and May. Again and again, as we raised our kids together, we kept each other from losing our marbles. Without our communal dinners, hikes and bikes, backpacking trips, laughing fits, and late-night phone consults and consolation, motherhood could have felt like a crazed and lonely journey.

My six brothers and sisters—and all their children and grandchildren—weave me in a web of family connection that sustains me every day. And finally, I'm grateful to my mother. Among her many gifts, she gave me her love of precise and beautiful language and her passion for good books. She never read most of these stories. But her heart and voice run through them all.

Credits

Earlier versions of some of these stories originally appeared in other publications. These essays have been revised, expanded, and retitled for *The Mama Sutra*. Grateful thanks to the following publications for their encouragement over the years and their blessing to include this material:

Sutra 2, originally published in *Yoga Journal* (March 2001) as "Into the Heart of Sorrow"

Sutra 5, originally published in *Tricycle: The Buddhist Review* (Summer 2003—Volume 12, Number 4) as "The Spice of Life"

Sutra 7, originally published in *Lion's Roar* (September 2005) as "Will I Die Too? Will You?"

Sutra 9, originally published in *Lion's Roar* (September 2006) as "The Big Questions"

Sutra 10, originally published in *Lion's Roar* (May 2008) as "Astronomy Lessons"

Sutra 11, originally published in *Perceptive Traveler* (September 2008) as "A Passage Back to India"

Sutra 12, originally published in *Tricycle: The Buddhist Review* (Summer 2006—Volume 15, Number 4) as "Fifteen Weeks of Dharma Dating"

Sutra 13, originally published in *Lion's Roar* (July 2011) as "The Best Laid Plans"

Sutra 14, originally published in *Lion's Roar* (January 2013) as "Dancing in Foam"

About the Author

Anne Cushman is a writer and meditation teacher whose work focuses on the intersection between spiritual practice and the wild, messy, heartbreaking, and hilarious details of ordinary life. She is the author of the novel *Enlightenment for Idiots* (named by *Booklist* as one of the best first novels of its year), the India pilgrimage guide *From Here to Nirvana*, and the mindful yoga book *Moving into Meditation*. She is a member of the Teachers Council at Spirit Rock Meditation Center, where she teaches regularly on retreats that emphasize embodiment, creativity, and women's awakening. She is the Director of Mentoring for the international Mindfulness Meditation Teacher Certification Program (from the Awareness Training Institute and the Greater Good Science Center at UC-Berkeley), and she offers individual mentoring sessions to students worldwide via video conferencing. Anne served as an editor and writer at both *Yoga Journal* and *Tricycle*, and her personal essays on contemplative practice in contemporary life have been widely published in venues that include the *New York Times*; the *San Francisco Chronicle*; *O, The Oprah Magazine*; and *Lion's Roar*. Her work has also been anthologized in *The Best Buddhist Writing 2004* and *2006*, *A Women's Path: Women's Best Spiritual Travel Writing*, *Traveling Souls: Contemporary Pilgrimage Stories*, and other books. The mother of a teenage son and a twenty-something stepdaughter, she lives with her family in Fairfax, California. To learn more about the author, visit her website at www.annecushman.com.